C000244016

JOURNAL FOUR

All material remains copyright of the authors and artists. Please contact them through the editor if you wish to re-use any of their work. We have tried to ensure that no copyrights have been breached by our use of visual or written material. Please contact us if you feel that original material in your possession has been used inappropriately.

Acknowledgements

Innumerable people have provided their support in making *Strange Attractor Journal Four* happen. As well as all the contributors to this volume, we would particularly like to thank: Ned Bagg, Richard Bohane, Louise Burton, Ralph Cowling, LSD, Sylvia Hutchinson, The Little Shoppe of Horrors, John Lundberg, Neil Mortimer, Hannah Westland.

Contributions

Strange Attractor welcomes proposals for written and visual contributions to future editions of our *Journal*. Please send any such materials to the editor via email or to the postal address below.

mark@strangeattractor.co.uk

Strange Attractor Journal

BM SAP, LONDON
WC1N 3XX, UK

www.strangeattractor.co.uk

ISBN 9780954805463

Journal Four

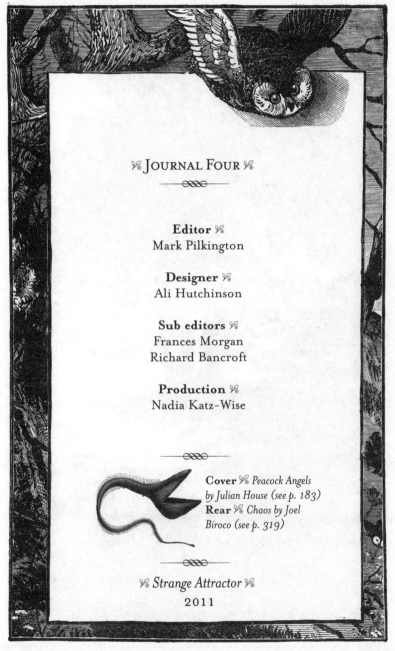

Editor
Mark Pilkington

Designer
Ali Hutchinson

Sub editors
Frances Morgan
Richard Bancroft

Production
Nadia Katz-Wise

Cover *Peacock Angels by Julian House (see p. 183)*
Rear *Chaos by Joel Biroco (see p. 319)*

Strange Attractor
2011

Journal Four

Introduction

TEN YEARS since we began organising live events, four years since the publication of *Journal Three* and seven years since the appearance of *Journal One*, we are still here.

But what, after all this time, is Strange Attractor?

It is points of intersection and transition; it is the syncretic filaments connecting culture and nature, science and magic, past and future; it is the relationships between secrets and mysteries, humans and animals, us and not us, and the questions that arise from those relationships.

With these eighteen new contributions we continue to celebrate unpopular culture; charting uncertain territories, unearthing improbable histories, exploring fragile realities and seeding further possibilities.

Join us.

Journal Four

Contents

Looking for LIBERTALIA

by DAVID LUKE

Men who were born and bred in Slavery, by which their Spirits were broke, who, ignorant of their Birth-Right, and the Sweets of Liberty, dance to the Musick of their Chains, would brand this generous Crew with the insidious Name of Pyrates, and think it meritorious, to be instrumental in their Destruction. Self-Preservation therefore, and not a cruel Disposition, obliged him to declare War against all European Ships and Vessels.

A General History of the Pyrates
Captain Charles Johnson (1728)

I PULLED UP alongside the small decrepit dock in our deflating inflatable and dropped off the harbourmaster, an immigration official and some other guy half dressed in combats, who I guessed was from the military. They were all clinging to their life jackets in dread as they clambered onto the shore, like shaken kids getting off an amusement park ride. Due to their terror of going across the bay in our little dinghy it had taken some financial persuasion to get them all to come out to our anchored ship for an inspection, rather than us having to dock the ungainly monster and make it vulnerable to a host of unknown harbour parasites – cockroaches, rats, thieves, that sort of thing.

Clambering out of the dingy the harbourmaster bid us farewell and then as an afterthought told us casually that there had just been a tsunami warning from Jakarta and that we should take all the necessary precautions before the wave's imminent arrival in about three hours. 'What should we do?' I asked. 'I don't know,' he said, 'I've never seen a tsunami here before. We're evacuating the port region. Your captain will know what to do.' I looked at him in disbelief as he turned to catch up with the others who were fast disappearing into the darkness. 'Nice meeting you, I hope you are still alive tomorrow', he offered limply, and then he legged it.

I bounced back across the vast natural harbour of Antsiranana to our ship, the only one anchored there still afloat. The great bay was a graveyard of sunken vessels whose old masts and hulls jutted out everywhere, the carcasses of forgotten battles and ancients storms. I clambered on board and made my way down to the command room and broke the good news to the captain. 'The small boat's got a puncture, there's been an earthquake of 8.4 on the Richter scale somewhere near Jakarta and we've been issued with an imminent tsunami warning, oh, and we're out of coffee'. 'What do you mean, we're out of coffee?' he asked, smiling wryly. I relayed the sparse comments the harbourmaster had dropped on us and he gave a tired sigh and turned to the chart table. 'OK, I think the thing to do is let out some more anchor chain, and just sit it out. It would take us three hours to raise the boat and the anchor and motor round to this other bay anyway and there's no time now to make it back into the ocean'. Propped up on the remnants of our precious caffeine supply he probably hadn't slept for more than a couple of hours in the last thirty-six. 'Let's raise the boat and make sure we're ready to go if need be. Shipshape everything good... Have you got a cigarette?'

It was early evening now and none of us had had any sleep

the night before. Approaching the coast of Madagascar, all our efforts had been sapped crossing what sailors call 'the washing machine' near the mouth of the Antsiranana Bay. It had taken three attempts to secure the anchor and then a tiring last-ditch effort to lower the small boat to greet the harbour officials. There was certainly nothing left in us for a tsunami.

It was September 2007; the ten of us onboard had just sailed non-stop for the last month across the South Indian Ocean in a fourteen-man Chinese junk ship. 82 feet of ferrous-cement, steel, wood and hemp, the *RV Heraclitus* was the three-mast floating dream of a collective of hippies, actors and a couple of engineers in Oakland, California, during the early seventies. Having little marine experience, two of them did a correspondence course in boat building while the others put on plays around San Francisco to raise the money for materials. All of them took a hand in the construction. The finished product was ocean-ready but naturally quite quirky, and it seemed to have been designed to make it as awkward as possible to get from A to B anywhere onboard. It was heavy and slow too, with all the stealth of a sinking cement mixer, but it had still somehow managed to scoot us along in the Southeast trade winds at up to nine knots. This unlikely speed had been largely due to the perpetual gale that had pushed us, and the ship, to our limits for the entire voyage. Everyone had been working like press-ganged naval skivvies under the whip for the last eight weeks, preparing the ship for the ocean crossing and then battling moody elements day and night in the Indian Ocean.

The current incumbents of the ship consisted largely of European adult runaways escaping life back home and seeking adventure. Almost all were novice sailors when they joined the ship, save for the German captain and chief. The journey had been exhausting, frequently painful, yet often hilarious as we bobbed along at alternating right angles, lumbering through swells as high as eight metres. It had been gruelling alright, but we had a dream to hold it all together. Our plan was to sail from the Indonesian paradise of Sumatra in Southeast Asia to the forgotten island of Madagascar off the east coast of Africa, much like the original settlers of Madagascar had done about 2,000 years ago.

We also shared the same vision of sailing the old junk ship to Madagascar in search of the mythic pirate utopia of Libertalia, to arrive as the buccaneers of old must have done and to find what fragments remained of the old renegade reverie. We intended to sing a sea shanty to the lost sailor Shangri La, and explore a country, by sea, that might still have a few vestiges of the liminal life the corsairs had led left clinging to its shores. We hoped we might still find something of this legacy in a country as undeveloped as Madagascar, which has no trains and less than half a dozen tarmac roads spanning an island twice the size of the UK. A place as weird as Madagascar where the dead are annually removed from their tombs, unwrapped, partied with, and then wrapped up and put back to bed as part of the traditional *Famadihana* (turning of the bones) ceremony.

But the dead I was primarily seeking the company of were the ghosts of pirate legends, who had lived the 'short but merry life', free of bondage to land or law. First described by Captain Charles Johnson in *A General History of the Robberies and Murders of the Most Notorious Pyrates* (1724-28), the legend of Libertalia describes an intentional pirate enclave in the north of Madagascar which, although the actual chronology is vague, flourished for several years at the turn of the sixteenth to seventeenth centuries. A kind of anarchist Arcadia made manifest, Libertalia was founded by the disgruntled Captain Misson, and a lewd, atheist Dominican priest, Father Caraccioli, who hoped to build a new egalitarian community based upon ideals of equality and liberty for all. Foreshadowing the American constitution by about 100 years, Caraccioli extolled that, 'everyman is born free, and has as much right to what will support him as to the air he respires'.

Ghosts of pirate legends

As a seaman, the Provençal Misson had been elected captain of the French manowar, *Victoire*, when, by chance, the original captain and officers were killed in an engagement with a British ship in the Mediterranean. With the help of Caraccioli, Misson persuaded the remaining crewmen to come with him and start a 'new marine republic' against all forms of governance, telling them, 'That he might with the

Ship he had under Foot, and the brave Fellows under Command, bid Defiance to the Power of Europe, enjoy every Thing he wish'd, reign Sovereign of the Southern Seas, and lawfully make War on all the World, since it would deprive him of that Liberty to which he had a Right by the Laws of Nature'. And so they set sail for the South Indian Ocean under a white flag bearing the motto '*A Deo a Libertate*' (for god and liberty).

Having high humanitarian ideals far in advance of European or US law pertaining to slavery and its abolition, Misson's mission also encompassed attacking slave ships, freeing all the slaves and prisoners, and offering them a new life in Libertalia. In a speech to the crew the good captain argued that:

> *the Trading for those of our own Species, could never be agreeable to the Eyes of divine Justice: That no Man had Power of the Liberty of another; and while those who profess'd a more enlightened Knowledge of the Deity, sold men like Beasts; they prov'd that their Religion was no more than a Grimace.*

After various piratical escapades and some time in the Comoros Islands – where, on the way to generate Libertalia, the captain and crew stopped to liberate their genitalia, and found for themselves devoted wives – Misson finally settled in Antsiranana, in northern Madagascar. This unique haven is still considered the safest, largest and most beautiful natural harbour in the entire Indian Ocean. Truly cosmopolitan, the settlement soon became home to French, English and Dutch sailors encountered in raids, and even old enemies like the Portuguese, along with a large contingent of Comorons, native Madagascans, and many freed African slaves. A new universal language evolved and the colony began trading booty as far away as New York via the famous pirate Captain Tew, who also joined the self-styled 'Liberi' as admiral of the fleet. Other passing pirates also fell for the lure of Libertalia, Captain William Kidd supposedly lost half his crew to Misson's dream after stopping there to make repairs to his ship.

All went well in the pirate utopia for many years until Misson's humanity finally unravelled the dream it had woven. Against advice he opted to exile rather than kill prisoners and almost caused the immediate demise of the republic when some of them returned with a Portuguese war fleet and were narrowly beaten off. Misson then resolved to form a council to settle disputes about the governance of Libertalia, thereby driving Captain Tew off across the bay to start his own truly anarchic settlement. It's then that the Madagascan tribespeople in the surrounding hills took advantage of the Liberi's diminished numbers and attacked them. Caraccioli and many others were killed and Misson escaped, found Tew, and they both put to sea, but Misson's ship disappeared in a storm and the legend of Libertalia disappeared into Captain Johnson's bureau as the now missing Misson manuscript.

Sailing to a physical location is one thing but trying to find what, if anything, remains there of an ideology from a time long since past was likely to be more slippery than grasping a jellied eel in a Greenwich pie shop. To make matters worse there are numerous contentions and mysteries concerning the identity of Johnson and the very existence of Misson and Libertalia. John Robert Moore, Professor of English at Indiana University, dropped a literary cannonball when, in 1932, he announced to the Modern Language Association that Captain Charles Johnson was actually an alias of Daniel Defoe, author of the English language proto-novel, *Robinson Crusoe*. However, even this remains unproven, and of the 500 works attributed to Defoe, he only ever signed his name to less than a dozen of them. It wasn't until 1961, over 200 years after the publication of *A General History of Pyrates*, that Maximillian Novak added more oil to my jellied eel and suggested that the story of Libertalia was one of Defoe's 'most remarkable and neglected works of fiction' and that Misson had been wholly fabricated by Defoe as much as Robinson Crusoe. Yet Novak's accusation has a strange whiff of truth about it because an anachronism in Johnson's story puts Misson's death in 1694 even though he is supposed to have taken part in an action with the French Navy in 1708. Such an inaccuracy has cast the truth of Libertalia into the murky light of possible fabrication, but champions to lost causes and lost utopias, such as Peter Lamborn Wilson, have defended the Libertalian myth.

Wilson acknowledges that there is no surviving evidence for Libertalia, and that the Misson manuscript upon which Johnson supposedly based his story of Libertalia has never materialised either. Yet he reminds us that fact may be stranger than fiction by pointing out that their absence does not necessarily make them fictitious and that alternatives to the now popular 'pure fiction' faction are possible. As much as Robinson Crusoe was based on the real character of Alexander Selkirk, Misson may not have been purely fictitious either, speculating that the anomalies may have been poetic license exercised by Johnson/Defoe to obscure Misson's true identity (especially after the real hermit Selkirk became mobbed by Crusoe fans). In any case various shades of truth exist between pure fact and pure fiction and the story of

Libertalia lies somewhere between the two because much of Johnson's book has already been corroborated and is still considered the leading historical text on South Sea pirates – though certainly it was written for popular appeal and may have been sexed up here and there for better reading. Nevertheless, Wilson also points out that Johnson obviously interviewed many pirates whilst researching his book and yet no one contemporaneously pointed the finger at Johnson for fabricating Libertalia when the book was first published. Obviously, this doesn't qualify it as definitely real, but it was at least highly believable at the time, and for good reason.

Following the decline of the golden age of piracy towards the end of the seventeenth century and with the subsequent ousting of pirate enclaves in the Caribbean, such as Tortuga in Hispaniola, many buccaneers and pirates turned their attentions elsewhere. Madagascar at that time remained un-colonised by Europeans and the many native Malagasy tribes stood divided. Much of the island also remained quite inaccessible by land, as it still does, particularly the bay of Antsiranana which was cut off from the rest of the country by mountains (indeed, the first complete paved road from the capital to Antsiranana, a major

Madagascan town with an airport, had only just been completed at the time of writing). The island of Madagascar also offered the perfect location with which to attack trade ships to the Orient as they rounded Africa, and it is known that there existed many genuine pirate enclaves and mini-kingdoms along the Madagascan coast at that time, though none as utopian as Libertalia.

Around 1695, the English Captain Henry Avery used the north eastern Madagascan Bay of Antongila as the base from which his fleet of six ships captured the imperial Moghal dhow en route from India to the Hajj, taking the Moghal princess onboard as his wife and becoming a mock king in the process, proclaiming himself Ruler of Antongila. In southern Madagascar, Abraham Samuel, a Jamaican pirate, set up camp in the abandoned French stronghold of Fort Dauphin around 1696 and was heralded as King Samuel by the natives. Similarly around 1719, in the northeast, near the Bay of Antongila, James Plaintain crowned himself King of Ranter Bay (now Rantabe), a place that probably took its name from the British radical revolutionary sect, the Ranters, who denied the authority of the church and the existence of sin – a sentiment sympathetic with the plight of any pirate. So certainly anarchist pirate utopias and self-styled kingdoms in Madagascar were known to genuinely exist at that time, and though most of these were short lived – Hakim Bey's Temporary Autonomous Zones (TAZs) in every sense – some thrived for many years.

Anarchist pirate utopias

In 1691 the former buccaneer Adam Baldridge set up a trading post across the water from Ranter Bay on the Madagascan island of Sainte-Marie, which by the beginning of the eighteenth century had become a flourishing pirate enclave under the command of the British Captain Nathaniel North. Captain Kidd is known to have traded here in 1698 and visitors to the island can still see a pirate church and cemetery with a curious monument dated 1834, apparently in honour of Captain Kidd. Speaking to the locals in Île Sainte-Marie I was told that there were once 1,000 pirate ships on the island and stories of their exploits, apocryphal or not, still abound. An expatriated German sailor told me over a drink that on one occasion a prize ship full of whiskey had caused 500 men to perish in the ensuing fights over drinking rights.

Although Île Sainte-Marie and its thriving booty trade was certainly no Libertalia, its influence lasted long after the original pirates had gone. Kevin Rushby, who is probably the only writer on Libertalia to have actually travelled to Madagascar, spoke to direct descendents of pirates from the coast around Île Sainte-Marie. It is known that many pirates had married local women and made a mixed offspring called the *zana-mulatto*, for whom a cemetery still exits near the old pirate fort in Fenoarivo. According to one of Rushby's informants, one such pirate was Adam James, their ancestor, who arrived around 1720 and fell in with the local chief, Ratsimilaho. Befriending many pirates, the chief united the various groups of the region into the Betsimisaraka tribe (those who stand together), later dominating the whole northeast region, including Ranter Bay, the Bay of Antongila, Fenoarivo, and Île Sainte-Marie. Ratsimilaho's daughter and heir, Princess Bety, married a shipwrecked Frenchman and was given Île Sainte-Marie as a wedding gift but later handed over sovereignty to the King of France after Ratsimilaho's death in 1750. Nevertheless the Betsimisaraka, some having descended from pirates, later took up the black flag in their own style and from 1795 onwards organised war canoe raiding parties of up to 10,000 men that sacked the Comoros Islands and the Mozambique coastline, making slaves of the inhabitants.

A far cry from Misson's emancipatory Libertalia, the legacy of the pirates of Madagascar's east coast at least certifies the genuine existence and longevity of pirate communities in that region. It also adds weight to the idea that Libertalia was real, because so many pirate havens existed in that area at the time. The location of our supposed pirate utopia, Antsiranana, offered the safest natural harbour in the Indian Ocean and was remote from 'civilisation' by both land and sea. Any sailor worth his rum could look at a chart of the waters around Madagascar and pinpoint Antsiranana as an ideal ocean anchorage, and few would doubt that pirates would have settled there, if anywhere at all.

Madagascar's old charms – safe anchorage, isolation, lack of government, cheap rum, pretty natives, etc – never really disappeared and it still seems to hold its charm to sailors as a great place to exchange one's national identity for the pirate lifestyle. On the north coast, a little further west of Antsiranana, Russian Bay takes its name from a twentieth-century Russian warship, the *Vlotny*, which was posted there in 1905 during the Russo-Japanese war, but never returned. Upon arrival, having clapped eyes on the beautiful land and its native women, the entire crew lost the will to return to Russia, and made their home there. Keeping with tradition, they briefly took to piracy before running out of fuel and then scrapped the ship for bits to trade. They might well have chosen Antsiranana as their bay of choice but it was the Madagascan base for the operations of the French Navy at the time. Nevertheless, it is interesting to note that, much like Misson's Liberi, the Russians never integrated themselves with the local Sakalava people and so died without heirs, quite unlike the pirates and the Betsimisaraka people in the northeast. Trawling the bays and bars of Madagascar for salty characters I didn't have to look far to meet many expat sailors, none of whom could be said to be outright pirates, but some of whom made a nefarious living trading and smuggling throughout the region, and flew a black flag in their hearts.

It's also easy to see why any sailor would want to abandon everything for a life in Madagascar. Aside from its legendary invisible man-eating plants, this forgotten island has no dangerous flora or fauna in its wide and exotic taxonomy (something like 80-90% of which are endemic), and there is an abundance of indigenous fish, fruits and spices upon which to feast. In the rural areas the locals say that even the poorest people never go hungry. The country also boasts some of the cheapest and tastiest rum on the planet, and for us Europeans the local women are frighteningly beautiful. Having finally arrived in Madagascar after our three thousand mile voyage and survived the welcoming tsunami (which, in the end, only amounted to a brief three foot swell), it was with great anticipation that our crew first debarked on the port of Antsiranana (known as Diego-Suarez), home to the mythic Libertalia.

Weirdly enough, a few days before arriving there I'd had a disturbing dream that twenty gorgeous naked black women were standing waist-deep in the ocean by the beach, luring me towards the land with whispered promises of yet more beauties ashore. I'd hailed 'hard to port' to the helmsman but had then had the worrying realisation that the women were probably sirens and awoke with a start thinking I'd driven the ship upon the rocks at the sight of forty naked breasts. It soon surprised me to find that that my Ulyssean dream wasn't that far from the truth. During the following days, the captain had a job keeping focus among the male crew who largely abandoned their concern for repairing and maintaining the ship in favour of getting to know the locals. It seemed that, like Kidd, we would lose half our crew to what remained of Libertalia, and so we set sail – prematurely some would say.

Yet we almost didn't make it out of there, and I'd feared we wouldn't when I heard from a local guide that the young women consulted the spirits, the tromba, and used love magic to win themselves husbands out of white foreigners, vazaha, who they rightly perceived to be much richer than themselves. He wasn't wrong either: I found a recent anthropological study of Madagascar that indicates that the use of love magic to charm victims is currently considered an immoral magical pandemic by the Malagasy. It looked like the sirens were winning when the ship failed to exit the bay on its first attempt (much to the thinly-veiled joy of many of the crew) because the combined wind and swell pushed us backwards into what the expedition chief described as the birth canal of Diego-Suarez bay.

We anchored up by the entrance of the bay for the night and I used my turn on watch to improvise a ritual to the Chinese junkmen's favourite god, 'Lung Wang, the Dragon King, chief of the gods of water and rain', to whom I'd been mumbling propitiations ever since we left Sumatra. Appropriately enough I'd picked some leaves of the Dragon Tree (*Agavaceae dracaena*) whilst on shore because I'd read in a dodgy

The Bliss Tree

guidebook that the local Malagasy called it the Bliss Tree, considered it sacred, and chewed its leaves for psychoactive effect. So I munched on the bitter green leaves while calling on Lung Wang for favourable winds the next day. No bliss or altered state was forthcoming, though I shouldn't have been surprised because I later learnt I was chewing on a common European houseplant. However, the dragon responded in our favour and we were able to sneak out of the calm bay early the next morning, avoiding actually washing up on the rocks in the wind as we nearly had the day before. The sirens' spell was broken.

Fortunately, before departing I'd had the opportunity to explore Antsiranana and the surrounding area, finding many ruins of old unidentified buildings all around the immediate coast, and was informed of vast unexplored cave systems near the mouth of the bay. Yet there remained no solid evidence of the Liberi pirates, even though their legacy lingered everywhere, parodied in the paintings of buccaneers on the town walls and in the obligatorily named bar, Libertalia (many of which can be found in Madagascar). Indeed, oral histories, albeit of unknown origin, of Misson's visit were still available on the Comoron island of Anjoun, according to Kevin Rushby. More than that though, the spirit of Libertalia seemingly remained here, loosely speaking, in the personality of the people. The women seemed fiercely independent, and the men appeared happily nonchalant and apparently cared for little more than a merry life. On the whole the Malagasy we had met were happy, bawdy and bold.

Nevertheless, whether Libertalia was real or not its anarchic spirit also seems to have somehow percolated into the people in the form of local politics, or the apparent lack of them. Having recently been sacked from Yale, seemingly for his own anarchist views, anthropologist David Graeber has illustrated how the contemporary Malagasy are almost defined by their outright distrust of politicians. Such an attitude appears to have been fostered since the abolition of slavery when the native aristocracy and commoners were financially levelled through colonial-induced poverty. Among the people, to be trusted to make any kind of legitimate political decision requires that you must first have been dead for several years, with most important decisions being made solely by the ancestors. Conveniently this is done through spirit mediums. To the Madagascan people, all forms of power exerted by the living have come to be associated with slavery. Consequently, Madagascar has remained virtually static as a developing nation because the people's passive resistance to any type of hierarchical coercion has rendered the government practically impotent – anarchy through applied apathy. In Madagascar, the only good politician is a dead one, and preferably dead for a long time.

Misson would no doubt have been proud of present day Madagascar, a nation of relative equality, the population largely descended from slaves (and occasionally pirates), anarchic and apparently emancipated from the sexual repressions of religion. It's a place where almost anyone is capable of surviving on the bounty of the land, and where the only trusted politicians have long been dead. In fact it is a place that could live up to the title ascribed to it by the English utopianist, Walter Hamond, who visited it in 1640 as a ship's

surgeon and wrote a tract entreating people to come here entitled *A Paradox Proving That the Inhabitants of the Isle called Madagascar… are the Happiest People in the World.*

Misson and Libertalia might not have existed, but the idea of Libertalia had beckoned me to sail there as surely as it did Tew and his crew and those of Captain Kidd. Aside from whatever islands of hope have emerged here from the foggy sea of historical mystery, all I can really go on is the feeling of the place – even if searching for Misson and Libertalia now might amount to nothing more than hunting for the long dead ghosts of fictitious characters, imagined by a fictitious author.

Viva Libertalia!

Revolutionary Spirit Wars in Contemporary Haiti

Text and photographs by
JOHN CUSSANS

The Case of the Monumental Pig

N December 2009 I was a participant in the Ghetto Biennale, an event organised by Leah Gordon and the Atis Rezistans group from the Grand Rue area of Port-au-Prince, Haiti. I had been invited because of a number of texts I had written about western representations of vodou; the history of zombies; and a complex set of correlations that linked the writings of the French surrealist philosopher Georges Bataille to the revolutionary history of Haiti. My interest in Haiti derives from the images of voodoo that made their way to me through the vectors of mainstream mass media and popular horror during my childhood in 1970s Britain.[1]

The diabolical seeds that were planted during my regular Friday night 'Appointments with Fear' led me on an a twisted academic path that found me, in the 1990s, writing a doctoral thesis about the 'video nasty' controversy from a theoretical perspective based on the writings of Bataille (or 'the Ian Brady

1. It is interesting to note how closely the representation of the vodou ceremony in Freddie Francis' *Dr. Terror's House of Horrors* (1965) – a film which deeply impressed my childhood imagination and kept me awake for weeks to come after watching it – coincides with one of the first ethnographic accounts of a vodou ceremony reported in Moreau de Saint-Mery's *Descriptions of the French Part of the Island of Saint Domingue* (1787) (translated by Spencer as *A Civilization that Perished – The Last Years of Colonial Rule in Haiti* (1985)).

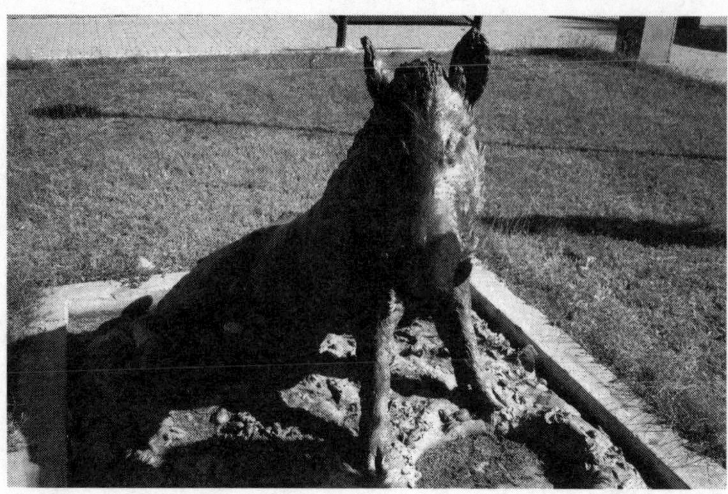

of social theory', as one of my supervisors memorably and unfairly referred to him).

It was towards the completion of my thesis that Haiti came to the fore of my research interests. I had been trying to understand how Bataille's theory of sacred revolution – understood as a massive, *acephalic* (headless), collective expenditure of social wealth, triggered by sacred ritual – could be applied to commodified representations of violent excess such as those incarnated in videos like *Cannibal Holocaust* (1980) or *I Spit on Your Grave* (1978), which had been banned in the UK in the 1980s amidst fears about their detrimental influence on young people.[2]

The clearest correlation I could find was in the metaphor of mass (mediated) contagions of destructive delirium which was

2. Video Nasty was a popular term used by the British tabloid press to identify a number of low-budget, very violent horror films available in rentable video formats in the 1980s. The films were considered to be in breach of the Obscene Publications Act (1959) which was being circumvented by the new media format. The campaign led to the prosecution of 39 films for obscenity and the establishment of the Video Recording Act of 1984.

characteristic of both Bataille's theory of revolution and the fears expressed by censors who believed that video nasties were capable of transforming 'suggestible' young people into sociopathic delinquents who could bring British society to the brink of moral chaos.[3]

Bataille's 'base materialist' theory of revolution insisted on the fundamentally dualistic nature of the sacred, moving between the poles of pure, ideal, productive and 'Good' elements and the abject, base, destructive and 'Evil' ones. For Bataille the deeply contagious energy of the sacred is constantly 'channelled' for the maintenance of social order.[4]

Energy of the sacred

It was the magnetic metaphor underpinning the left and right-handed polarities of the sacred, along with Bataille's insistence of the materialist foundations of his theory, that orientated me in the direction of 'animal magnetism'. I traced fears of 'diabolical' mass-mediated contagion back through nineteenth century theories of crowd psychology and mass influence (which accompanied the emergence of the mass media) to the work of Anton Mesmer in the late eighteenth century.

In Henri F Ellenberger's *The Discovery of the Unconscious* – a classic account of Mesmer's life, the subsequent history of Mesmerism

3. In *The Video Nasties: Freedom and Censorship in the Media* (1984) Martin Barker points out that these claims were influenced by the social unrest that followed in the wake of the Brixton riots in 1981. Although there was no causal link between the two phenomena an imaginary association was made by the government and popular news media at the time.

4. In *Theory of Religion* Bataille argues that the archaic dualism of the sacred undergoes a fundamental alteration with the development of monotheistic militarism and imperialism. The two poles of the sacred are clearly separated such that the divine is imagined to be the domain of the pure, ideal and transcendental aspects of the sacred while the base, sinister and malefic elements become associated with materiality and profanity. It is the forces of malefic sacred materialism that Bataille believed must be activated against the universal moral order of Reason and Divine Right which reduces all human beings to servicing its delusional productive ends.

and hypnosis, and their role in the development of dynamic psychiatry – I came across the following quote:

> *In Saint Domingue (pre-Revolutionary Haiti) Magnetism degenerated into a psychic epidemic amongst the Negro slaves, increasing their agitation, and the French domination ended in a bloodbath. Later Mesmer boasted that the new Republic, now called Haiti, owed its independence to him.*

Mesmerism in Haiti

Mesmerism[5] was brought to Saint Domingue by the youngest of three brothers from the aristocratic Puységur family. Count Chastenet de Puységur arrived in Saint Domingue in July 1784 on a cartographic mission to plot the coast of the island. His two elder brothers were already famous devotees of animal magnetism in France. Armand-Marie-Jacques (Marquis de Puységur) is widely credited as the inventor of 'artificial somnambulism' or hypnotism. He is also reputed to have developed a means of magnetizing trees on his family estate enabling collective healings of his workers, a practice significantly similar to the vodou rituals which take place around sacred Mapou trees in Haiti.

On arrival in Saint Domingue the young Count Chastenet immediately set to work demonstrating the virtues of animal magnetism at the poor house in Cap Français. The miraculous successes of these demonstrations (and the 'sensational' effects of the cure amongst the women of the colonial administration) led to the rapid spread of Mesmerism throughout the northern part of the colony. Enthusiastic slave-owners reputedly used the practice to re-

5. Mesmer's theory of animal magnetism was based on the assumption of a vital, ethereal fluid permeating all physical bodies, from planets to molecules, which, when blocked, caused ailments of all kinds. The Mesmeric system combined new, 'scientific' theories of magnetic conduction between physical bodies with social networks of involuntary behavioural contagion induced by 'action-at-a-distance'. The theory and practice of animal magnetism resonated with radical political and philosophical ideas that would go on to shape the French Revolution.

invigorate their depleted slave properties in order to extract further profit from them (McLellan, pp.176-178). At precisely the same time, back in France, Mesmer and his Societies of Harmony had gained a reputation for being hotbeds of revolutionary fervour (see Darnton's *Mesmerism and the End of the Enlightenment in France*) and were subject to an investigation by a Royal Commission intent on discrediting the practice by 'scientifically' disproving the existence of magnetic fluid. The authorities in Saint Domingue, aware of these investigations, cast a sceptical and cautionary eye over the practice as it spread through the colony. Once the practice passed out of the hands of the white elites and into those of the mulattos and blacks, the authorities were quick to act.

The first historian of the colonial period, Moreau de Saint-Mery (whose early 'ethnographic' accounts of vodou were mentioned above) reported that in 1786, in the northern parish of Marmelade, a mulatto named Jérome and his black assistant Télémaque promoted a version of Mesmerism combined with 'magical treatments'. The colonial authorities, no doubt still very concerned about the legacy of Mackandal (an influential herbalist, poisoner, vodouist and leader of a series of rebel Maroon uprisings against the French plantation owners in the 1750s) aggressively suppressed this new brand of 'Creole Mesmerism' (McLellan's term), condemning Jérome to the galleys and Télémaque to public pillory. According to his biographer, DM Walmsely, it was due to events at this time that Mesmer made his notorious claim that the black slaves' confusion of animal magnetism with 'black magic' had led to their revolutionary uprising.

Mesmer's claim coincides perfectly, from a Bataillian perspective, with the accepted story of the foundational event which triggered the first slave-uprising of the Haitian revolution: the ceremony of Bois Caïman. This signal event in the history of Haitian independence took place on 14 August 1791 in Alligator Woods, on the northern plains of Saint Domingue, the site of Mackandal's sermons before his capture and execution by the French authorities in 1758. During a secret gathering of rebellious slaves and their leaders, presided over by the priest and former slave-driver Dutty Boukman, a vodou ceremony was enacted in which a black pig was sacrificed and a blood oath sworn to the god of the black slaves and to the spirit of Liberty.[6]

The idea of an historical coincidence between a religious ceremony involving blood sacrifice and the channelling of the contagious 'left-handed' forces of the sacred in the name of liberation from slavery with a materialist healing practice channelling blocked, corporeal matter-energy contagiously through human groups was about as Bataillian as a revolutionary historical event could get. And it was in pursuit of this mythical-material and historical coincidence that I found myself in Haiti.

The Story of the Monumental Pig

The designated residence for the international participants in the Ghetto Biennale was the Hotel Oloffson (made famous by Graham Greene's novel *The Comedians*). On my first day there I struck up a conversation with Cameron Brohman, a Canadian artist who was participating in the Biennale with the Brandaid project he had co-founded in 2009.[7]

When I explained to Cameron my reasons for being at the Biennale he recounted a story he had been told by Reginald Jean François, a Haitian-born deportee from the US with whom he was working, about a ceremonial ritual performed by a unit of United Nations military personnel on a sculpture of a pig in downtown Port-

6. There is some controversy concerning the historical facts and cultural significance of the Bois Caïman ceremony, a debate which has been recently re-kindled due to post-earthquake accusations made by Evangelical Christian leaders that Haiti is cursed by God because of a pact made with Satan at that time.

7. Brandaid is a non-profit 'micromarketing' project that supports and promotes the work of artisans in developing countries. At the time of the Biennale Cameron was developing a project which involved establishing a sustainable community of young artisans in the Cité Soleil district of Port-au-Prince who will produce model Tap-Taps – the brightly decorated local buses in Haiti – made from materials gleaned from local landfills.

au-Prince during the early phase of their occupation. After consulting with Reggie, Cameron offered to take me to the site where Reggie could recount the story.

The following is an annotated transcription of the video documentation I shot at the Plaza Italia, Port-au-Prince, on 14 December, during our visit to the monument of the ceremonial pig:

Reggie – So what else do you want to know about the pig?

John – *I'll tell you what I want to know about the pig... there are some things I know about the pig... I know the stuff about Bois Caïman.*

R – Bwa Kayiman?

J – *Bwa Kayiman, oui.*

R – What about it?

J – *Well, that they killed a pig and that set the whole thing off...*

R – No, they ain't killed a pig. The vodou spirits sent the pig for them to sacrifice. The pig couldn't get killed. It was an offering to the demon gods in order for this thing to work, for liberty and freedom and a contract had to be signed.[8]

Nobody killed a pig. The pig was an offering.

J – *By Boukman, right?*[9]

8. The Christian Evangelical notion that Haitians made an historical pact with Satan is popularly referred to as 'The Contract' in Haiti. The story is widely promoted by churches and missionary organizations as a pretext for anti-vodou campaigns there.

9. Dutty Boukman (which translates as 'Dirty Bookman') was a Jamaican born houngan (voudou priest) who presided over the ceremony of Bois Caïman. He was killed by the French shortly after the uprising and his head was displayed to try and dispel rumours about his invincibility among the insurrectionary slaves.

R – Was it by Boukman Cameroon? Boukman was a slave that the French people couldn't kill. They were shooting him, they were sticking knives in this man, they were tying him up, he was always coming out the chain, he was going to war with a big… you know back in the day their handcuffs or their kneecuffs weren't as proper and small as what we have now… they had some big ugly looking stuff with a big ball of iron lead, heavy ball, I mean it could be at least three to four hundred pounds heavy, to move around. So he was very amazing. They ended up killing him though… they figured he couldn't die.[10]

J – *So people know and recognise this pig? Is it the same pig?*

R – It's the pig. You see that pig, if you notice, the pig that we have here right now is not the pig we're going to see now. Coz that's a boar. It has tusks. I don't know what president it was but around thirty something years ago they claimed that all these wild boars we had weren't good for the people of Haiti because they had worms and ate children.[11] But at that time we had no problem with our pigs. So it was

10. Stories about the invincibility of voudou-inspired slave leaders are most strongly associated with François Mackandal who organized mass poisonings of food and water supplies and created a network of secret rebel slave organizations in the 1750s. Haitian folklore tells of how, when the French tried to burn the captured Mackandal, he escaped death by transforming himself into a mosquito. The wave of yellow fever that helped decimate Leclerc's forces during France's attempt to regain control of the colony in 1804 is believed by some to have been the work of the spirit of Mackandal. In 1758 a law was passed to prohibit the use of makandals, one of the terms used by the French authorities to describe 'magical weapons', pwens or 'body-guards' (McAlister, p.121).

11. In 1978, during the Presidency of Jean-Claude 'Baby Doc' Duvalier, the indigenous Haitian pig was diagnosed as having African Swine Fever and, under pressure from the US government, the population was almost entirely eradicated and replaced by an American pig that cost as much to feed as a Haitian human. See Leah Gordon's 1997 documentary film *A Pig's Tail*.

a way that the American government was trying to destroy the Haitian meat programme. These pigs could survive on anything. They won't get sick and we could eat them and we wouldn't get sick. So they said that we don't have enough knowledge. But it's a lie though. You guys have got cameras right, we've had that. It's all in the voudou. I have a mirror and I can conjure a spell and I want to see where you are and I can see you through that mirror from the invisible realm. And these guys said we weren't good enough, we were stupid, we were ignorant, we didn't know Jack Diddly about anything. So they have white magic, which is that, and we have black magic, which is something else that they can't understand.

J – *So you think this [the video camera] is a power tool?*

R – Of course! Do you have the brain to create something like this? You have to be inspired by something invisible and it's called the white magic. It comes from the white man. Do you have the brain to create a satellite to roam the space and having a solar panel on it to keep it energised? This is not things from men. This is from spirits with powers, from angels, and they will give you the knowledge, the know-how, just like they give us the know-how to do things with the mirror. So it's the same world. It's just a different way of doing things. Us, we have a lot of smell, a lot of perfume, and a whole lot of things from the ground, and that mirror will have to be a real secret mirror that no one can see except for the purpose of seeing where your mum or your enemies are. So now they've got it with satellite dishes. This is a real crazy world. The modern world and our world are two different worlds. If you see Richard [Morse] the owner of the Oloffson, he's into white people's art, and he knows the difference between white magic and black magic.

White art & black magic

J – *He's a smart guy.*

R – Richard? Yeh, genius man. The man can see things from another way. If the American CIA want someone to speak all they have to do is put something in their water and start asking them questions and they'll answer. If the Haitian wants you to speak all they have to do is get a demon in you and you'll start speaking. You're going to tell the truth. It's the same thing. They just have different ways about it. That pig down there, that big boar, they said let's get all them pigs out of here. Guess what. The new pigs we have, they can't survive in that garbage. Before you know it they get sick and die, they need shots, they need doctors, they need all sorts of stuff. They can't eat garbage. Our old pigs could eat all that and stay strong and ask for more. The new one won't. For real! Our old pig would get in that garbage and eat all that up. Just like a goat can eat anything, the old pig eat more than anything.

J – *So people are aware of this. So what are the UN doing?*[12]

R – The UN are more aware of the Haitian history because the Haitians are not educated.

So they won't go the library and pick up a book and start reading about their history. But, what our parents will do is this: they will tell us about the story, from word to word, from way back till now. The reason they are calling us a third world or fourth world whatever – a dimensional different world from the real world – is that we're still living two hundred years ago, like we're here two hundred years later, that's our mentality.

Cameron – *So what did the UN do?*

R – The UN? They came over here…

12. In February 2004, shortly after the 2nd ousting of President Jean Bertrand Aristide, the UN drafted a Security Council resolution to send a multi-national force to Haiti for three months 'to help to secure and stabilize the capital, Port-au-Prince, and elsewhere in the country' (UN Security Council resolution 1529). This was followed by the creation of MINUSTAH (United Nations Stabilization Mission in Haiti) in June 2004.

C – *With the pig.*

R – With the pig?

C – *Yeh.*

R – Well… we have the Sri Lankans, the Jordanians, the Bangladeshis who came to war here in 2004 with the Chimeres.[13] The UN said 'Hold on. These guys have vodou!' They couldn't understand why they couldn't stop a bunch of untrained guys with guns, roaming the streets and warring with them when they're well-equipped and well-trained. So what the Sri Lankans did was go down to the pig

13. The term Chimere was used after the ousting of President Aristide in 2004 to describe armed gangs of his supporters from the poor neighbourhoods of Port-au-Prince. It is a very controversial term in the recent politics of Haiti. Traditionally a deeply pejorative swear word meaning violent 'monster', 'ghoul' or 'ghost', it was widely used in Haiti to describe the worst kind of person. It was also used specifically by the wealthy elites as a derogatory term to describe very poor and unemployed people. In 'Epithets without Borders' Richard Sanders claims that the term was part of the military linguistic arsenal used to vilify and dehumanize the enemy during the ousting of Aristide.

monument with drums, guitars, violins and rattles and all sorts of stuff and they started singing to the pig. And after they started singing to the pig, they put strange markings on it, weird markings.

See that's the ceremonial pig right there.

You see all them strange markings on him? They were never there. The American folk they destroy all that pig. They're like 'this pig is bad pig'. So they gave us new pigs. But the new pig is not that strong. They can't survive the heat. But this pig survive everything, except human beings. So humans killed the pig. But when the UN came here in 2004, the Sri Lankans came in military clothes and robes, like the Arabs does, and they came here and started singing and playing drums to the pig, and we were all around looking at this, and to me this was strange because these guys have a gun mission, to come here with the guns, stop the bad guys, kill 'em, put them to jail and then go back home. But these guys were doing some strange stuff. See that, that's a cross and that's a mark on the ear. They're tying this pig up because they believe the monumental pig[14] still has certain powers that have the Haitian folks going crazy. Look around the leg. They're tying it up with their mystical powers. You see the back? This is a cross in red graffiti. When it was fresher you could see better the other stuff they put on. They want the pig to slow down. They cornered the pig down, all four sides. They're not playing. They're stopping the pig from the North, East, West and South. To them this pig exists right here in the spirit world. That's why it's got its monument here.

14. The sculpture is one of several bronze replicas of the Florentine Boar (or *Il Porcellino*). The sculpture in the Mercato Nuovo in Florence is itself a replica of the original, which was a bronze copy of a Hellenistic marble original. Visitors to *Il Porcellino* put coins into its mouth for good luck and rub its nose to ensure their return to Florence. I have not been able to ascertain how and when the replica arrived in Haiti and whether or not the monument is associated by local people with the pig sacrificed in the Bois Caïman ceremony. However some Evangelical accounts about 'The Contract' claim that Haitians worship an iron effigy of the pig. I have as yet found no evidential support for these claims.

So that's the story of the pig. This guy here he's blind right. He's going round the pig and he wants some money. See if I was lying I'd be dying by now because I can see what happened in 2004 and he's doing it now. It's no coincidence that they keep playing music to the pig. Believe me man! It's straight jacket. And not just them. We had some Baptist missionaries who came around 1988/9. They were playing Christian music to the pig and they were putting their hands upon the pig and cursing it: 'In Jesus' name you big fat pig get out of here! We're chasing you off.' If you think I'm lying this is where I sell mahogany and wood carving, right there. I'm here 24/7, except three or four months from now. I haven't been around lately, coz I'm doing work over at the airport. But this is where my shop, my paintings, my mahogany and things go, right there.

He ain't gonna stop until you pay him for that pig man. That thing is real.

BIBLIOGRAPHY

Martin Barker (Ed.) *The Video Nasties: Freedom and Censorship in the Media* (1984) Pluto: London

Georges Bataille. *Theory of Religion* (1989) Zone Books: New York

Robert Darnton. *Mesmerism and the End of the Enlightenment in France* (1968) Harvard University Press: Cambridge, Mass

David Geggus. *Haitian Revolutionary Studies* (2002) Indiana University Press: Bloomington

Elizabeth McAlister Rara. *Vodou, Power and Performance in Haiti and its Diaspora* (2002) University of California Press: Berkeley

James E McLellan. *Colonialism and Science – Saint Domingue in the Old Regime* (1992) John Hopkins University Press: London

Moreau de Saint-Mery. *A Civilization that Perished – The Last Years of White Colonial Rule in Haiti* (1985) Translated, Abridged and Edited by Ivor D Spencer, University Press of America

DM Walmsley. *Anton Mesmer* (1967) Hale: London

THE UNDERWORLD OF THE EAST

BEING EIGHTEEN YEARS' ACTUAL EXPERIENCES OF THE UNDERWORLDS, DRUG HAUNTS AND JUNGLES OF INDIA, CHINA, AND THE MALAY ARCHIPELAGO

N FIRST encountering James Lee's 1935 memoirs *The Underworld of the East*, with their alluring subtitle, the modern reader can be forgiven for entertaining doubts about their authenticity. Too many details and incidents seem contrived with a twenty-first century sensibility in mind; episode after episode reads like a deft modern pastiche or postmodern hoax. It is not merely that Lee's most distinctive trope, his enthusiasm for drugs, fits so much more closely with our times than with his own. In between his accounts of smoking, swallowing and injecting as many mind-altering substances as he can find, he strolls between deliriously exotic escapades: one moment pitted against a man-eating tiger, the next forming the first motorcycle gang in Calcutta. Even on returning to dismal and repressed Edwardian England, he finds himself demonstrating sterile needle techniques to cocaine-addicted prostitutes before hallucinating a turbanned Hindu gentleman in the ticket queue at Piccadilly Circus station. Throughout his narrative, he carries the sulphurous whiff of a character from William Burroughs' fictional rogues' gallery: the insouciant junkie

by MIKE JAY
Illustration by NATHALIE TAYTON

explorer, the hard-bitten colonial renegade trailing his native wife and opium pipe. Indeed, the suspicious reader might even recall that Lee, the maiden name of Burroughs' mother, was the *nom de plume* under which he originally published his first book, *Junky*.

The improbable sense of modernity is enhanced, too, by the way that Lee seems to have escaped from the straitjacket of his era's prejudices. From the moment he arrives in the East, Lee ignores the colonial form of distancing oneself from the locals 'by affecting to consider them as inferiors'; he shows a ravenous appetite for immersing himself in the local culture, and promptly marries a local woman whom he subsequently treats just as he would a European wife. The standard racial epithets of the period, such as 'nigger' or 'coolie', are conspicuous by their absence, and his comparisons between cultures are mostly to the disadvantage of the West. 'These people work for no-one', he observes in India, while back home 'the greater part of our population are wage-slaves, at the beck and call of their masters… of what benefit is our civilisation to ninety percent of the people, if it brings them barely enough of the coarsest food and cheapest shoddy clothing?'

But it is his refusal to conform to his contemporaries' attitudes to drugs that has guaranteed *Underworld*'s survival. Most drug literature of the late nineteenth and early twentieth centuries offers meagre rewards to the modern reader, consisting as it does of polite variations on conventions that had formed half a century previously, and had only become more anaemic in the interim. Typically, dark hints of the subject matter are relied on to sustain the reader's curiosity; when drugs appear, they are whisked on and off stage in a moment, discreetly draped in the paraphrase of 'forbidden acts' or 'unmentionable vices', after which their ruinous consequences are hammered home in moralising narratives of temptation and self-destruction. Lee, by contrast, is frank, even forensic in his testimony. His goal is to describe the administration and effects of all the drugs he takes as explicitly as possible, to develop his theme that 'the life of a drug taker can be a happy one, far surpassing that of any other, or it can be one of suffering and misery; it depends on the user's knowledge'.

Dark hints & forbidden acts

His failure to engage with the self-censoring conventions of Victorian drug literature is, more than likely, because he never bothered to read any of it. Lee was not a man of letters but a jobbing technical engineer from the industrial heartlands of northern England. His is not the work of an author aspiring to a literary career, but of someone who believes the maxim that everybody has one book in them. The familiar drug literature of the period tends, either self-consciously or reflexively, to follow the templates of Thomas de Quincey and Charles Baudelaire in the assumption that only those already possessed of a spark of genius can expect it to ignite under the influence; but Lee has no urge to demonstrate that he is more interesting than the next man, simply to share the fact that he's having a more interesting time. In de Quincey's famous formulation, the pains of his Faustian pact are doomed always to outweigh the pleasures, just as for Baudelaire drugs are a 'forbidden game' that can only lead to self-destruction. Lee's mission, by contrast, is to separate the pleasures from the pains, to pass on to his readers the techniques that will allow them to do the same, and to put drugs aside painlessly when the time comes to do so. As William Burroughs observed in 1990, Lee's cheerful pragmatism is 'a refreshing departure from the repentant whine of cured addicts'.

The insistently practical tone of his book is consistent with his line of work, which is also what led him to his travels in the East. Born in Kirkleatham in Yorkshire in 1873, James Sidney Lee worked as a draughtsman in the steelworks of Sheffield and Teesside before, in 1894, deciding that the life of a British worker was not for him. 'I was getting fed up with life in England', he tells us. 'There was too much sameness about it: a place where there is little real freedom, and one had to do just as the next fellow did. To wear the same kind of clothes, with a collar and tie, and talk about football or horse-racing or be considered no sport… these were just some of the things that I found irksome'. He applied for jobs on engineering and mining projects in the colonies, and it was on his first posting, to Assam on the north-east Indian frontier, that he discovered morphine and cocaine, opium and hashish, and began to cultivate his drug use as a 'hobby' that led him to curious and fascinating experiences, both cultural and psychic, and around which he increasingly structured his peripatetic career.

It was certainly unusual for someone of Lee's background to publish a forthright account of his drug use, but its existence makes it seem likely that he was not alone in such pursuits, and that adventures of his type are underrepresented in the historical record. The ease with which he encountered drugs in the colonies and the interest they held for him suggests that his sanguine self-medication may have been more widespread at the time than the familiar sources imply. These sources are heavily skewed towards literary accounts, obedient to the conventions of the genre and often produced by authors with no first-hand experience of the drugs about which they were writing. Even those who wrote from experience were a self-selecting sample, well aware of the accepted boundaries of taste in the literary market.

But his account is atypical in more than literary terms: it stands in arresting contrast to the portrait of drugs that was being assembled in the wider worlds of medicine and politics, and from which the criminalisation of these substances was shortly to emerge. Throughout the nineteenth century, mind-altering drugs had been thoroughly investigated by writers, artists and scientists, and opium, cocaine and cannabis had been widely available from pharmacists and liberally included in household medicines. But it was precisely during the period spanned by Lee's adventures, from the 1890s to the First World War, that they were reconceived in terms of plague and degeneration, and serious attempts to prohibit their use began; and it was precisely in Lee's *milieu*, where working men and women rubbed shoulders with foreign cultures in the colonies of the East and the ports, slums and Chinatowns of the West's cities, that such anxieties were most acutely focused.

As the nineteenth century drew to its close, the images generated by the fear of 'Oriental contagion' crowded upon one another and became a staple of mass popular culture. It was the opening of

'I was intoxicated *in an entirely new and strange manner and was looking forward to some new experience in the spirit world...'*

Charles Dickens' *Edwin Drood*, serialised in 1870, that first introduced to British readers the vision of the opium den concealed in the grim tenements of Limehouse and Poplar, around London's docks: stinking alleys, crowded hovels, lice-infested bunks, British, Chinese and Lascar sailors huddled together while an old hag, who had over long years of debauchery 'smoked herself into a strange likeness of the Chinaman', tends the pipe and smears opium dross across its bowl with a filthy brooch-pin. Similar scenes were elaborated across hundreds of fictional and faux-documentary accounts, by popular writers from Oscar Wilde to Arthur Conan Doyle, and luridly illustrated by the likes of Gustave

Doré. The opium den became a terminus of the damned: the free-falling West End roué committing slow suicide a world away from his gambling debts and extra-marital scandals or, increasingly, the chorus girl lured into prostitution and slavery by the Chinese underworld kingpin who found his fictional apotheosis in 1913 in Sax Rohmer's *The Mystery of Fu Manchu*, 'the yellow peril incarnate in one man'.

Such are the images of drugs and Oriental influence that we readily summon from the period today, yet the documentary evidence for them is at best elusive. Dickens' formative account and Doré's familiar image were both embroidered from a visit to the home of a well-known Anglo-Chinese couple in Shadwell, and thereafter the Chinese opium den took on a fictional life of its own. Although opium was widely available in potions and tinctures on every high street, the spectre of Europeans corrupted into the drug habit by shadowy Orientals functioned as a symbol for wider concerns. Religious temperance campaigners feared the prospect of an urban underclass surrendering to narcotics along with cheap gin; doctors feared the self-medication regimes of the ignorant running out of control in the free-for-all marketplaces of the metropolis; missionaries warned of Chinese revenge for the predatory British role in the Opium Wars; and the urban middling classes were terrified by the teeming, unfamiliar, multicultural ports and red light districts proliferating on their doorsteps. The use of drugs – along with their alarming new technology, the hypodermic needle – was indeed spreading, not least among doctors and their clientele; but the image of contagion through the vector of foreign and 'inferior' races gave urgency to the view that such drugs needed to be prohibited before they could infect the healthy mainstream of society.

Oriental contagion

It is against this background that James Lee offers such an intriguing corrective to the received image. His first contact with drugs occurs shortly after his arrival in Assam, where he is working as mechanical engineer in a coalmine, maintaining outdated hauling machinery while guarded by a company of Gurkhas against hostile Naga hill tribes. Suffering a bout of malaria, he is attended by 'a fat and jolly Hindoo of about forty years of age' whom he refers to henceforth as Dr Babu. The doctor produces an object Lee has never seen before, a hypodermic syringe, and slides it into his patient's arm. 'I will never forget that first injection', Lee recalls; 'I was simply purring with content'. Dreamily, he asks Dr Babu what the medicine is, and receives the reply: 'It is morphia, the most useful medicine in the world'.

Babu's approach to prescribing is decidedly liberal. He leaves Lee with a syringe and a tube of quarter-grain tablets, explaining the need for clean needles to avoid septicaemia but apparently not bothering to mention the risk of addiction. Within a few weeks, Lee is accustomed to his relaxing morphine shot in the evening after work, but has also developed the junkie's perennial curse: chronic constipation. This, combined with his increasing doses, makes him decide to curtail his habit; but he soon discovers that this is easier said than done. 'Pride and fear made me stick to my intention', he records, but the fidgets, pains, cramps and insomnia eventually send him back to Dr Babu. 'Sir', Babu elaborates, 'Morphia is a very strange medicine, it is both Heaven and Hell. It is very difficult to give up, but it can be done'. At which he pops Lee's arm with half a grain of cocaine.

The effect of this is immediate euphoria, 'joy and good spirits'; the doctor leaves him with more, and the instruction to replace the morphia gradually with cocaine until he is weaned from it. This is the controversial 'cocaine cure for morphinism' that was widely touted in the 1890s, and indeed had been pioneered in 1886 by the young Sigmund Freud, who had attempted to cure his friend Ernst Fleischl's morphine addiction in this way. Fleischl, a chronic and nervous addict, had spiralled into chaotic cocaine use, and Freud's reputation had been badly tarnished as a result; but for Lee, impatient to get rid of an inadvertently acquired dependency, the regime was an effective one. Its main drawback was that cocaine interrupted his sleep, but for this the resourceful Babu had another answer. 'Perhaps because I treated him differently from the way most Europeans treated the educated Indian', the doctor invited Lee back to his home to smoke a few pipes of opium, which 'procured a sound and refreshing sleep'.

Lee settled into an equilibrium with these three drugs, shuttling between periods of use and abstention from each, and permitting himself the occasional 'regular binge' on cocaine. Over the next few months he saw a great deal more of the subcontinent, and discovered more drugs. He took a trip to Calcutta, where he immersed himself in the crowds and markets, and to Benares, where he found the Ganges a remarkable sight but the magic of the fakirs rather tawdry ('the Indian rope trick is a fable, and never has been done and never will be done, and the man who says he has seen it is a foolish person'). In Lucknow, he found opium eaten rather than smoked ('a very crude habit') and also discovered hashish with which, in large doses combined with cocaine, he gradually achieved the ability to hallucinate vividly and at will.

An unusual body of knowledge

As Lee continued his travels, he came to realise that his body of knowledge was an unusual one, combining as it did the Oriental familiarity with drugs and the Western scientific understanding of them. The medical knowledge he had acquired from Babu he passed on to others, both European and Oriental. Posted to Sumatra and assigned to turn a mangrove-choked river into a loading wharf, jetty and rail-head for a coalmine being opened in the interior, he spends a long rainy season with a Chinese trader who smokes opium every morning and moans about his miserable addiction every afternoon. Lee frees him from his 'living death' by introducing him to new drugs, 'and soon he was like a new man; full of life and happiness; eating well; and then he sent to Singapore for a new wife'. But Lee was also conscious that much of what he was seeking from these drugs was outside the medical frame, and required him to formulate his own rules by self-experiment. He began to suspect, too, that places like the jungles of Sumatra might be home to entirely novel plant drugs, equally outside the scope of Western science and Oriental lore.

Here, then, is a full and thorough account of a member of the

British working classes acquiring the drug habit from Oriental sources, and it differs from the familiar narrative in almost every respect. In place of 'contagion' we find informed curiosity; in place of exploitation, a respectful reciprocity; in place of degradation, a complex and mutually beneficial cultural exchange. By the same token Lee's story, as it develops, challenges the familiar assumptions about the reasons for taking these drugs, and the uses to which they are put. The drug 'habit' is not his doomed destination, but a pitfall to be avoided if the pleasure he derives from them is to be maintained; the danger they present to him is not uncontrolled craving but boredom and over-familiarity. He is not seeking oblivion: his interest is not in the drugs themselves but in their power to intensify his engagement with life, and to reveal and explore unsuspected dimensions of mind. As his story progresses, brief chapters with titles such as 'Strange Waking Dreams' and 'Strange Thoughts and Visions' record the peaks of such experience, and the philosophy of life that begins to emerge from them: an 'Evolutionary Law' whereby all organisms, including human societies, tend towards greater aggregation and complexity, and through which Christian morality, Oriental *karma* and secular rationalism are all ultimately destined to fuse together into a single ethical principle: 'there will be only one sin, the doing of an injury or injustice to another'.

Strange thoughts & visions

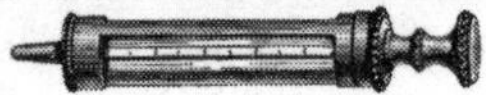

By the time he wrote *Underworld of the East* in the early 1930s James Lee had, by his own account at least, abandoned his use of drugs. 'When the Dangerous Drugs Act came into force' in 1920, he informs us drily, 'I gave up using all drugs, because the danger and risk of obtaining them was too great. The paltry quantities, about which the authorities make such a fuss, were of no use to me, and I was able to give them up without any trouble or suffering'. His 'hobby' had been a discreet activity, but not a shameful one: a personal voyage of discovery, encouraged by some doctors and disapproved by others, to be undertaken without advertisement to society at large. The prospect of immersing himself in

Crucified by Dacoits, *above, was one of several plates included in the first edition of* The Underworld of the East *(1935). They appear to have been included by the publisher rather than the author: most are stock shots of villages, cities and 'natives' with only a vague relation to the text. This is by far the most arresting, and accompanies Lee's narrative of a motorcycle and camping trip through the wilds of north-east India, during which he apprehended a grease-smeared robber (dacoit) stalking through the camp at night ('I knew that it was not a drug-induced vision, as I was not in the right condition for seeing these').*

a criminal underworld to pursue it had limited appeal.

An unspoken tragedy

There is, however, an unspoken component to the final act of his story which, despite its gravity, Lee mentions only in passing. His wife Mulki, whom he met shortly after his arrival in Assam – before Dr Babu, and the beginning of his drug career – is a silent but steadfast presence throughout his narrative. He marries her, rescuing her from the choice between an arranged marriage or a life of hard labour in the mines, and she accompanies him on many of his travels. She joins him on his most isolated posting in the Sumatran jungle; she returns to England with him on several occasions, and even meets Queen Victoria outside Buckingham Palace: 'Queen Victoria spoke to her in Hindustani, and asked all particulars… she talked quite a while with the Queen, who finally ordered one of the attendants to give Mulki a five-shilling piece, and told her to make it into a brooch'. They tour England together: Mulki is rapidly bored by 'old places', but loves the amusements of Blackpool, 'which she never tired of talking about for ever afterwards'. But all these adventures are overshadowed by Lee's bald statement, on the reader's first acquaintance with her, that 'Poor girl, she died suddenly in London, while we were staying at a small private hotel in Bow Lane, Cheapside in 1915, from an overdose of some drug, I think morphia'.

This is a tragedy that hovers over the rest of the book, but is not mentioned further beyond a promise to discuss it in a second volume that was never to emerge. Yet it is also mysterious: Lee's vagueness about the drug responsible is uncharacteristic at the best of times, and particularly in the context of his wife's death. However, the coroner's report of the inquest into her death, which took place in London on 30 November 1914, suggests that Lee's reticence was due to the highly charged circumstances that surrounded it. Only a few months earlier, hardening medical attitudes to drug use had been given statutory force with the criminalisation of opium, morphine and cocaine under the wartime emergency powers of the Defence of the Realm Act, and Mulki's death is an early and devastating example of their human cost.

In his deposition to the inquest, Lee laid out his and his wife's shared history of drug use. Although he keeps her at arm's length from his 'hobby' throughout his book, explaining at one point that 'she had not learned to use drugs, although she had begged many times for me to allow her, and I was afraid that when I was away she would start with opium, as everywhere around there were natives using it', Mulki had, it transpires, begun using morphine and cocaine in Singapore and had continued, along with Lee, to do so intermittently for the next twenty years. In the autumn of 1914, while they were living together in Cheapside, Lee had found that despite the recent ban there were still several chemists in London selling both drugs, and he had bought a supply from Ray's pharmacy in Holborn without any questions asked. Back at the hotel, Mulki had just injected some cocaine when 'she suddenly lost consciousness'. Lee 'carried her downstairs to the office and saw the manager', but 'a doctor could not be got'; after attempting to bring her round with artificial respiration and brandy, he drove her to the local Boots chemist, but he 'could not do anything' either. Lee then took her on to St Bartholemew's Hospital, where they saw a doctor named William Thompson, who decided to inject her with more morphine and cocaine. At this point, according to Lee, she was 'alive and breathing'; but within minutes she was dead.

Dr Thompson's deposition disputes this sequence of events. According to him, Mulki was already dead on arrival, having 'died perhaps on the way'. Lee was 'very upset and giving her artificial respiration'; Thompson gave her morphine and cocaine, he claims, on her husband's request, though Lee makes no mention of this and his knowledge of their effects makes it seem unlikely. In the doctor's stated opinion, she died 'of heart failure' rather than from his injection: 'her habit of injection of these drugs cocaine and morphine would quite account for it'. The coroner's eventual verdict was misadventure – 'cardiac failure, result of her habits of injecting morphine and cocaine' – rather than medical malpractice.

Lee, it seems, did not take the matter further, and chose not even to air it in his book twenty years later. If his sequence of events is correct, however, Mulki was killed by the injection of a doctor who understood the drugs in question less well than his patient, and used their illegal status to absolve himself from blame. But Lee must have recognised that the word of a habitual drug user against that of a medical professional could only lead to one conclusion; and indeed the verdict, once delivered, was swiftly patched into the familiar template. The following day's edition of *The Times* reported the doctor's version of events, stressing that 'like nearly all Indians' Mulki 'was in the habit of taking drugs', adding that Lee 'had himself been taking drugs since 1895', and floating the possibility of suicide. In the public record, the end of Mulki's life would become simply another entry in the sad catalogue of such fatalities, and further evidence for the need to prohibit dangerous drugs.

Lee himself would live to a ripe old age. He seems to have remained single, and never to have had children: the scattered records of his later life show him living with members of his family in Redcar on Teesside, and his will left a modest estate of £775 to his sister, brother and their descendents. He eventually died in London in 1951, at the age of seventy-seven, of a carcinoma of the liver – a condition most likely generated by earlier liver damage, and quite possibly related to his drug use, but one that seems not to have significantly shortened his life.

For details of James Lee's biography I am greatly indebted to the researches of James Gilman and Martin Kelly, who have tracked his life through official documents including birth and death certificates, ships' passenger lists and the extraordinary coroner's report on the death of Mulki, and through interviews with surviving relatives.

From Atlantis to Mars: The Dream of Venus

by KEN HOLLINGS

I. Twilight of the Idols

HE VAMPIRE IS dead, a wooden stake driven through his heart by fearful, determined hands. For centuries he has fastened himself upon this barren mountain region, slowly draining the life out of it. His hunger was legendary, and his powers the stuff of folklore and superstition. Now his reign of terror is over. It will be dawn soon. All of his victims will quickly fade with the coming of a new day. The camera pulls back slowly to reveal the first pale beams of sunlight filtering in through the ruined walls of Castle Dracula. The long nightmare is finally at an end. There should be music playing. The old laboratory, where strange flesh was once given life, is now an empty shell left to gather the dust of ages in weary silence. Its giant transformers, mysterious coils and bulky generators have long since been dismantled and taken elsewhere. The villagers who live in this desolate region can return to their former pursuits, safe in the knowledge that the Mad Baron will no longer be able to continue his foul, ungodly experiments. Even the superstitious old peasant women who once sat around the fire

> *The dream takes us back again to the distant states of human culture and gives us a means by which to understand them better.*
>
> *Friedrich Nietzsche* HUMAN, ALL TOO HUMAN: I, 13

late at night crooning and mumbling to themselves have gone, taking their curses and cries for vengeance with them. It will be some years before anyone hears a werewolf howling at the full moon in Mitteleuropa again.

Over on the other side of the Atlantic, America's love affair with the horror movie dies a quick and painless death in the closing moments of World War II. Calling upon all the monsters at its disposal, Universal Studios bring the cycle to a bloodless conclusion with *House of Dracula* in 1945, the *House of Frankenstein* having already collapsed the previous year. Within a few short months of the Allied victory over Nazi Germany, it is as if Central Europe had never existed on a Hollywood back lot. The sets are struck, the ornate scenery dismantled. Nothing now remains of those quaint foreign villages but their quaint foreign names: Goldstadt, Ingolstadt and Karlstadt. As the camera pans across the abandoned soundstage, illuminated by a few naked spotlights, a last sad and desperate tune is heard fading in on the soundtrack: some final theme of renunciation as Valhalla crumbles to nothing.

Finality is such an inexhaustible concept: it just keeps on coming, revealing how pliable a sense of ending can be. Nobody, as a consequence, remembers the victims of horror movies. The audience always saves its last shudder for the monster. Should it be any different now? Monsters have always served as a warning to others: as portents of what might have been or must never be. In April 1945 Hitler and Goebbels commit suicide in their command bunker located beneath the ravaged streets of Berlin; their bodies are immediately cremated after their deaths. The last of Germany's defences, the ramshackle 'Werewolf Squadrons' made up of young boys and old men, have been unable to hold back the Soviet tide. Atlantis has fallen. In one last, self-destructive gesture of defiance, Joseph Goebbels has ordered the Berlin subway tunnels to be flooded as punishment for the hundreds of families who had sought refuge there. 'The masses need something for the imagination,' Hitler once decreed, 'they need fixed, permanent doctrines. The initiates know that there is nothing fixed, that everything is permanently changing.'

Atlantis has fallen

Endings leave long trails of debris behind them. Folklore and superstition can have no place in this new world of ruins, defeat and plans for the future. Modernism for the masses requires new myths: ones that will distance them from those of the past. From Atlantis to Mars: transition is a means of deferring an unresolved conflict. Caught between the old and the eternal, the modern represents only a moment of temporary respite. The true initiates work the cameras, record the dialogue and edit the final film. It's entirely probable that, when cinema has ceased to maintain itself as an art form, it will continue to survive as music. In this way, its influence will still be felt long after the unstoppable torrents of today's digital regime have swept film away, leaving only a set of downloadable audiovisual components in its wake. Friedrich Schelling's observation, 'Architecture is a frozen music', will acquire new meanings, especially in a world where movie soundtracks outnumber actual movies.

II.

And even in Atlantis of the legend
The night the seas rushed in,
The drowning men still bellowed for their slaves.
– Bertolt Brecht, 'A Worker Reads History', 1928

New eras begin where old ones end. That, at least, is how it should go. As early as 1844, Ralph Waldo Emerson surveys Manhattan's busy skyline and declares that 'America is the country of the future.' The thrusting skyscrapers of New York and the other major cities along the Eastern Seaboard soon become the heroic expression of this vision. Collectively they constitute a citadel of progress, not just for the United States but for the rest of the world as well. They also share a drowned counterpart hidden away below the Atlantic waves. In 1866, as recounted by Jules Verne, the *USS Abraham Lincoln* sets off for its fateful encounter with Captain Nemo's *Nautilus* from the Brooklyn Navy Yard. First published in 1870, Verne's *20,000 Leagues under the Sea* describes an undersea world of wonders, including Red Sea coral reefs, Arctic ice shelves and, most strikingly, the 'long lines of sunken walls and broad deserted streets' of Atlantis – a 'perfect Pompeii escaped beneath the waters', according to the novel's French narrator. Plato's account of an advanced civilization of engineers and architects perishing in 'a day and a night' thousands of years before recorded history haunts the imagination of the industrial age.

Atlantis has always been an unfinished story with a legendary ending, preserved in the deep waters of unconscious memory. American congressman Ignatius Donnelly publishes his best-selling account *Atlantis, the Antedeluvian World* in 1882; the following year Krakatoa erupts, throwing out tidal waves and columns of volcanic ash. By century's end there are already sixteen novels in print that deal with the myth of Atlantis. Although her first major work on religion and science, *Isis Unveiled*, contains only one page on the lost civilization, Madame Blavatsky's *The Secret Doctrine* is a commentary upon 'The Book of Dzyan', a sacred text composed in Atlantis which reveals that humanity is the fifth 'root race' following the Atlanteans in an upward spiritual ascendancy towards more ethereal states of being. In 1896 W Scott-Elliot traces a similar line of evolution from matter to spirit in *The Story of Atlantis*. Two years later, the Martians arrive out of a darkening sky. HG Wells' account of London reduced to an uninhabitable wasteland of stone, glass and steel by invaders from Mars proves too much for *The Boston Evening Post*, which publishes a pirated edition of the novel. Entitled *Fighters from Mars: The War of the Worlds In and Near Boston*, it details the summary defeat of advanced Martian technology by Yankee engineering and knowhow. As if to emphasize the point, a sequel is commissioned from astronomer Garrett P Serviss: *Edison's Conquest of Mars*, in which the great American inventor equips a punitive expedition to Mars with 'electric ships' and disintegration rays. A science reporter for various US newspapers, Serviss packs his thrilling narrative with thinly disguised references to Atlantis. The lifeless remains of Luna, an ancient and advanced civilization, are discovered on the Moon; while the Martians, it transpires, have been busy breeding an Aryan super-race with humans abducted from the 'Vale of Cashmere', a mythical paradise celebrated by the American songwriter Thomas Moore for 'its temples, its grottoes, its fountains as clear, as the love-lighted eyes that hang o'er the wave'. As a native New Yorker, Serviss will no doubt have recalled that the Vale of Cashmere also lends its name to an area of Prospect Park in Brooklyn.

The canals, temples and harbours of Atlantis, not to mention its palaces with indoor 'hot and cold' fountains, find their reflection in the nineteenth-century citadel of progress. No city can be considered modern without a showing of glass, steel and heated water. Industrial plumbing and glazing techniques create exotic public environments such as parks, zoological gardens and aquariums; the fish tank becomes a standard feature in the Victorian home. The mermaid, the water nymph and the lobster serve as reminders of a lost world that the industrial revolution has helped to create. Defined in terms of the technology that sustains it, the exotic transforms culture into a pathological condition. Even as the art critic Walter Pater speaks of the aesthetic intelligence's 'intense diamond hard flame', his image is derived from the plumber's blowtorch. Perverse and ideal, lifeless yet rhythmic, the art nouveau line freezes architecture into strange new forms, prompting Walter Benjamin to describe its German counterpart, *Jugendstil*, as 'the dream that one has come awake'. Caught between Brooklyn and the Atlantic Ocean, Coney Island is by the start of the new century a wildly

Inhabitants of the Deep

hallucinatory expression of that dream. 'It is marvellous what you can do in the way of arousing human emotions by the use you can make architecturally of simple lines,' declares Frederic Thompson in 1903. Decorated with over a million electric lights, his Luna Park invites its visitors to step onto the surface of the Moon in search of pleasures 'not of this Earth', making it one of Coney's most successful institutions. Its main rival is Senator H Reynolds' Dreamland, whose main attractions include a submarine ride, 'Inhabitants of the Deep', 'the End of the World' and 'the Fall of Pompeii'. Access to these delights is granted by passing beneath the vast plaster sailing ships at its entrance, suggesting that only by submerging themselves beneath the waves can the public reach Dreamland. Dismissed by socialist author Maxim Gorky as a 'cheap, hastily constructed toyhouse for the amusement of children', Coney Island combines magic and engineering to transform itself into an Atlantis Risen for the masses. At the height of its busiest season, the police come by regularly at dawn to clear the corpses off the beach.

In 1911, set ablaze by a stray electric spark, Dreamland takes just three hours to burn to the ground. Three years later Luna Park also goes up in flames. By then Frederic Thompson has gone on to stage a spectacular new revue at the Hippodrome, the vast theatre complex he has established on New York's Sixth Avenue. *A Yankee Circus on Mars* tells of a stranded theatrical troupe invited to 'remain permanently and to become inhabitants of that far-away planet'. The show's climax is an amazing piece of aquatic choreography in which 64 'diving girls' descend a staircase in squads of eight into the Hippodrome's vast artificial lake; they 'walk into the water until their heads are out of sight', an effect so moving that 'men sit in the front row, night after night, weeping silently.' On Easter Sunday 1917, the Hippodrome is the chosen venue for a performance of Berlioz's *Requiem* – conducted by Edgard Varèse, making his US debut – as a memorial to those lost in the sinking of the *SS Vigilante* by a German submarine. Five days later United States Congress votes to go to war with Germany. That same year US Navy recruit Buckminster Fuller examines water bubbles forming in the wake of his ship outside Brooklyn's Naval Yards and wonders how they manage to form perfect spheres without calculating pi. 'All true insight forms an eddy,' notes Walter Benjamin. 'To swim in time against the direction of the swirling stream.'

III. Engineer Hero

The flooded antediluvian structures of Atlantis seem to be simultaneously as empty and as full as the transparent skyscrapers of tomorrow. When Fritz Lang first conceives of his silent classic *Metropolis*, detailing life in the city of the twenty-first century, it is the glittering towers of New York he has in mind. Extending itself vertically both above and below the ground, Lang's Metropolis is mostly set in a subterranean twilight of tunnels, pipes and corridors. At what point in their development did cities start this expansion deep into the earth? With no middle-class suburban sprawl to absorb the forces of progress and social unrest, no wonder the greatest threat to Metropolis is the deliberate flooding of its lower depths, where the workers' homes are allowed to disappear beneath the water. 'That vertical city of the future we know now is, to put it mildly, highly improbable,' HG Wells writes disapprovingly in his review of Lang's film. 'Even in New York and Chicago, where the pressure on the central sites is exceptionally great, it is only the central office and entertainment region that soars and excavates.' At the same time visionary architect Hugh Ferriss starts sketching out the gigantic vertical labyrinths which he confidently predicts will overwhelm the American skyline, 'In the future,' Ferriss claims, 'with the evolution of the cities, New Yorkers will literally live in the skies.' Unfortunately, the colossal bunkers and looming towers which he devises in one heavily-shaded rendition after another only serve to reduce the heavens to a tiny grey blur, neither empty nor full, glimpsed from below.

Works of engineering are myths of transition. Following on from Edison's defeat of the Martians, publisher Hugo Gernsback includes science-fiction tales in such technical journals as *The Electrical Experimenter* and *Science and Invention*. In 1926, just as *Metropolis* is released to the general public, he launches *Amazing Stories*, which contains nothing but 'scientifiction'. It is courtesy of *Amazing Stories* that

Buck Rogers has his earliest adventures in the twenty-fifth century. A syndicated comic-strip starring Buck Roger appears in 1929: the first to feature rocket ships, atomic blasters and journeys to other planets. That same year Hugh Ferriss publishes *The Metropolis of Tomorrow*, his grand design for life in the future. However, the Stock Market Crash of 1929 also means that his 'Visions of the Titan City' are never realized. Skyscrapers are now for jumping off: not completing. Meanwhile the Great Depression throws up some unlikely new heroes, such as Alfred W Lawson whose Direct Credits Society wins an extraordinary mandate from the huddled masses. A professional baseball player, aviator and the inventor of the first commercial airliner as well as a 'trans-oceanic float system', Lawson is less a chieftain of industry than one of its more inspired berserkers, denouncing modern mathematics as 'a cheat's invention used by people to defraud one another'. As economic theory, Direct Credit may be worthless, but it is nothing compared with 'Lawsonomy', a detailed and highly complex body of knowledge which will, its creator boasts, explain 'everything about everything to everybody'. In such self-published books as *Manlife* and *Creation*, Lawson outlines a cosmology based upon the universal forces of 'Suction' and 'Pressure', which finds a curious echo in the theories of Viennese engineer Hans Hörbiger. Declaring objective science to be a 'pernicious invention' and mathematics 'nothing but lies', Hörbiger propounds a Doctrine of Eternal Ice in which the universe responds solely to the forces of 'Attraction' and 'Repulsion'. A series of ice moons have thereby been irresistibly pulled down from the sky to earth, he argues, drastically altering the planet's gravitational field and producing huge tidal waves, one of which caused the watery destruction of Atlantis.

Throughout the twenties and thirties Edgar Cayce, the Sleeping Prophet of Virginia Beach, describes in great detail daily life in ancient Atlantis. Going into a deep trance, lulled by the sound of the Atlantic waves, he warns that the poles of the planet will one day be violently reversed, allowing the sunken towers of Atlantis to rise again. American newsstands are now heaving under an increasing

number of science-fiction magazines such as *Air Wonder Stories*, *Science Wonder Quarterly*, *Astounding Stories*, *Startling Stories*, and *Marvel Science Stories*. Can the amazed, the astounded and the startled keep pace with progress? 'It is scarcely an exaggeration to say that any contemporary consciousness that has not appropriated the American experience, even if in opposition, has something reactionary about it,' writes Theodor Adorno of his stay in Los Angeles with fellow Frankfurt School theorist Max Horkheimer. In 1931 a 'Fête Moderne: A Fantasie in Flame and Silver' is held at New York's Hotel Astor to celebrate the future; among the skyscraper replicas, science fiction costumes and space-age decor, one woman comes dressed simply as the 'Basin Girl', complete with faucets, pipes and mirror. The bathroom has replaced the fish tank in the modern household as its principal watery medium. The plumber, the architectural designer and the structural engineer are now the heroes of the future. At the 1933 Chicago World's Fair, while the United States climbs out of the Depression, Buckminster Fuller demonstrates his new Dymaxion car, and the first Buck Rogers film is premiered: a ten-minute epic entitled *An Interplanetary Battle with the Tiger Men of Mars.*

By satisfying each new desire which it arouses, progress sells itself to the masses. But progress also has its discontents. There are those who quickly grow dissatisfied with such thrusting materialism. The masses will always be in search of something more. Joining Fritz Lang in his self-imposed exile from the Nazis is a growing Hollywood colony of German writers and directors. Among them is Curt Siodmak, who scripted *FP1 Does Not Answer*, a futuristic melodramatic set aboard a gigantic floating platform similar to the one invented by Alfred

Lawson, and *The Tunnel*, about a subterranean motorway linking Europe with America. Both tales are transatlantic in location, feature engineers, aviators and industrialists as their heroes and look towards America for their future. However, it is Atlantis that has truly become one of the regular stops along the way to tomorrow. As a sequel to *The Problem of Atlantis*, Lewis Spence publishes *Will Europe Follow Atlantis?* Written during the Nazi rise to power, it argues that the moral excesses of the modern world may well lead to a second deluge. By now even Buck Rogers has visited the watery ruins of Atlantis.

IV. *To make in ourselves a new consciousness, an erotic sense of reality, is to become conscious of symbolism. Symbolism is mind making connections (correspondences) rather than distinctions (separations). Symbolism makes conscious interconnections and unions that were unconscious and repressed. Freud says symbolism is on the track of a former identity, a lost unity: the lost continent, Atlantis...'*

- Norman O Brown, *Love's Body*

During the twentieth century, the masses are treated as an imperfect medium for the realization of ideas. The World's Fair consequently becomes an industrial machine designed for the processing of crowds, giving the public direct access to such concepts in modern living as futuristic architecture, high-speed trains, prefabricated homes, multilane highways and robots. The 1939 New York World's Fair, located outside Manhattan at Flushing Meadows, has 'Building the World of Tomorrow' as its theme. Visitors to the Westinghouse 'Hall of Electric Living' are invited to marvel at 'Elektro the Motoman' as he performs mystifying feats of deduction or thrill to the 'Battle of the Centuries' between a frowsy-looking housewife and an automatic dishwasher. Elsewhere General Motors' Futurama pavilion presents life in year 1960, while RCA proudly displays its first television set. Located outside the beaux-art symmetry of the main attractions, impassively arranged around the abstract forms of Wallace Harrison's Trylon and Perisphere, is the fair's Amusement Zone. Notable among its many sideshows offering 'streamlined festivity for the World of Today and the World of Tomorrow' is 'Dalí's Dream of Venus': a combination dime museum, fun house and surrealist art show that represents, so its instigators claim, 'an attempt to utilize scientifically the mechanisms of inspiration and imagination'. Even so, the fair's original contract, drawn up with Dalí's New York dealer Julien Levi and architect Ian Woodner, calls for a work entitled 'Bottoms of the Sea'. A separate business deal with a US manufacturer of a new kind of soft rubber that keeps its shape underwater helps to establish the exhibit's theme, while a newspaper report claims Dalí's real interest to be the 'bottom of men's minds and everyone knew that there was no end to them'.

A surrealist fun house

Unlike the Perisphere, inside which a scale model of 'Democracity: the Metropolis of the Machine Age' is concealed, 'Dalí's Lovely Liquid Ladies' are housed within a lopsided structure of distended coral formations and marine accretions set in white plaster. Spines and teeth are mixed with splayed legs and bared breasts beneath a giant reproduction of Botticelli's *Venus* rising serenely from the sea – the fair organizers having firmly rejected Dalí's idea of replacing her face with a monstrous fish head. Inside the architecture of a horror movie is revealed: Aphrodite's grotto set in Dracula's castle. An 'Aphrodisiac Vampire' prowls in the shadows while a half-naked Venus reclines, surrounded by lobsters and bottles of champagne, upon a seemingly endless bed. In a deep sleep, her dream takes an underwater form, which is what the public have come to see. 'A long glass tank,' *Time* breathlessly reports, 'is filled with such subaqueous decor as a fireplace, typewriters with fungus-like rubber keys, rubber telephones, a man made of rubber ping-pong bats, a mummified cow, a supine rubber woman painted to resemble the keyboard of a piano. Into the tank they plunged living girls, nude to the waist and wearing little Gay Nineties girdles and fishnet stockings.' The enrobing of 'Dalí's Nude Aquarium' represents a complex series of mythological transformations. The birth of Aphrodite, emerging unclothed from the bloodied water after her father's castration, already has a twentieth-century incarnation at the World's Fair. DuPont's Wonder World of Chemistry has a 'Princess of Plastics' emerging from a giant test tube dressed entirely in nylon: 'lace evening gown, stockings, satin slippers and undergarments', a press release reveals. Meanwhile publicity shots for 'Venus's Prenatal Chateau beneath the Water' show Dalí tricking out naked women in such undersea finery as oysters, eels and mussels. One model sports a lobster in her hair with another lain across her lap; a second has a lobster curled over her mound of Venus, evoking art nouveau nightmares. 'Like the lobster of the deep, I am dressed in my skeleton,' the goddess intones on the 78 rpm disc released to promote the Dream of Venus show. 'Within is the rose-coloured flesh of dreams, more gentle than honey.'

The old-fashioned corsets, garters and fishnets worn by the women as they swim about the glass tank also evoke memories of the 'Dive Show', an aquatic form of burlesque featuring live mermaids and Edwardian bathing belles. So popular is this entertainment that George Méliès feels impelled to include half-naked sea nymphs in his 1907 film adaptation of Verne's *20,000 Leagues under the Sea* (*opposite*). While planning their Surrealist sideshow, Levi and Woodner are offered some

free advice from Billy Rose, creator of the Aquacade, a synchronized swimming display staged at the fair's Fountain Lagoon. 'Anything writ in water will succeed,' the old showman confides, 'lagoons fountains, aquacades, ice coolers anything you please but the public is disposed towards water.' Transformed through the medium of water, Hörbiger's Doctrine of Eternal Ice and Lawson's principles of Suction and Pressure stand revealed as Dalí's paranoiac-critical method played out on a cosmological level. 'Here is what we can still love,' the painter writes approvingly of art nouveau architecture, 'the imposing block of those rapturous and frigid structures scattered across all of Europe.' Images ripple and bend within the Dive Show's glass tank, rendering it empty and full at the same time – imitating 'the world of the hardened undulations of sculpted water' Dalí claims to have discovered in the *Jugendstil* line. Like some ancient dream, a swirling assemblage of cultural flotsam and jetsam is brought erotically to life by the presence of the half-naked female divers, 'seen at close range and a trifle water-magnified' as *Time* reports. As if to validate the introduction of indoor plumbing to the modern home, Dalí's chorines swim in pure New York tap water. 'This isn't water,' complain one parcel of tourists, thinking they have seen through this trick, 'it's compressed air.'

Except that the water in the tank is murky on opening night. Dye from the bathing belles' gloves dirties the water of the unconscious mind; plus, as a backdrop to the girls' gyrations, Dalí has painted Vesuvius erupting, burying the ruins of Pompeii under a cloud of volcanic ash. Dalí himself has fled his own dream and is already back across the Atlantic, working with the Ballets Russes on the staging of *Venusberg*, a ballet inspired by mad King Ludwig II of Bavaria. Very soon the world as reflected in the arrangement of pavilions at Flushing Meadows will no longer exist. In May 1939 US Navy submarine *Squalus* sinks off the New Hampshire coastline. Having been denied an official presence at the World's Fair, Germany demands the Czechoslovakian exhibit be destroyed after the Nazi invasion of that country. A public subscription keeps it open until the fair closes in 1940. By then 'Dalí's Dream of Venus' has been renamed '20,000 Legs Under the Sea'; and Walter Benjamin has taken his own life by swallowing morphine while attempting to reach America on papers arranged for him by Max Horkheimer.

V. Ice Cosmology

Meanwhile Curt Siodmak finds himself working at Universal Studios in Hollywood, busily updating the past rather than dreaming of the future. By the outbreak of World War II the horror movie is such a firmly established genre that it allows little room for innovation. It presents its best dramas in black and white. The only shades of grey it recognizes are to be found in the swirling vapours which help to hide the monster from view. More importantly, like the war itself, the horror movie is distinctly foreign in nature. Preying upon a ruthlessly divided class system, Baron Frankenstein and Count Dracula plainly have no place on Main Street. Siodmak's script for *Son of Dracula*, directed by his brother Robert and released in 1942, makes it clear that Dracula's son has grown tired of the thin blood on offer in 'decayed-ent' Mitteleuropa and has come to the 'virile' United States to find fresh supplies of victims. 'My land is dry and desolate,' he confesses. 'The soil is red with the blood of a hundred races. There is no life left in it. Here, you have a young and vital race.' Judging by the way Lon Chaney's sturdy American bulk has to be wedged into the title role it is hard to imagine a creature less in need of extra nourishment.

He has come to the land of indoor plumbing only to find himself in a stretch of Louisiana swampland, surrounded by the gloomy remains of a terminally ailing Southern aristocracy. Posing as 'Alucard' – a darkened reflection of the family name – Dracula's heir claims to be conducting valuable scientific research and therefore cannot be disturbed during the hours of daylight. This, however, doesn't fool the local doctor, Harry Brewster. A canny, straight-talking family physician played by J Edward Bomberg, Dr Brewster is smart and practical where Count Alucard is mysterious and devious. Both exude authority, but of very different kinds. Alucard's is an inherited superiority which he considers to be his by birth, while Brewster's has been earned: the certificates hanging on his surgery wall say as much. The good doctor has a fairly good idea of the mumbo-jumbo being smuggled in from the old country under the guise of 'science'. In fact, in Alucard's case, it is barely worthy of the name: merely an excuse for nocturnal blood-letting. The reeking night mists of the Bayou, the call of the wild beasts and the odd gypsy's curse may persuade us that Count Alucard has found himself in a waterlogged version of Transylvania, but Harry Brewster knows that this is America, not Europe. What is most significant about the clash between Alucard and Harry Brewster is not so much its successful resolution as the subtle ideological twist which Curt and Robert Siodmak bring to it. The Manichean struggle between good and evil which lies at the heart of the traditional Hollywood horror movie has become one staged between opposing bodies of knowledge and the different worlds they represent. On one side of this unequal conflict is educated pragmatism and informed expertise: on the other, questionable notions of natural superiority and the darkly extravagant claims of an unfathomably weird science.

Nocturnal blood-letting

By the time *Son of Dracula* is released, there is enough evidence to suggest that such a contest is already taking place. Hermann Rauschning, the ex-Nazi leader for Danzig, has fled Germany for

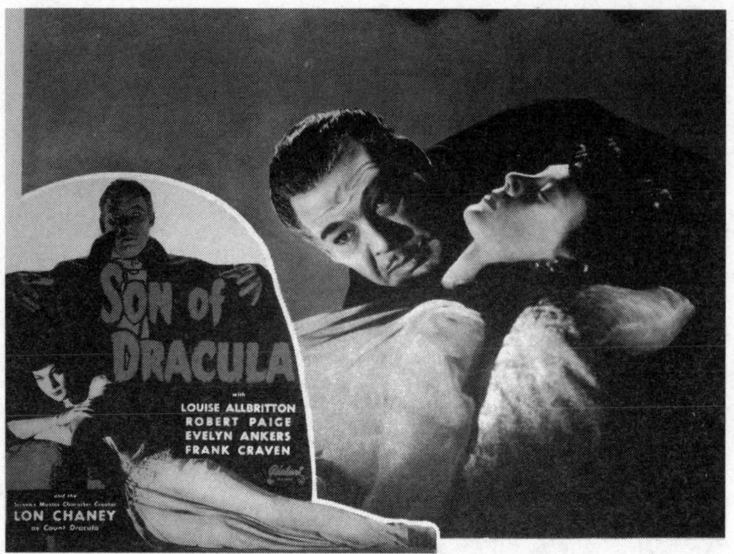

America, bearing strange tales of what goes on inside the Führer's brain. Between 1939 and 1941 he publishes a series of astonishing revelations. 'It is impossible to understand Hitler's political plans,' Rauschning cautions his readers, 'unless one is familiar with his basic beliefs and his conviction that there is a magic relationship between Man and the Universe.' Siodmak's engineer heroes are being dismissed in favour of the most apocalyptic belief systems. Scientists and physicists are now signing up to Hörbiger's Doctrine of Eternal Ice. Among them are Hermann Oberth and Willey Ley, co-founders of Germany's Society for Space Travel whose membership includes a young Wernher von Braun. 'We are often abused for being the enemies of the mind and spirit,' Hitler likes to boast. 'Well, that is what we are, but in a far deeper sense than bourgeois science in its idiotic pride could ever imagine.' These are the kind of words to echo around a mad scientist's laboratory. 'It's strange to hear a man of science calmly admit that he believes in a superstition so fantastic!' Dr Brewster exclaims as rampant vampirism starts to assert itself on American soil. Europe's culture is both corrupt and corrupting; what remains is cold, ancient and decayed. *Son of Dracula* has made its point. How pure can the blood of one who drinks the blood of others be? What place is there in the future for the timeless, the immortal and the undead? From an American point of view, the rise of Nazism exposes the great lie once and for all. 'Our revolution,' Hitler asserts, 'is a new stage, or, rather, the final stage in an evolution which will end by abolishing history.' Or as Herr Rauschning puts it: 'At bottom every German has one foot in Atlantis.'

VI. *Among the stylistic elements that enter into Jugendstil from the iron construction and technical design, one of the most important is the predominance of... the empty over the full.*
– Walter Benjamin, *The Arcades Project*

There is only one future. We tend to assume we're the only culture or society that trembles on the edge of destruction, but this is a fear which constantly updates itself. Planting a foot firmly in the World of Tomorrow, the Westinghouse Corporation buries a time capsule containing memorabilia of the 1939 New York World's Fair beneath Flushing Meadows. Its contents are not to be unearthed until the year 6939: five thousand years into the future. The company deposits a second capsule, ten feet away from the first, at the close of the 1964 New York World's Fair, which is also held in Flushing Meadows. This one is scheduled to be opened, along with the first, in 6939. How much time does change require to take effect? Atlantis, after all, disappeared in a single night. Westinghouse is not alone in optimistically repeating itself twenty-five years after the first New York World's Fair. General Motors reinvents its Futurama pavilion, now depicting the world of 2024, while Walt Disney offers the public a revolving 'Carousel of Progress' which, as it name implies, also requires constant updating. Emblematic of this modern encroachment upon the present is the Unisphere, a hollow steel representation of the Earth as seen from space, its oceans little more than empty outlines upon its surface. Built on the foundations of the 1939 Perisphere, it stands in the middle of a large reflecting pool,

MAGIC NAMES!

Are you interested in the almost forgotten past of the Earth? If you are, here is the wonder book of all time concerning the great catastrophe which destroyed the civilization of 24,000 years ago!

"I REMEMBER LEMURIA!"

by RICHARD S. SHAVER

This is an incredible story of a Pennsylvania welder who began to receive strange thoughts from his electric welder. At first he thought he was going mad, but then, when the astounding story of Lemuria came to him, he realized that here was something more than mere madness. His experiences convinced him that what he was hearing was true. Whether his "memories" are true or not is for you to judge. Thousands of people have already claimed "I Remember Lemuria!" and its sequel of 10,000 years later, "The Return of Sathanas" is a revelation. The evidence of its truth is self-contained for those who will read, and think!

Particularly recommended to Students of the Occult

Limited edition. Get your copy now. The price is $3.00 postpaid. Only prepaid orders accepted.

VENTURE PRESS

305 STUDIO BLDG., 1718 SHERMAN AVE., EVANSTON, ILLINOIS

surrounded by a ring of fountains designed to draw attention away from the pedestal supporting it. Not surprisingly, Robert Moses, the man in charge of the 1964 World's Fair, is also responsible for placing an aquarium over Dreamland's charred remains on Coney Island.

The unsupported sphere floating in empty space is part of a new post-war cosmology. Dedicated to 'Man's Achievements on a Shrinking Globe in an Expanding Universe', the Unisphere looks outwards where the Perisphere turned in upon the model city displayed at its centre. By 1964 the Soviet cosmonaut and the US astronaut have come to represent the masses both on this planet and beyond it. Updated and transformed, memories of the past linger on, however. Having introducing readers of *Amazing Stories* to 'Mantong' – an original dialect of Atlantis incomprehensible to existing language experts who 'operate on incorrect principles' – Richard Shaver goes on to relate memories of his former life in 'Sub-Atlan', a city located miles below the fabled lost continent. In this earlier incarnation, Shaver reveals, he was a descendant of ancient, god-like creatures, known as the Atlans and the Titans, who had come from space 150,000 years ago to colonize Atlantis and Lemuria. Both races soon discovered that the sun was beginning to emit poisonous radiation which ravaged their bodies and stripped them of their immortality. Some returned to space in search of another Atlantis to colonize, while others burrowed deep into the bowels of the earth to create vast underground cities accessible only through caves located on the planet's surface. Published in *Amazing Stories* at the end of World War II as a true account of actual events, Shaver's tales of Sub-Atlan and its terrible legacy prepared the American public for the first reported sightings of flying saucers in the spring and summer of 1947. That, however, is another tale for another time. It is enough to note here that, as human achievement in an expanding universe becomes a distinct possibility in the World of Tomorrow, industrial myths such as Atlantis, the Martians and the Vampire appear increasingly transitional in nature. How will they survive in the vacuum of empty space?

Worlds in collision

A former student of Freud's pupil Wilhelm Stekel, Immanuel Velikovsky arrives in the USA on a temporary visa in 1939 just as war breaks out in Europe. He subsequently becomes a permanent resident of New York City, where he studies Hans Hörbiger's Doctrine of Eternal Ice before abandoning it for a theory of his own devising, published in 1950 under the title *Worlds in Collision*. A retelling of the old industrial myths in the name of a new cosmology, Velikovsky's book argues that the planet Venus was pulled out of Jupiter's enormous mass by a passing comet, which went on to drag Mars into its present orbit and cause all manner of cataclysmic events here on Earth. The floods and tidal waves that have swept through human memory are, his argument implies, but dreams based on actual incidents. Hotly contested by the scientific establishment, avidly read by the general public of the time, Velikovsky's theories are another example of how the rapids and debris created around it can often seem more impressive than the waterfall itself. Buffeted by unimaginable forces and cosmic alignments, the human image stands exposed in the middle of the twentieth century as a twisting column of water: a dynamic and complex form constantly shifting in space. To accommodate such instability will require new structures and facilities directly modelled upon the modern miracle of indoor plumbing; even before the fountains are switched on in Flushing Meadows for the 1964 World's Fair, the third issue of the radical architectural journal *Archigram* goes into circulation. Partially inspired by the utopian design theories of Buckminster Fuller, the magazine's contents are categorized under three separate headings: 'Bathrooms', 'Bubbles' and 'Systems'. These together will form the architecture of the Space Age.

Haunted Soundsystem

by STEPHEN GRASSO

As a voodoo practitioner and record obsessive, it was only a matter of time before those two interests collided head-on and I began to explore the strange world of Voodoo recordings on vinyl. The influence of African Diaspora magico-religious traditions can be heard in music from the Caribbean, Latin America and the Southern States of the US – everywhere that the horrific transatlantic slave trade deposited its human cargo. Music and dance are central to African religious practice. The sound of drums calls the spirits to be present, and the activity of dance invites possession by the ancestral gods. The ancient drum rhythms of the gods of Africa were never crushed, despite armed efforts to eradicate them. The rhythms of Voodoo simply mutated and found their way onto a diversity of turntables around the globe, and that old black magic endures.

When you look at the various African Diaspora traditions, one clear theme that emerges is the way in which the overseas colonies of Catholic nations were a more fertile ground for preserving African religious beliefs than the colonies of Protestant nations. The presence of Catholic saints provided an ideal framework for disguising the African deities, so the West African god Legba became St. Anthony, Ogun became St. George, Danbala became St. Patrick, the principle female deities of Africa were each masked behind a different image of the Virgin, and so on. Worship of the ancestral religions could continue under the guise of devout Catholic prayer, whereas under Protestant rule, there was no convenient structure for preserving a clandestine religion and anything resembling African worship was punishable by death.

In this way, areas such as Haiti, Cuba, Brazil and New Orleans (originally a French and then Spanish colony) have produced extremely cohesive New World religious forms with the deities of Africa at their heart. In Protestant colonies, the traditions that emerged are less likely to have an emphasis on the African deities, yet the same spiritual impulse finds its expression through other channels. Most notably, it survives in the remembrance of folk magic practices, often divorced from their original context; and in the form of outwardly Christian revivalist groups and spiritual churches that draw inspiration from the Old Testament but are nonetheless heavily influenced by African spirituality and forms of worship.

Black Cat Bone

Hoodoo conjure is a tradition of folk magic deriving from the Southern states of the US, predominantly practised by African Americans, but with Native American and European strains of influence feeding into its complex melting pot. The many references to hoodoo in early blues recordings are well documented, as is the famous urban legend about the bluesman Robert Johnson selling his soul to the devil at the crossroads in order to acquire his skill on the guitar. Robert Johnson did record a song about the crossroads, but it was actually his friend and contemporary Tommy Johnson who claimed to have been gifted his skills in this way. The story was later attributed to Robert Johnson by a music journalist, presumably because the latter was a better known musician.

Harry Middleton Hyatt's exhaustive five volume work *Hoodoo-Conjuration-Witchcraft-Rootwork* – a compendium of oral accounts of hoodoo practice collected between 1936 and 1940 throughout the southern US states – contains many folk references to visiting the crossroads at midnight to acquire skill at music or gambling. While the mysterious personage at the crossroads is sometimes referred to as 'the devil', he is more frequently depicted as 'a big black man'. This figure in African American folklore appears to derive from folk memories of the ubiquitous west African trickster and messenger god, Eshu Elegbara, whose domain is the crossroads. Known variously as Papa Legba, Papa Limba, Ellegua or Exu, his role is to open the way for communication to occur between our world and the world of spirit. He is intimately concerned with magic, and practitioners of Voodoo would speak to him at the crossroads about matters of luck and opportunity. He is by no means an evil deity, but in his role as trickster, accuser and upsetter, he can be ambivalent and ambiguous – and for these reasons he sometimes becomes syncretised with the image of 'the devil'.

Lost gods of Africa

In my own experience of these matters, he is far more interested in rum and cigars, than in the acquisition of souls as payment for his work, and the oral histories recorded by Hyatt tend to bear this sort of transaction out. The gods of Africa may have been lost in a religious context by the slaves transported to the United States, but they endured in the imagination and became sublimated into folk characters such the devil at the crossroads. Similarly the folk hero John Henry, the railroad worker who raced against a steam-powered hammer and won, bears more than a passing resemblance to Africa's Ogun, the god of iron. Henry the 'steel driving man' has been the subject of recordings by Leadbelly, Big Bill Broonzy, Mississippi John Hurt and others too numerous to mention.

Another recurrent folk character in the litany of the blues is the unstoppable badman Stagger Lee or Stackolee. His tale, like John

Henry's, is based on a real life incident. In 1895, Stagger Lee Shelton shot William Lyons in cold blood for stealing his hat. This incident seems an unlikely basis for a legend, but something in the character of Lee struck a note in the popular consciousness. He belonged to a notorious and flamboyant gang of pimps in St. Louis called 'The Macks', and the casualness of his crime somehow cemented him to the archetype of the dangerous and unpredictable black man who defies white authority. There is perhaps something of the character of the god Shango – the Yoruban god of fire, passion and machismo – reflected in this image, as if the character of Stagger Lee became a vessel to contain and transmit something of Shango's mysteries in a secular form.

Most hoodoo references in blues music date from the pre-war era, which means the original recordings exist in the 78 format, although there have of course been many represses on LP over the years. Willie Dixon's 'Rub my Root' is one of many blues tracks to reference High John the Conqueror root, a staple of hoodoo practice, said to bring luck and associated with male virility. Memphis Minnie's 'Black Dust' finds her discovering a cursing powder along the lines of goofer dust on her front doorstep, left by a jealous rival. There are many recipes for goofer dust, but a common base is graveyard dirt, powdered sulphur and salt, to which other assorted nastiness might be added. Lightnin' Hopkins' 'Black Cat Bone' refers to a hoodoo talisman said to bring luck or even invisibility. To get one, you have to boil a black cat alive until the flesh peels easily from its bones, and then look at each bone in a mirror. The one with no reflection is the one you need to retain for your dubious purpose.

Hoodoo conjure is such a persistent theme in so many blues recordings that it could be regarded as a primary source for understanding this tradition of magical practice. The references are often characterised by a matter-of-factness that suggests these practices are not an anomaly at the edges of the culture, but an aspect of everyday life encountered on a daily basis. A hoodoo frame of reference, almost magic realist in its negotiation of life's turbulence, permeates the blues and its folk litany. It's a world where red brick dust laid out on your threshold keeps away people with ill intent, and the imprint left by a someone's shoe in the earth can be used to work wickedness against them.

LE GRAND ZOMBI IN CONGO SQUARE

The Holy City of New Orleans is not like the rest of the South, or anywhere else in the US. It is both the birthplace of jazz and of a unique form of Voodoo, related to but distinct from the Vodou found in Haiti. Tracing the influence of New Orleans Voodoo upon jazz is not as clear cut as spotting references to hoodoo conjure in the lyrics of the blues. You will rarely find direct references to African spiritual practices in early jazz recordings – and for good reason.

The golden age of Voodoo in New Orleans began before the American purchase of Louisiana in 1803, and had its heyday in the years before the US Civil War decimated the South 60 years later. During this period, the issue of race in the city was more complex than elsewhere in the south. Various factors – such as the system of *plaçage*, where it was culturally accepted that a white man would marry a white woman, but also take a black mistress and look after her children – resulted in a strong Creole culture, where a significant proportion of the population was of mixed race.

In pre-war New Orleans, not all black-skinned people were slaves, and not all slaves were black-skinned. 'Free people of colour' often owned slaves themselves, and while they were not permitted to attain the same degree of power and status as their white-skinned counterparts, there were nonetheless many wealthy and powerful Creoles of African descent. Many people with African heritage would pass as white, and many Caucasians – like Marie Laveau's white husband Christophe Glapion – would pass as Creole, pretending to an African heritage in order to circumvent the indignity of *plaçage* and legally marry the person they were in love with.

This was the climate in which Voodoo flourished in the Crescent City. Marie Laveau could hold open ceremonies for the spirits in Congo Square attended by upwards of 500 celebrants and experienced

YEMANJÁ

UMBANDA

only limited interference from the authorities. The urgent drums of the Calinda and the Bamboula would sound out in the night, and the priestess of the mysteries would lead the proceedings, dancing with her great serpent Le Grand Zombi draped about her as she moved to the ancient rhythms of African magic. Voodoo was practised openly, with many Conjure Doctors and Voodoo Queens operating in the city, selling herbs, fixing gris-gris, and telling fortunes. The Bayou was a hotbed of Voodoo, with large scale midnight ceremonies taking place deep in the swamps on St. John's Eve and other important dates in the Voodoo calendar.

Conjure doctors & voodoo queens

All of this, of course, attracted much negative attention from the typically ignorant and racist press, who can never resist an opportunity to fill column inches with lurid depictions of African traditional religions. The primal fear that the Voodoo gatherings provoked – and the theme of many feverish newspaper headlines – was that they wilfully did not observe the colour line. The somewhat covert liaisons of *plaçage* were one thing, but these 'temporary autonomous zones' in the city attended by black, white and mixed race celebrants were something else entirely. Much like the media hysteria that would later surround jazz, the overwhelming fear of the day was that Voodoo provided a social setting where the lines of racial segregation were dissolved; and specifically, that such mixed gatherings might lead to sexual relations between black men and white women.

Despite these attacks by the press, Voodoo remained a cultural force in New Orleans, but this was to change radically following the Civil War and the failure of reconstruction. Although slavery was abolished in the US, it was replaced by the pernicious Jim Crow segregation laws and the purposeful creation of an underclass. Once wealthy and influential Creoles – if they were fortunate enough not to have lost all their holdings in the war – now found themselves subject to the 'one drop' rule, where their mixed race heritage greatly reduced their civil rights and eradicated any social position they may have attained. The Jim Crow laws were in force right up until the 1960s when the Civil Rights Movement successfully campaigned to have them overturned, but their legacy of disenfranchisement continues to this day.

The South was brought to its knees during the Civil War, with many cities burned to the ground and the confederate currency rendered obsolete. This desperate landscape contributed to the rise of the Ku Klux Klan's power throughout the Southern States, to the point where openly celebrated Voodoo ceremonies – of the sort held in Marie Laveau's lifetime – were no longer a plausible proposition. During Jim Crow, anything that drew too much attention could and regularly did end in a lynching, and the great tradition of Voodoo in New Orleans came to an end – or at least it appeared to.

The Voodoo of Congo Square not only administered to the spiritual needs of its congregation, but served an important social and community-building function. Something as vibrant and deeply embedded in the social fabric as this does not simply disappear when it is outlawed. Voodoo went to ground – its nebulous spirit, creativity and social release flowing into the jazz clubs of Storyville and Treme; and its religious practice finding new expression behind the closed doors of the African Spiritual Churches of the city.

New Orleans Jazz came out of nightclubs in the same tiny area of the city where Congo Square is located. When the Voodoo dances were outlawed, that energy soon found a new secular expression in the rhythms of jazz. Black musicians learned how to play instruments left behind by the marching bands of the civil war, employing an African syncopation that emphasises the off-beat, not unlike the Petro rhythms of Haitian Vodou. The influence of Voodoo on jazz is implicit, but necessarily covert in a region where the Klan had a stranglehold, so there are few overt references to these matters in early recordings. Yet there are some anomalous nods to it here and there. For instance, Charlie Barnet – a white jazz man and son of a millionaire banker, who faced little danger of being lynched by the Klan – made several overtly Voodoo-themed recordings in the 1930s, such as 'Ogoun Badagris', named for the Haitian war god, and 'Xango' named for the ever popular god of fire and thunder. Barnet was one of the first bandleaders to integrate his band, a notorious party crew on the jazz circuit, and his repeated tips of the hat to Voodoo deities suggests an interest if not an active involvement in the practice. The story of Voodoo is suffused with such secret histories.

JOCOMO FINO AH NAH NAY

If jazz and its emergent culture provided one home for the disenfranchised spirit of New Orleans Voodoo, a Wisconsin-born spiritualist called Mother Leafy Anderson was instrumental in providing another. Anderson was the founder of the African American Spiritual Church movement in New Orleans during the 1920s, an outwardly Christian church that included the veneration of spirit guides such as Black Hawk, Queen Esther and Father John. Black Hawk was a historic Sauk American Indian chief who lived between 1767 and 1838 in Anderson's native Illinois. He was vehemently opposed to ceding Native American land to white settlers and their governments, and fought in several wars against the US colonial powers.

In Anderson's Spiritual Church, Black Hawk was called upon as a spirit of resistance to authority and protection against persecution by authority. He is known as a 'watcher on the wall' who notifies of breaches in one's spiritual defences; and in New Orleans Voodoo a plaster effigy of an Indian chief is often placed in a bucket of earth or sand and positioned near the perimeter of a property for protection and fed with offerings of fruit and cigars.

Anderson's original church movement was vocal in distancing itself from Voodoo, and was careful to position itself as a respectable Christian organisation taking its lead from the Bible; nonetheless its services still involved spirit possession and were inspired by distinctly African religious worship. After Anderson's death in 1927, the movement fractured into many denominations who were not all so squeamish about the V-word, and went further in blurring the lines between the Spiritual Church movement and the hidden currents of New Orleans Voodoo. Anderson's successor, Mother Catherine Seals, was much less conservative than her predecessor and freely incorporated elements of rootwork and Southern hoodoo conjure into her church services.

The presence of a Native American spirit in an African Diaspora religious context is not without precedent. The disenfranchised original occupants of the Americas and Caribbean were often great allies to the transported Africans, offering shelter to escaped slaves and teaching African healers and sorcerers about the magical and medicinal properties of the alien landscape to which they had been relocated. Haitian Vodou contains many non-African elements that are thought to be surviving remnants of Taino and Arawak belief. In Cuban Santeria, the Orisha Ochosi, deity of hunting and master of the forest and its medicine, is frequently depicted with a plaster image of a Native American Indian, not unlike the plaster images of Black Hawk. Similarly, in the Brazilian African Diaspora traditions, such as Candomble and Umbanda, the spirits of dead Native Americans are known as the Caboclo and considered powerful ancestral spirits of the land that will frequently possess celebrants to perform cleansings and give advice.

In New Orleans, this spiritual reverence for Native American tribespeople is also reflected in the city's Mardi Gras Indian masking traditions. More than a century old (around 200 years old according to some sources), and arising out of the same communities as the African Spiritual Churches, masking Indian for Mardi Gras is another instance of African Americans paying symbolic tribute to their indigenous benefactors. The Indian is a potent symbol of freedom, and masking Indian is a celebration of that freedom.

Big Chief, Spy Boy & Wild Man

Few in the black neighbourhoods could participate in the exclusive Mardi Gras parades and masked balls held in the city, so masking Indian became a homegrown way of celebrating the season. Numerous Indian tribes came into being throughout the city during Mardi Gras, each led by a Big Chief and accompanied by participants taking on the roles of Queen, Spy Boy, Flag Boy, Medicine Man, Wild Man and so on. In the early days of masking, confrontations between tribes would frequently be violent and often fatal. It was seen as a time to settle scores between rival gangs, taking advantage of the chaos and anonymity of Mardi Gras – where everyone in the city is masked and the police already have their hands full controlling the crowds near the main parades.

Since the 1940s, the Indian tribes have stopped killing one another when they meet in the street, and their confrontation is now played out through the medium of elaborate costume, song and dance. When two Big Chiefs come face-to-face, each will perform a theatrical display of chants and dances until one party concedes defeat to the other. It's a display of showmanship and machismo that recalls the mysteries of Shango, who rules over drums, dance and masculinity. Indian costumes can cost thousands of dollars to construct, and require months of planning and preparation to make happen. A new costume is required each year, but often beaded patches – much resembling the sequined flags of Haitian Vodou, believed to contain spirits, and often passed down from older retired Indians – are incorporated into the new year's costume.

Mardi Gras Indian music is a rich tradition, with the first known musical reference being Louis Dumaine's 1927 instrumental 'To-Wa-Bac-A-Wa', named for the Indian Creole chant 'Two-Way-Pocky-Way'. However the first recording to popularise Mardi Gras Indian chants was Sugar Boy Crawford's 1953 recording 'Jockomo', which tells of a Spy Boy's encounter with a Flag Boy of another tribe, and the ensuing threats of violence. The song later resurfaced, to much bigger acclaim, as The Dixie Cups' 1965 hit 'Iko Iko' which incorporated many of the same elements as Crawford's original but in a style more reminiscent of the Mardi Gras Indian sound.

Both versions revolve around the chorus: 'Iko Iko, Iko Iko An Day, Jockomo Fino Ah Nah Nay, Jockomo Fi Na Nay'. Crawford claimed to have written down individual Indian chants and put them together to make the chorus. He claimed that 'Iko' was used as a victory chant, and 'Jockomo' was a battle cry, but had no idea what the words actually meant. The Dixie Cups claimed to have heard their grandmother sing the chants, but similarly had no idea of the meaning of the Creole patois. Theories abound, but there is no clear consensus, and 'Jockomo Fino Ah Nah Nay' remains a New Orleans Voodoo mystery that has passed into the litany of funk. It appears on a 12" version of Afrika Bambaataa and Soul Sonic Force's 1983 Afrofuturist track 'Renegades of Funk', alongside the recognisable Cuban Santeria chant 'Alafia Ache Ache'. Somewhat less credibly, 'Iko Iko' has even been covered by Rolf Harris.

Professor Longhair's 1964 recording 'Big Chief' picks up a Mardi Gras Indian theme, with the vocal version making reference to Spy Boys and Flag Boys. Professor Longhair, or Fess, has something of the air of Robert (or Tommy) Johnson's story to him, in that he previously made his living as a street hustler and only started playing piano seriously when he was in his thirties – yet his sound almost singlehandedly defines something quintessential about New Orleans music and inspired everyone from Fats Domino to Allen Toussaint. Every note that Fess plays is alive with the fevered rhythms of New Orleans Voodoo and Congo Square. Following his death in 1980, a shrine to Fess was constructed in the New Orleans nightspot Tipitina's, named for one of his signature tracks and created as a venue for him to play in his later years. The shrine is well-tended with lit candles and offerings of fruit, smokes and liquor. A similar Voodoo shrine exists for R&B legend Ernie K-Doe (famous for the hits 'Mother-in-law' and 'Here come the girls') at the Mother-in-Law Lounge in Treme, near Congo Square, opened by his late wife Antoinette. The bar features a life-size mannequin of K-Doe, which is equally well-tended with candles and offerings. These bar-side shrines to dead musicians are a clear illustration of how an instinctive Voodoo practice permeates the culture of New Orleans.

'Handa Wanda', a heavy funk 7" released in 1970 by Big Chief Bo Dollis and the Wild Magnolias, was the first recording by an actual Mardi Gras Indian tribe to draw wider attention to the sound. It features the familiar Creole patois Indian chants and references to Spy Boys (et al), and was shortly followed by a full-length album *The Wild Magnolias* in 1973. The tribe played support slots in full Indian costume with Aretha Franklin and Gladys Knight & The Pips, carrying the Indian sound beyond the confines of the city.

Another Indian tribe, The Wild Tchoupitoulas, also released an eponymous record in 1975, backed by The Meters and produced by Allen Toussaint. The Meters are widely considered one of the progenitors of the New Orleans funk sound, and their frontman Art Neville happened to be the nephew of George Landry, AKA Big Chief Jolly of the Wild Tchoupitoulas tribe. Masking Indian is a family business, and in addition to bringing his own band in on the session, the recording also featured his brothers Charles, Aaron and Cyril Neville – playing together for the first time before they ever found independent success as the Neville Brothers. There's perhaps no clearer example of the intimate relationship between the origins of funk and the Mardi Gras Indian traditions, themselves steeped in New Orleans Voodoo, than the Wild Tchoupitoulas record.

The musician Mac Rebenack, recording as Dr John The Night Tripper, has undoubtedly done the most to export the idiosyncratic Voodoo sound of New Orleans to a global audience, with a series of recordings in the late 1960s that interpreted NOLA Voodoo through a psychedelic lens. The three LPs *Gris-gris*, *Remedies*, and *The Sun, Moon & Herbs* are steeped in references to this culture, replete with Spy Boys, swamp witches, Indian chiefs, gris-gris bags, High John roots, gator teeth, and some stone graveyard business. The original Dr John, after whom Rebenack is named, was a Congo Square drummer, conjure man and contemporary of Marie Laveau. Like the legendary Voodoo Queen herself, he may be a composite of more than one person, combining in an image of the archetypal New Orleans witch-doctor.

Dr John's commercial success opened the doors for other artists with a similar Voodoo flavour to their performance, notably Tony McKay who recorded under the name Exuma and released a series of albums in the early 1970s. A native of the Bahamas, Exuma eventually settled in New Orleans, but at the height of his career was a part of the same Greenwich Village folk scene in New York that produced Bob Dylan and others. His sound was an unclassifiable mix of Bahamian carnival ('jonkanoo') music, acoustic folk and raw blues, and his first eponymous LP features tracks such as 'Exuma the Obeah Man' and

'Dambala', named for the Haitian snake god. The latter track was covered by Nina Simone on her 1974 record *It Is Finished,* which also features a stripped down cover of 'Obeah woman', an Exuma produced funk 7" from 1973 with a vocal by Patricia Rollins.

Voodoo, in its many forms, is a continuously recurrent background presence in almost every genre of African American music. Often it is sublimated or manifests in a new form conditioned by the specifics of the landscape and the experience of the people living there. But the same mysteries are alluded to, and the same emergent spirit of Voodoo inhabits everything from Howlin' Wolf's 'Smokestack Lightning' to Afrika Bambaataa's 'Shango Message'.

Homenaje a los Santos

Meanwhile, elsewhere in the New World, the ancient gods of Africa had not been so effectively written out of the picture (or at least masked over) as they had been in the US. Within the Catholic colonies of the Caribbean, notably Haiti, Cuba and Brazil, the African religions merged and continued to be practised, taking on the form of a cult of the Saints. All of the African Diaspora religions are unique, but they share a certain DNA and have much in common, despite their differences in form and emphasis.

The dancer Katherine Dunham played an important role in introducing Caribbean and Latin American Voodoo sounds to a western audience. Akin to Nina Simone, Dunham had the air of a displaced Voodoo Queen raised in a hostile culture, who nonetheless found a way to inhabit her role. She is renowned as the first lady of African American dance and had one of the most successful dance careers of the twentieth century, touring internationally with the only self-subsidised black dance troupe of the day. She was also trained as an anthropologist and widely published throughout her lifetime.

She set up the Katherine Dunham School of Cultural Arts in New York, which was attended by Sidney Poitier, James Dean, Gregory Peck and Eartha Kitt among others. The fact that an Eartha Kitt track exists titled 'Shango', where Kitt prays to the Yoruban god

KATHERINE DUNHAM
PRESENTS
a study in hi fidelity sound
DRUM RHYTHMS OF
HAITI CUBA BRAZIL
THE SINGING GODS
audio fidelity

Lyrichord Stereo LLST 7341
DIVINE HORSEMEN
THE VOODOO GODS OF HAITI

of thunder during the spoken word introduction, is almost certainly inspired by her time as Dunham's protégé. In the mid-sixties, Dunham was appointed cultural ambassador to Senegal, where she trained the Senegal National Ballet; and she later served as an artist in residence at Southern Illinois University, where she collaborated on education projects with the visionary futurist architect Buckminster Fuller.

After years of training and involvement in the traditions, Dunham ultimately took the asson (a magical gourd rattle) as a Mambo of Haitian Vodou, and was also crowned a Santera in Cuban Santeria. Dunham was a powerhouse of transformative change, almost equally regarded as a dancer, an academic and an activist. In 1992, when she was in her eighties, she went on a 47-day hunger strike to protest US mistreatment of the Haitian boat people, which drew much international publicity towards the cause. She only stopped her protest after the then Haitian President, Jean-Bertrand Aristide, and the civil rights leader Jesse Jackson visited her and asked her to stop risking her life for this. Dunham stated, 'My job is to create a useful legacy'.

Divine Horsemen

It was Dunham who inspired her personal secretary, the dancer and experimental filmmaker Maya Deren, to visit and study the dances of Haiti. Deren's interest and involvement in Haiti resulted in the book *Divine Horsemen*, which half a century later remains the definitive account of Haitian Vodou, blending anthropological reportage with experiential elucidations of the religion's mysteries. Deren also recorded 18,000 feet of film, edited into a posthumous documentary in 1977 by her former husband. Audio extracts from these recordings were pressed on vinyl, first in the Fifties, then in the Seventies and remain one of the best ethnographic recordings of Haitian ritual, containing the drum rhythms for almost all of the central pantheon of Vodou. The sound quality is remarkable, considering the primitive car-battery powered recording equipment she had at her disposal, that involved strapping a microphone to the *Poteau Mitan* (or centre pole) of the Vodou temple.

In 1956 Katherine Dunham released an exotica record called

The Singing Gods, which featured musicians from Haiti, Cuba and Brazil. Among the Cuban artists was the Santero and master drummer Chano Pozo, who Dunham took on tour with her dance group, and who ultimately settled in New York. Chano Pozo was a devotee of the thunder god Shango, and throughout his life would carry a red scarf to signify his relationship with the Orisha. Typical of a child of Shango, Chano Pozo was a huge man with a formidable prowess for fighting, dancing, drumming and popularity with women. He was rumoured to have worked as a leg-breaker for a local gangster, and was killed during a fight in New York over the quality of some marijuana.

While living in New York, Pozo was introduced to the jazz trumpet player Dizzy Gillespie, and went on to become a full time member of his band, playing with them at Carnegie Hall and on a European tour. The marriage of Dizzy Gillespie's bebop style, and the Santeria-based AfroCuban drum rhythms that Chano Pozo brought to the mix, set the foundation for what would ultimately become known as AfroCuban Jazz. Examples of their material from this period include the tracks 'Cubana be Cubana bop' and 'Tin Tin Deo'. Gillespie was intentionally trying to bring together these two traditions of music that had a common origin in Africa, but had developed along independent lines following the forced exodus to the New World.

The 1930s Cuban bandleader Xavier Cugat was another musician who played an important early role in exporting Cuban rhythms to the US. A flamboyant character, he would perform on stage holding a conductor's baton in one hand and a miniature chihuahua in the other. Cugat was among the first musicians to introduce Latin dance music like the rumba and tango to an American audience, but among his early repertoire were two songs written by the Cuban composer Margarita Lecuona entitled 'Babalu' and 'Tabu'. Lecuona was the sister of the better known songwriter Ernesto Lecuona, whose influence on Cuban popular music could be compared to the influence of George Gershwin in the US. Margarita Lecuona's song 'Babalu' is a hymn to the very popular Cuban Orisha Babalu Aye, the god of smallpox and disease, syncretised with St. Lazarus, who is called upon for his great healing power. The Spanish lyrics describe a spiritual service for Babalu, involving offerings of Aguardiente (a cane liquor popular in Cuba and a staple of Santeria practice), money and tobacco, along with seventeen lit candles arranged in the shape of a cross (seventeen being the sacred number of Babalu).

The song was initially a hit in Cuba for the popular singer Miguelito Valdes, a protégé of Cugat, and a good friend of Chano Pozo. Valdes was so associated with the song that he became popularly known throughout Cuba as Mr Babalu. His performance of the song was later lifted wholesale by another protégé of Cugat, the musician Desi Arnaz, who would go on to marry Lucille Ball and star as her screen husband Ricky Ricardo in the hit 1950s TV show *I Love Lucy*. Arnaz played a fictionalised version of himself, and would frequently perform a lively rendition of 'Babalu' on the show at the venue Club Babalu, which his character owned. So this hymn to the African god of smallpox became a mainstay of 1950s Americana. The song 'Babalu' has since been covered by everyone from Yma Sumac to Johnny Mathis, and has entered into the lexicon of popular culture to the extent that it spawned such bizarre follow-ups as 'Babalu's Wedding Day' by The Eternals, a Fifties doowop group and contemporary of The Drifters; and 'Babalu Boogaloo' by the Puerto Rican musician Willie Rosario.

The other Margarita Lecuona song in Cugat's repertoire, 'Tabu', contains a verse that shouts out to 'Obatala, Shango, Yemaya' in its earliest versions, including Desi Arnaz's cut of it where he slightly changes the roll call of Orisha included – as if he's namechecking his own relationships with the Orisha as opposed to those of Cugat. 'Tabu' has been much covered and became a big band and exotica standard for many years, with all reference to the Orisha gradually excised from the lyrics as it became more popular.

Other successful Cuban musicians such as Perez Prado, Tito Puente and Celia Cruz have been rumoured to have an interest or involvement in Santeria. Cruz, the queen of salsa, denied that she was an initiate of the religion and claimed to be exclusively Roman Catholic, yet she recorded three albums of devotional music for the

Orisha: *Homenaje a los Santos, Volumes 1 & 2* and *Homenaje a La Madama*, the latter dedicated to the spirit La Madama – a sort of matriarchal African ancestor spirit. La Madama is commonly made out of a black plastic doll stuffed with herbs and other items, and is called upon for protection and for help in reading the playing cards. The cover of the record shows a possessed spirit medium reading the cards, surrounded by a La Madama effigy, a statue of St. Lazarus and other spiritual items. Cruz's best known Orisha song is a hymn to Yemaya, the goddess of the sea and motherhood. Despite her public claims to have no involvement with Santeria, Cruz's public persona was that of an archetypal child of Yemaya. She would frequently perform dressed in blue, Yemaya's sacred colour; and her catchphrase 'Azucar', meaning sugar, recalled a traditional offering to the sea goddess.

Other Cuban musicians were more forthright in proclaiming an allegiance to the spirits. The percussionist Mongo Santamaria, an initiate of the religion and child of Shango, most famous for his recording of 'Watermelon Man', cut a track dedicated to his god called 'O Mi Shango' on his 1976 record *Sofrito*. The track opens with one of Shango's drum rhythms and prayers chanted in Yoruban, then radically shifts style and tempo into a sort of proto-disco Latin funk workout peppered with shouts of 'Cabio sile', the traditional greeting to the god of fire. In places it sounds exactly like a Blaxploitation movie soundtrack, and you can imagine split screen images of Shango playing the drums, dancing, fighting, seducing women and walking through fire.

Similarly, the Cuban pianist Eddie Palmieri released a record in 1978 titled *Lucumi Macumba Voodoo*, composed of tracks dedicated to the Orisha. The cover of the record is a slightly cheesecake close-up of a woman's bare neck and shoulders, adorned with eight strings of multicoloured beads. The beads are known as *collares*, and are the first step of initiation into Lukumi, the religion more widely known as Santeria. Interestingly, the beads depicted are not the most commonly given *collares*, but relate to some very specific roads of the Orisha. For instance, the recurring red beads in the blue necklace for Yemaya and the white necklace of Obatala, denote that they are dedicated to particular warrior roads of those Orisha. The liner notes of the record contain a bafflingly complex description of African melodic patterns written by Palmieri:

> *Cellos alone play glissando harmonics, followed by the piano solo in E-flat minor that introduces the call letters of the god Ozain and eventually states a theme derived from a variation of chord structures of the same. For example: the call letters or numbers of Ozain are 636 737 699 636 in the mythology. With mathematical application, using the E-Flat as zero extension, one being E-natural, working in semi-tones ascending, my first root number, six, converts to A-natural, three is C, six is F-sharp. 737 thus becomes D-flat, E-natural and B-natural. The call letters being twelve numbers, they become twelve musical tones, voice-led to avoid repetition of notes.*

Black Orpheus

The music of Brazil follows a similar pattern to that of Cuba. Brazil has produced several African Diaspora traditions including Candomble and Macumba, Umbanda and Quimbanda. An eBay search will occasionally turn up obscure recordings of religious music related to these traditions, often privately pressed or on tiny labels, and most commonly LPs dedicated to popular Orisha such as Shango and Yemaya. While the form of the music may be drum-led and involve a choir of singers performing call and response patterns - as per the religious music of Haiti and Cuba - the execution is unmistakably Brazilian. It's easy to hear the origins of the samba and bossa-nova in the rhythm and cadence of the devotional songs.

As per the parallel example of Cuban Orisha music, the African Diaspora religious traditions of Brazil exert a strong influence on more outwardly secular areas of Brazilian culture and music. The 1959 film *Orpheu Negro* (Black Orpheus), directed by Marcel Camus, presents such a depiction of Brazil's traditions and their music. With a soundtrack by Antonio Carlos Jobim, who wrote 'The Girl from Ipanema', the story is a retelling of the Greek myth of Orpheus and Eurydice set in Rio de Janeiro during Carnival. On the soundtrack record, the song 'Felicidade', Jobim's beautiful bossanova signature track for the film, is almost completely lost beneath a mountain of Carnival sounds, drums and chaotic background noise. At the climax of the film, Orpheus's journey to the Underworld is depicted in a scene where the lead character is led down many flights of stairs to a basement where a Candomble or Macumba ceremony is being held. During the service, an elderly woman smoking a huge cigar is possessed by the spirit of his lost Eurydice, and he converses with her from beyond the grave.

The bossanova musician Sergio Mendes, who found international acclaim during the Sixties for a series of albums recorded with his band Brazil '66, released an album with his later line-up, Brazil '77, called *Primal Roots*. It is essentially the Sergio Mendes Voodoo record, arranged by Mendes, but incorporating many elements of Brazilian folk music and African Diaspora religious themes. The record opens with 'Promessa de Pescador' (promise of a fisherman), written by the Bahian composer Dorival Caymmi. It tells the story of a fisherman's appeal to the sea goddess Lemanja (known elsewhere as Yemaya) for the safety of his son while he is at sea. The record also features other songs dedicated to Lemanja, the Caboclo Indian spirits, and the spirit Pomba Gira.

More recently, in 1992, the singer Maria Bethania, sister of the musician Caetano Veloso, released *Olho d'Agua* which contains several tracks with Orixa themes. Both Bethania and Veloso were strongly associated with the Tropicalismo art movement of the late Sixties, which produced many examples of Brazilian psychedelia and encompassed musicians such as Os Mutantes, Gilberto Gil and Gal Costa. An interest or flirtation with Afro-Brazilian magico-religious traditions simmers beneath the surface of Tropicalia, with Os Mutantes recording a song called 'Bat Macumba', and Gilberto Gil making a record with Jorge Ben called *Ogum Xango*, named for the two Orixa. The short-lived Tropicalia movement, which expressed resistance to the 1964 right-wing coup in Brazil, saw many performers arrested, tortured by the government, forced into 'psychiatric care' or exiled from the country. The centre piece of Bethania's *Olho d'Agua* is the track 'Louvacao a Oxum', a beautiful hymn to the goddess Oxum (known elsewhere as Oshun), who rules over rivers, pleasure, love, sex, joy and luxury. Bethania appears on the album cover looking every bit the child of Oxum, with her gold arm bracelet, dark hair and captivating eyes, and the back cover depicts a waterfall, where Oxum is traditionally believed to bathe.

Obeah Man Style

The survival of African magico-religious traditions in Jamaica, as a Protestant colony, follows a broadly similar pattern to their survival in the United States. An indigenous folk magic survives in the form of obeah, which could be readily compared to the hoodoo conjure of the US South; whereas the African religious impulse is expressed through various 'revival' groups that take their lead from the Old Testament, but incorporate drum-led services and spirit possession in a way that is not unlike the African Spiritual Churches of New Orleans.

The drum was made illegal in Jamaica during the days of slavery, as a specific measure to suppress African religious practice. It was thought that such gatherings could provide a catalyst for a slave uprising, and as the Haitian revolution went on to demonstrate, they were right. However, certain traditions of African religious drumming such as the Burru and Kumina styles did survive this oppression in an underground form. The West African Burru tribal group maintained strong elements of their culture intact through slavery and colonial rule; whereas Kumina is the musical component of a revivalist religion called Pocomania, which has its roots in Ghana and involves drum-led spirit possession by the ancestors. Both of these African patterns of drumming formed the foundation for the music that would later emerge out of the Rastafari camps of the 1930s, and went on to influence the development of reggae.

The colonial suppression of Voodoo-style gatherings in Jamaica has certain thematic parallels with the consequences of outlawing the Congo Square dances in New Orleans. An argument might be made that the rise of the very secular soundsystem dances in Kingston in the 1950s were as much an expression of a distinctly African holding of space as the jazz clubs of Treme. The soundmen who held the dances came to serve a role in their community comparable to that of the Houngan in a Voodoo temple, providing financial aid, legal help and advice on all matters to the locals who followed their sound. The soundmen's dances created a free African space, and provided ghetto sufferahs with a celebratory territory that existed beyond the frequently desperate realities of colonial oppression and post-colonial turbulence. A local soundsystem was followed with the same fervency as any Vodou peristyle, and the clashes between rival soundsystems were just as deadly as Vodou Society disputes. During the mid-Sixties rude boy era where violence in Kingston escalated due to severe economic problems, it was soundmen such as Prince Buster who took the responsibility of speaking out against the escalating gangster culture. Buster released a series of records where he took on the persona of Judge Dread, a stern African judge giving out heavy sentences to badmen in the community, coming on like the voice of the ancestors cut onto a dub plate 7".

A free African space

In Haitian Vodou, the Lwa Loco is considered the first Houngan. He is syncretised with St. Joseph, both for his role as nurturing protector of the infant Christ, and for his profession as a carpenter. Loco is concerned with the structure and integrity of the temple, and ensures the solidity and stability of a Vodou house. It is perhaps then fitting that Sir Coxsone Downbeat, one of the primal forces of Jamaican music, was a carpenter by trade and first got into running a soundsystem because his carpentry skills allowed him to build his own speaker boxes and other equipment. Similarly, the great New Orleans funk and R&B producer Eddie Bo was originally a carpenter, and when Hurricane Katrina destroyed his restaurant, Check your Bucket, he rebuilt it himself by hand despite being in his seventies.

The music played on the Jamaican soundsystems was initially New Orleans R&B, before the development of uniquely Jamaican musical forms such as ska, and later rocksteady, roots reggae, dub and dancehall. One of the earliest ska records was 'Oh Carolina', performed by the Folkes Brothers and produced by Prince Buster, a cover version of which was later a hit for Shaggy in the Eighties. Buster wanted to create a sound that didn't just emulate American R&B, but brought something of Jamaican culture into the mix, so he sought out the Rasta master drummer Count Ossie to play drums on the record. Count Ossie's rhythms were heavily influenced by Burru and Kumina patterns, and his inclusion in the session was extremely controversial as Rastafarians were at the time considered social pariahs in mainstream Jamaican society. In this way a sweet love song becomes a revolutionary fire. The soaring drums on 'Oh Carolina' ring out like an urgent message from Africa, and the 7" captures the moment at which the emergent JA soundsystem dances came into contact with the underground African spiritualities that had survived and mutated into Rastafari. Prince Buster's desire to cross-fertilise the New Orleans R&B sound with an indigenous Jamaican musical tradition has parallels with Dizzy Gillespie's impulse to marry US jazz with Afro-Cuban drum rhythms, and the end result similarly defined a new genre of music.

The folk magic traditions of obeah tend to take a hammering in many Jamaican recordings. Examples of this include 'Obeah Book' by The Ethiopians, 'Black Candle' and 'Voodooism' by Lee Perry, 'Obeah Man' by Welton Irie, and 'Fire pon Obeah' by Capleton. On the surface of things, you might assume there to be hostility between Rastafari and competing traditions like obeah. However, the vocal denouncement of obeah on these tracks is perhaps more in the spirit of Mother Leafy Anderson's efforts to disassociate her New Orleans Spiritual Church from a popular concept of Voodoo as evil magic. Historically, Rastafari was much denigrated in Jamaican society and the difference between a Rastaman and an obeah man was perhaps not so well-defined in the popular imagination, as both looked to Africa for inspiration and strongly resisted colonial culture.

The twilight profession of the obeah man tends to attract

many charlatans and unscrupulous con men, as well as those who are legitimate in their beliefs and practice, but predominantly work evil magic in return for cash. Many, if not all, reggae tracks that take an anti-obeah line concern themselves specifically with this issue. Lee Perry's 'Black Candle' is addressed to an obeah worker who is burning a 'bad lamp' on the song's protagonist. The vocal defiantly proclaims, 'You can burn black candle little more, iniquity worker, you can't hurt I' as the righteous power of Jah is stronger than any 'evil science'. The Ethiopians track takes a similar line, affirming: 'I'm not an obeah man, I am a rasta man, I am the righteous one. I do not study iniquity. I do not act wickedly'. Welton Irie bemoans the experience of visiting an obeah man who turns out to be a con man: 'spread a white sheet, with rice and goat meat, and when you not look, it's him who go and eat, and when you turn round, he say a duppy do it, you get so fed up you just kiss your teeth.' In all these instances, the word 'obeah' is essentially just a synonym for malicious witchcraft and the anti-social mindset that seeks to work evil magic on others for personal gain. Hence the anti-obeah sentiment in reggae is very similar to the hoodoo references in early blues recordings that deplore the practice of harmful magic, and does not necessarily indicate an antagonism between reggae and African magico-religious traditions *per se*.

Malicious witchcraft & the anti-social mindset

For instance, Capleton's 'Fire Pon Obeah' is as blistering an attack on the practice of evil science as has been committed to vinyl, but it opens with the dancehall MC voicing the words 'tell them Shango, tell them'. Capleton, while a vocal adherent of the Bobo Ashanti denomination of Rastafari, chooses to go by the stage names 'King Shango' and 'The God of Fire', among other titles, which suggests at least some degree of appreciation and endorsement of Yoruban tradition and theology alongside his Rastafari beliefs. One of the defining principles of Rastafari is its notion of Africa as a sacred landscape, so it would seem somewhat at odds with this pan-African perspective to assume that these records were denouncing African spirituality as a whole, rather than malicious magic specifically. Across the African diaspora, the diverse traditions of Africa frequently tend to merge organically when they encounter one another, so it seems highly unlikely that there are not points where traditions such as Pocomania, Rastafari and obeah inhabit a common ground.

The ideal of the righteous Rastaman has certain parallels with the concept of Moses as 'The Great Voodoo Man of the Bible', which is an important trope of US hoodoo. In both instances, the magic of the Old Testament sits in as a substitute for the outlawed magic of Africa. In hoodoo, Moses' command over snakes, his parting of the Red Sea and role as a spiritual leader of his people make him a perfect fit for the lost role of Houngan. Many blues recordings reference the story of Moses and imply a spiritual comparison between the Jewish exile and the forced African Diaspora. Rastafari picks up this same theme, and depicts the displaced African people as the Biblical lost tribe of Israel, forced to dwell in Babylon and yearning to return to Africa. Lopez Walker's 'Send another Moses' is a prime example of

this trend, calling on the Biblical personage to smite corrupt rulers and 'whip them with the Rod of Correction'. The Maytals' 'Six and Seven Books of Moses' makes the hoodoo connection explicit, as the song is named after an eighteenth-century German grimoire that purported to be the lost writings of Moses detailing how he performed his feats of magic. The book became popular among African American hoodoo practitioners, and later spawned another sequel *The 8th, 9th and 10th Books of Moses*, written by Henri Gamache in the 1940s. Gamache penned a lengthy introduction to this work, clearly inspired by the ideas of Marcus Garvey who was writing in the same period, where he portrayed Moses as a black African sorcerer. The Maytals' record namechecks the first five books of the Bible and then states 'the sixth and the seventh book, he wrote them all' – as if to affirm the reality of this pan-African interpretation of Moses and his magic.

In his book *Bass Culture*, Lloyd Bradley argues that the experimentation of dub can be traced back to the principles of obeah. In obeah practice, a human being is thought to be comprised of various spiritual components, the influence of which can be increased or decreased by the obeah professor to create a more healthy balance.

Bradley draws a parallel between this philosophy, and the dub producer who considers the component parts of a song and manipulates them to create something new out of the existing pattern. It's a principle common to all Voodoo practice, where a violent man might need the volume turned down on their Ogun, or a loveless woman might need their Oshun brought up louder in the mix. In Bradley's view, certain dub producers such as King Tubby and Lee Perry may not practice obeah in the traditional sense, but their work in the studio can be considered a part of the same continuum, crafting X-Ray music shot through with echo, sound effects and abyssal caverns of dread.

'Obeah Man Style' by Lone Ranger bucks the trend of denigrating the folk magic practice, and positions obeah as an empowering force along similar lines to gunman lyrics. Equally, Peter Metro's 'Obeah in America' ends with the refrain 'hugging up the big obeah man' echoing the closing lines of The Maytals' 'Monkey Man'. Yellowman's 'Obeah' eulogises the ability of Jamaican singers, DJs and producers to 'work dem obeah' in the studio; and Lee Perry, with typical idiosyncrasy, changes his tune about the practice on the Adrian Sherwood-produced track 'Obeah Room' and relates how he intends to work his obeah on George Bush and Tony Blair.

Pocomania, the estranged grandmother of Rastafari, often sits in the background of reggae and occasionally makes her voice heard. Lee Perry's 'People Funny Boy' was directly inspired by the rhythms of Pocomania. In an interview, Perry shared the song's origins: 'One night me walking past a Pocomania church and hear the people inside a wail. And me catch the vibration and say boy! Let's make a sound fe catch the vibration of them people!' Pocomania later became a recurrent theme of Eighties and Nineties dancehall, beginning with Lord Sassafras's 'Pocomania Jump' where he recounts an obeah-type ritual involving a basin of water, offerings of fruit and parchment paper sprinkled with vinegar, and proudly proclaims 'Lord Sassafras has the best obeah.' On the cover of the record he appears in full Pocomania shepherd garb wielding a crooked stick. In the early Nineties, Gregory Peck (the dancehall MC, not the actor) released a hugely influential track called 'Pocoman Jam', which spawned many other cuts over the same riddim. Chalice and Lovindeer's 'Pocomania Day' was another popular Nineties hit, where the narrator laments his girl's decision to 'jump revival in a country church on Pocomania Day', leaving him to 'jump revival in a lonely way', and poignantly reminds her that when she feels the spirit, he 'was always around to stop her from falling down'.

The global influence of JA soundsystem culture can't really be overstated. During the 1970s, Jamaican-born DJ Kool Herc exported both the mobile soundsystem concept and the Jamaican DJ practice of toasting over riddims to the Bronx, and in the process became one of the founding fathers of hip hop. Meanwhile in the UK, *Empire Windrush*-era soundmen such as Duke Vin and Count Suckle set up the first soundsystem dances in 1950s London and laid the foundations of what would ultimately become the drum & bass/garage/hardcore/grime/dubstep continuum. The music might mutate over time, but what all such free spaces have in common is their creation of a predominantly African, or at least strongly African-influenced, temporary autonomous zone that is conjured into being for a time, and exists beyond the sanction and control of any ruling government or authority. There is something inherently threatening about the existence of soundsystem dances that puts a shiver of cold dread down the spine of mass Western culture and those who profit from it.

In his 1972 satirical novel, *Mumbo Jumbo*, the author Ishmael Reed portrays this Voodoo-esque force as 'Jes Grew', which he describes as an anti-plague that enlivens the host 'as electric as life, and characterised by ebullience and ecstasy... it is the delight of the Gods', proliferating uncontrollably through Western culture and infecting everything it touches. As Jes Grew spreads virulently over the globe, another force characterised by Reed as 'The Wallflower Society' continually attempts to suppress it. In this spirit, perhaps a symbolic line can be drawn between the outlawing of the dances at Congo Square, and present day restrictions of civil liberties such as the racial profiling and heavy-handed police clampdowns on grime nights in London that have made it virtually impossible to experience the music live.

BRIXTON BASS PRESSURE

African Diaspora magic remains as prevalent a force in the contemporary urban landscape as it has been in any other time or place. Scrape beneath the surface of London and the living pulse of Voodoo sounds out like a bass echo. Libations of rum at the Four Aces in Dalston. Honey and oranges left by the Thames for Our Lady of Charity. Shango statues and Seven African Powers candles stare out of window displays selling rosaries and spiritual supplies in Brixton's covered market. Veves of the spirits tagged on railway sidings and bus shelters. Voodoo mutates and adapts itself to the environment in the same way that its music does. Its job is to reflect the landscape and living experience of its children and administer to the specific needs of time and place. Concrete pressure and broken promises. Postcode killings and skeng man menace. Destitute girls six months pregnant forced to take their chances sleeping rough in Victoria Park, while a pack of parasitic leeches reward their own failure with fat bonuses and duck islands. Wild creation pillaged and exploited for temporary profit, while the vulnerable are left to suffer at the sharp end. The foundations are shaken, economies in freefall, ecosystems in collapse, but still well-heeled vultures circle round to pick the last meat from the bones of the impoverished and call it something else. Spindoctor bokors work their wicked science, casting a glamour while they reach in your pocket to rob your dreams and dignity. Voodoo takes up an axe and calls the thunder to earth. It's the heart that's pierced but does not bleed. The dance of the Calinda. The living spirit that won't bow down. The skull in the top hat that calls the wicked to account.

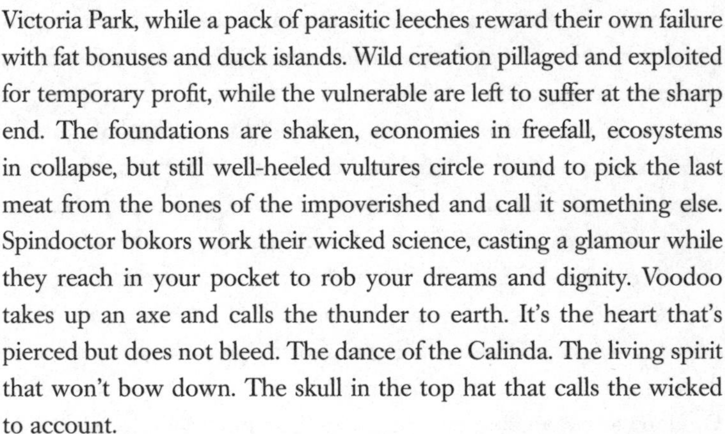

London has its dread Voodoo soundtrack, versioned and reversioned through the fluid medium of time. It's in the swing of the first New Orleans jazzmen playing Congo Square rhythms in the West End. It's in the blues parties and shebeens of the 1950s, The Flamingo Club in Soho and The Roaring Twenties on Carnaby Street, where Jamaican riddims first rang out and propagated post-war British soil with more fire. You can hear it in Papa Levi's 'Mi God, Mi King' and

The science of obeah

its righteous history lesson and unshakeable assertion of personal sovereignty, pitched against the blighted landscape and crippling inequality of Thatcher's Britain in the 1980s. You can hear it in Warrior Queen's 'Dem a bomb we', coming on like a fierce Erzulie Dantor, seething with rage among the blood and body parts of Tavistock Square, turning an accusatory eye upon those who bomb the innocent of their own communities in the name of fundamentalism. The science of obeah creeps into dubstep and its twilight excavation of haunted London, manipulating recorded sound to get under the skin of the urban wasteland and dig for fractured spirits. The ghosts of a thousand nightbus journeys across an endless terrain of South London badlands stretching into recursive oblivion. The phantom ambience and lost corridors of a crumbling inner city care home recorded onto tape after the patients have been put to bed. The mysteries of a carpark in Croydon. The sacred heart of Elephant and Castle in the rain. A backdrop of ruptured beats stolen from better times and called up to give testimony like a spectral reminder of lost nights and luminous dances long ago and in another life.

Turn the dial on the radio and Voodoo inhabits the liminal space between ghastly advertising jingles and talent show foulness. Pirate stations raise the Jolly Roger over east London and give cut-throat voice to urban pressure over towering sci-fi beats broadcast out of high-rise flats. Teenage MCs chat the mic about murder and count their dead. Carve out a space to nice up the dance. The grime of the city is shown as it is with nothing expurgated, holding up a mirror to the city as brutal and uncompromising as that carried by any vengeful Voodoo Queen. Voodoo casts its spell in London, and it uncoils slowly over time. Every dancehall is an outpost of the ancient temple, and every schoolkid spitting urgent bars about their life into a mobile phone is ridden by the spirit. You glimpse its reflection subtly, in the skulls, machetes, and coffin-shaped speaker boxes that adorn the cover art of The Bug's *London Zoo* album, a scathing dancehall attack on the city's ills and corruption; or in Grievous Angel's 'Lady Dub' a dubstep 12" dedicated to Erzulie Freda Dahomey, stamped with the image of the Mater Dolorosa, with whom she is syncretised. Erzulie Freda is the Lwa of love, beauty and sorrow. Champagne in the VIP area, French perfume and expensive lingerie. She feels the pain of the world but transforms it. She has many lovers but remains a virgin in her heart. She cries for the world because the grim realities of life down here can never match her perfect dream of beauty – but Erzulie is that capacity to dream of something better. Her tears wash away the fear and sorrow in which we can become mired, and bring a freshness of perception like the first morning in the Garden of Eden. Voodoo is this triumph. The gates of Congo Square are still open and the Kingdom of Shango was never conquered by the Black Iron Prison.

SELECT BIBLIOGRAPHY

HYATT, HARRY MIDDLETON. *Hoodoo-Conjuration-Witchcraft-Rootwork* (1970)

YRONWODE, CATHERINE. 'HOODOO IN THEORY AND PRACTICE': *www.luckymojo.com*

WARD, MARTHA. *Voodoo Queen: The spirited lives of Marie Laveau* (2004)

LONG, CAROLYN MORROW. *A New Orleans Voudou Priestess: The Legend and Reality of Marie Laveau* (2006)

MORGAN, THOMAS L. 'MARDI GRAS INDIAN INFLUENCE ON THE MUSIC OF NEW ORLEANS'. *www. jass.com/tom/next/indian.html*

CLARK JR, WILLIE W. 'A BRIEF HISTORY OF THE MARDI GRAS INDIANS': *www.mardigrasdigest.com/Sec_mgind/history.htm*

VEGA, MARTA MORENO. 'THE YORUBA ORISHA TRADITION COMES TO NEW YORK CITY': *African American Review*, SUMMER 1995

MCGOWAN, CHRIS AND PESSANHA, RICARDO. *The Brazilian Sound: Samba, Bossa Nova and the popular music of Brazil* (1994)

BRADLEY, LLOYD. *Bass Culture: when reggae was king* (2001)

Spinning with
SPIDERS' SILK

by ELEANOR MORGAN

IN THE autumn of 2009 a piece of golden coloured fabric went on display at the American Museum of Natural History in New York. It stretches 11 feet by 4 feet and was created entirely from the silk of the golden orb spider of Madagascar. Over four years, under the guidance of art historian Simon Peers, a group of Madagascan people collected approximately 3,000 spiders each day from trees and telegraph poles. The spiders were then handled by a group of women weavers, who extracted the silk from the creatures' spinnerets onto a spool from which it was woven on a loom. It is the largest known spiders' silk fabric in existence, yet it is not the first attempt to harvest silk from spiders.

Throughout our history people have experimented with spiders' silk to create fabrics and clothing. Most of these items have disappeared, and are perhaps still waiting to be found in various museums and attics. Simon Peers himself was inspired by the story of a nineteenth-century French missionary, Jacob Paul Camboué, who had woven the silk of the Madagascan golden orb spider into bed hangings. These were to be exhibited at the 1900 Paris Exposition, but there is no record

of them in the exhibition catalogue. As perhaps befits such a magical material, the history of people weaving with spiders' silk is intertwined with myths and vague accounts. Having researched the notes, letters and sketches of some of these individuals, I would like to present a short history of some spiders' silk collectors, the machines they created and the spiders they worked with. The prints accompanying this story are my own, created from historical written descriptions or drawings.

Fear of spiders is a common phobia, out of all proportion to their actual threat to us. Yet they also hold a particular mythical attraction. The Greek story of Arachne is one of many spider tales, in which the mortal Arachne's pride in her weaving ability leads to her being turned into a spider for all eternity by the goddess Athene. Another example is the spider Ananse, a trickster figure in West African and Caribbean tales, who was responsible for introducing stories and wisdom into the world. The enchanting, mythical potential of spiders lies in the fact that they produce what is perhaps *the* magical material: spiders' silk. Popularly held as being stronger than steel, it is also magnetic, water resistant and has 'shape memory', in that it can be stretched and return to its original size without any loss of tension. Such properties have made spiders' silk a versatile material for human uses. A nineteenth century naturalist records seeing women in Bermuda using spiders' silk for sewing; Australian aboriginal communities used it to make fishing nets and lines; and since the time of the Ancient Greeks, spider webs have been used to help heal wounds – a possibility still being explored today with artificial silk in biomedical research. More recently, strands of spiders' silk were used as crosshairs in gun sights and telescopes. There is also a story of the seventeenth-century Mughal Emperor Aurengzebe, who reproved his daughter for "the indelicacy of her costume, although she wore as many as seven thicknesses of spider cloth".[1] Examples of the practical uses of spiders' silk cannot

1. Henry Christopher McCook, *American Spiders and Their Spinningwork: A Natural History of the Orbweaving Spiders of the United States, with Special Regard to Their Industry and Habits* (Philadelphia: H. C. McCook, 1889), p. 84.

entirely avoid this sense of the fantastical and enchanting. Most of the collectors in this story recount being spellbound by the shimmering appearance of spiders' silk. Yet unlike silk worms, spiders have resisted all attempts at large-scale human harvesting. Even recent research into artificial silk has been unable to replicate the mysterious transformation of liquid protein to solid silk that takes place in the body of the spider. In this sense, the story of spiders' silk collectors can be considered as an example of the many enchantments and obstacles that occur in our encounters with animals.

The first recorded attempt to turn spider silk collecting into a commercially profitable activity was made by in 1709 by Monsieur Le Bon, President of the court of accounts in Montpelier. He collected spider's nests, which he boiled in water and gum arabic – a technique similar to those used for collecting silk from silk worms. Indeed, the interest in the commercial possibilities of spiders' silk was partly in response to the desire for a domestic European silk industry which would not rely on Asian imports, or on the delicate demands of the silk worm unsuited to the European climate and agricultural traditions. After boiling the cocoons, Le Bon dried and spun the silk into three pairs of spider silk stockings, two of which he presented to the Royal Academy of Sciences in Paris and the third to Sir Hans Sloane at the Royal Society in London.[2] In response to Le Bon's research, the Royal Academy commissioned the prolific scientist René Antoine de Réaumur to investigate the commercial possibilities of spiders' silk.

Using Le Bon's technique of boiling spider's nests, Reaumur concluded that spiders' silk could not be of any commercial value. He listed three limiting factors. The first was the difficulty of collecting and housing the spiders – particularly the problem of trying to prevent the spiders from eating each other. The second was supplying the animals with fresh prey, and the last was the inferior quality and yield of spiders' silk compared to that of the silk worm. However, in reference to this

2. Marquis de Bon, 'Translation of a letter from Marquis de Bon to Hans Sloane', 1739, EL/B3/41, GB 117 The Royal Society.

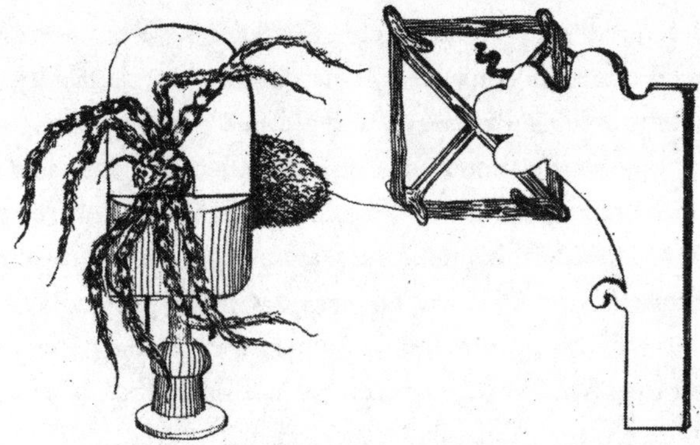

Fig.1 *Abbé Ramon de Termeyer's silk-gathering device*

final problem Reaumur had been studying the silk of spider's nests, a very fine material that most closely resembled that of silk worms. It was not until 1762 that a Spanish Jesuit priest discovered that the strongest silk came not from a spider's nests, but directly from her body.[3]

Abbé Raimondo (Ramòn) de Termeyer was a missionary and amateur naturalist. His wide and varied research included experiments on electric eels, a proposal for an antidote to viper venom and a short paper on how to keep eggs fresh during long journeys. But his main passion was spiders. His house in Milan was filled with thousands of them. They were suspended from separate canes all around the house, and were fed by a steady supply of flies that bred in the piles of rotten meat that Termeyer had put out for them.

Termeyer noticed that if he gave a fly to one of these spiders, it would quickly envelope it with silk from its abdomen. He went about devising a machine that could collect this silk directly from the spider's body. He came up with this contraption (*Fig.1*), in which the spider was held between two plates, while her silk was collected onto a spool.

3. Raimondo Maria de Termeyer, *Researches and Experiments Upon Silk from Spiders, and Upon Their Reproduction*. Translated and Revised by BG Wilder. Communicated to the Essex Institute. Extracted from the Proceedings, Vol. 5, p. 8. (Salem, Massachusetts, 1866).

Termeyer described the silk he collected as appearing like a mirror, or polished metal. He was convinced of its commercial possibility. He had solved the problems that Reaumur had listed – he kept his spiders on separate canes so they could not eat each other; they had a steady supply of food which was easy to provide and he had discovered that the silk they produced on his machine was stronger and more vibrant than that of the silk worm. He was now faced with the problem of how to spin the silk. It was too thin in its original form, so the strands had to be twisted together. Yet this led to the silk losing its lustre, looking more like white cotton than silk. In the end, he reverted to the tried and tested technique of boiling up the spiders' nests. He then spun the silk into pairs of stockings. Over the next 20 years, Termeyer sent these spiders' silk stockings to various monarchs, including Charles III of Spain, Catherine the Great and Archduke Ferdinand. He also sent some stockings to Napoleon and Josephine, in spite of the fact that his own house had been blown to pieces during the Napoleonic invasion of 1796.[4] Unfortunately, I have yet to find any record of what happened to any of these silk stockings.

Termeyer recorded his spider research in a small pamphlet, of which only one copy exists. It remained largely forgotten in a library in New York until 1866 when it was discovered by a US army surgeon.

But first, a quick stop somewhere closer to home – at 21 Friday Street, Cheapside, London, where in the autumn of 1829 Daniel Bransdon Rolt was struck by the beauty of the light on the spiders' webs in his garden.[5] He began to pull the silk from a spider, and was able to collect a few yards before the spider broke the thread with her legs. He proceeded to collect 100 of these garden spiders, and kept them in

4. M de Asúa, 'The experiments of Ramón M. Termeyer SJ on the electric eel in the River Plate region (c. 1760) and other early accounts of Electrophorus electricus.', *J Hist Neurosci*, 17 (2008), pp. 160–74.

5. Daniel B Rolt, 'Letter from Mr D Bransdon Rolt to the Royal Society of Arts, 29th November 1830', *Manuscript Transactions Vol 121 (1829–31) part 4 of 5, The Royal Society of Arts*.

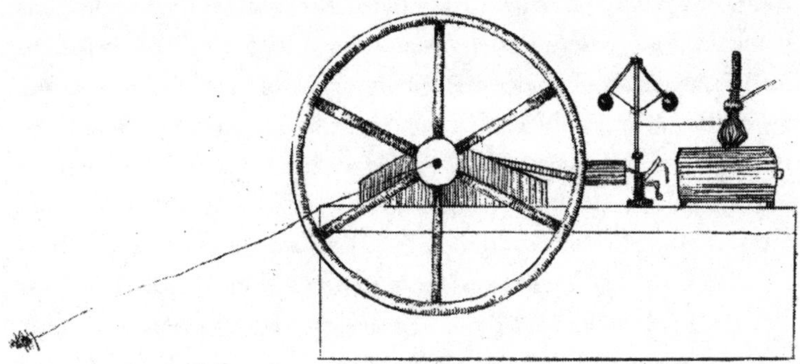

Fig. 2 *Daniel Bransdon Rolt's spider steam engine*

separate boxes in his room to prevent any cannibalism. Underneath the boxes was a large drawer containing rotten meat. This attracted flies, some of which would fly through tiny holes into the spider's dens above. He was thereby able to keep a large number of spiders alive while he devised a way of collecting their silk. In the end, he attached the individual spider to a steam engine, which he had borrowed from the factory in which he worked (*Fig. 2*). She was attached to a reel, which he turned at a rate of 150 feet per minute. Every 10 minutes he would change the spider for another. Over the course of two hours, he was able to collect 7,200 feet of silk. Rather than tying the spider down, as with Termeyer's machine, he simply let her crawl along the floor, or over his hands. Perhaps the rhythm and speed of the machine was such that the spider could not cut the thread with her legs.

Rolt submitted his findings, along with a scrap of silk and one of his spider houses, to the Royal Society of Arts, where he was presented with a silver medal in manufacturing, and praised for the novelty and ingenuity of his experiments.

I return now to the US Army Surgeon who found Abbé Termeyer's forgotten manuscript at the end of the American Civil War. His name was Dr Burt Green Wilder. In 1863 Wilder joined the 55th

Massachusetts regiment and was stationed on a marshy sandbar just south of Charleston, named Folly Island. To pass the time on Folly, he would explore its desolate terrain, and it was on one of these walks that he discovered a huge spider sitting in the centre of a golden coloured web, a web that stretched 10 feet between the trees. He collected the spider in his hat and carried it back to his tent. Here, he describes the scene:

> *The insect was very quiet, and did not attempt to escape; but presently, after crawling slowly along my sleeve, she let herself down to the floor, taking first the precaution, after the prudent fashion of most spiders, to attach to the point she left a silken line, which, as she descended, came from her body. Rather than seize the insect itself, I caught the thread and pulled. The spider was not moved, but the line readily drew out, and, being wound upon my hands, seemed so strong that I attached the end to a little quill, and, having placed the spider upon the side of the tent, lay down on my couch and turned the quill between my fingers.*

He continued at this for an hour and a half, after which time he had collected over 150 yards of "the most brilliant and beautiful golden silk I had ever seen". [6]

The spider that Wilder had found was the Nephila, or golden orb spider. Wilder was not the only soldier on Folly Island to have discovered this spider. Sigourney Wales, a lieutenant in the same regiment, had been passing the long hours on lookout duty by carving trinkets and mementoes, which he sold to the other men. He came across the Nephila, and like Wilder, realised that he could pull silk directly from the spider's spinnerets. He attached the thread to a spool and wound the yellow silk onto rubber rings, which apparently he was able to sell as real gold jewellery.

Wilder and Wales discussed their use of the spider, which led to Wilder's creation of a spider silk spinning machine, similar to that

6. Burt G Wilder, 'How my new acquaintances spin', *The Atlantic Monthly*, 18 (1866): p. 132.

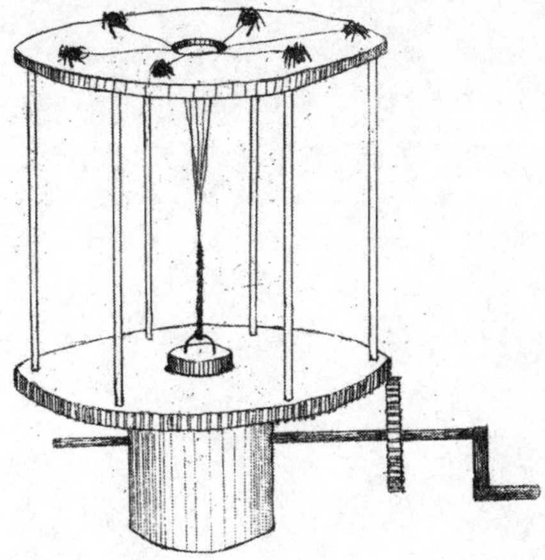

Fig.3 *Burt Wilder's silk-weaving drum*

of Termeyer. The spider was held in place upside down, which gave easier access to the spinnerets and was apparently more comfortable for the spider. In the autumn of 1864, while the union bombardment of Charleston was at its height, Wilder was able to wind almost two miles of golden silk on this machine.

After the end of the war, Sigourney Wales became a salesman in New York, while Burt Wilder became professor of zoology at Cornell University where he continued his investigations into spiders. He was interested not only in the biology of the spider, but also in the commercial potential of its silk. The thread was too thin to spin like cotton, so he tried various ways of twisting the threads together to make a thicker strand. In one of his attempts (*Fig.3*), he secured spiders to the top of a disk, and attached their silk to a stationary disk underneath. As the top disk turned, the silk was wound together. Using this process he was able to make a small strip of spiders' silk ribbon. In 1867, encouraged in his belief in the commercial potential of spiders' silk, he submitted a patent claim for his spider silk spinning machine.

I found Wilder's patent a few years ago while looking through old copies of *Scientific American*. I was already a spider silk spinner

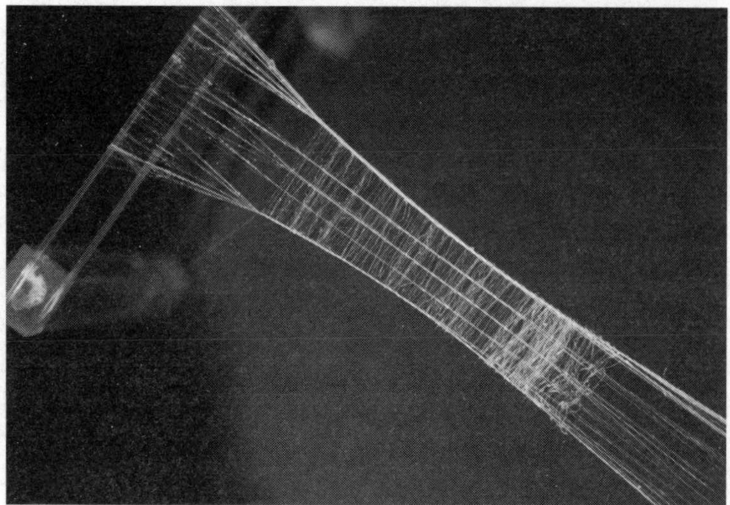

Fig.4 *Spider's silk woven by the author*

myself, but I did not know that there had been others. I collect silk from the European garden spider, which I weave into drawings or sculptures. It began in my studio, while I was staring at the many spider webs catching the dust and light in the corners of the room. I wanted to see what a sculpture made from spiders' silk would actually look like – could the strands of silk retain their magical glow when woven together? There were practical decisions to be made: How would I collect the silk? And once I had collected it, how would I weave such a fine material, better suited to spiders' legs then to clumsy human fingers? To begin, I constructed small wooden frames, which I placed behind the webs and pulled towards me, so that the strands of silk stuck to the frame. I then returned to my studio and tweezed apart the individual strands of silk. It was a slow and inefficient process, as I had to extract the dry, strong threads and discard the rest. I soon discovered a much better method. I found a huge web attached to the branches of a tree, with a European garden spider sitting in the centre. As before, I put my wooden frame behind the web and drew it towards me. The spider ran top right, off the web and onto a leaf. I turned the wooden frame, and the spider was still attached to the web with silk coming from her spinnerets. As I rotated the frame, I realised that I was extracting silk directly from her abdomen. I was able to collect at least two metres of silk before she cut the thread with her back legs.

It was unsettling to realise that I was extracting silk from a spider and could feel the bodily resistance of another animal through my hand. It is a moment that is described with amazement by many of the silk collectors. For me, the oddest experience is when I am weaving the silk on a loom. I stare at the silk for hours, and I can only see the threads clearly by using a strong spot light, so that when I close my eyes I can still see them as lines of light. At first I tried to work with tweezers, but the silk is more attracted to skin. So I hold and weave the silk between my hands. Often I cannot see it, so I seem to be gesturing at nothing, simply waving my hands in the air. I weave during early autumn, when spiders are at their largest. These are the 'gossamer' days, a name that originates from this time of year when all the bushes and trees seem to be covered in webs. After a day of weaving, I sometimes dream of the silk, the feel of it on my hands and the look of the strands on the loom. Perhaps these dreams are as close as we can get to the life of spiders.

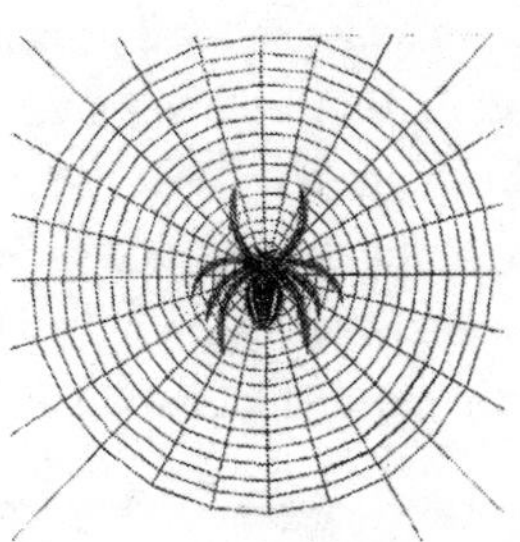

The Cult of Ku

a literary investigation into an ancient Chinese poisoning cult

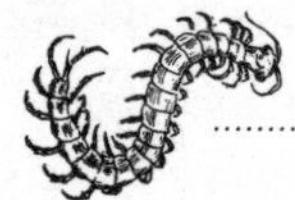

THE JUMP rhythms of Count Basie approximating Austin Spare's formula of the 'neither-neither'; John Levy's recordings of the Drukpa sect of Bhutan adumbrating the very qliphoth with their glissading shawms; the qabalistic significance of Bela Lugosi's name; GRS Mead's Theosophical analysis of a Mithraic ritual as mantric mimetic to approximate the arrival of the Outer Ones: these are just a few of the outré tentacles of Kenneth Grant's irreal research. His library of obsessions resides in some annex of the Miskatonic University founded on the most fragile precipices of reason – a glacial library with index cards sorted by the internal logic of a waking dream.

by ANDY SHARP *and* PHIL LEGARD *Illustration by* PHIL LEGARD

Grant's work is an extended conceit of occult humour, lost on academics and possibly lost on himself – 'the only difference between me and a madman is that I am not mad,' he quotes of Salvador Dalí. This is the nub for those who appreciate Grant for his obsessions rather than deride him as a lunatic: he is employing the Catalan master's paranoiac-critical methodology to magic.

One of the most exotic of Grant's fantasies involves a secret coterie of Chinese adepts known as the Cult of *Ku*. A faction supposedly existed in South London in the mid-twentieth century, though quite probably that faction operated in an ante-room of his own mythopoetic magickal lodge. Throughout Grant's Typhonian trilogies[1] *ku* surfaces as a touchstone of succubal preoccupations. Without doubt the opium waft of Sax Rohmer's pulp fiction drifts like yellow blossom on muddied waters between the Yangtse and a tributary of the Thames in Limehouse.

However, the roots of *ku* are very real and Grant's speculations in this region have their basis in an article which appeared in 1935 in the *Journal of the American Oriental Society*. It was entitled 'The Black Magic in China Known as Ku' and written by HY Feng and JK Shryock of the University of Pennsylvania.[2]

The article starts by defining *ku* as a specialised kind of 'black magic' that is used primarily to acquire wealth and secondarily as a means of revenge. Essentially, *ku* is a form of poison, which is extracted by placing venomous snakes and insects in a vessel until there is one survivor: a Darwinian form of dark alchemy. The surviving creature is called the *ku* and the poison extracted from it is then administered to the victim. Once the victim has died, their wealth will pass on to the practitioner of *ku*.

---

1. See for example *The Magical Revival* (London: Frederick Muller, 1972), *Aleister Crowley and the Hidden God* (London: Frederick Muller, 1973), and *Cults of the Shadow* (London: Frederick Muller, 1975).

2. 'The Black Magic in China Known as *ku*'. HY Feng, JK Shryock. *Journal of the American Oriental Society*, Vol. 55, No. 1. (Mar., 1935), pp. 1-30.

第十八卦 蠱 山風蠱 艮上巽下

KÛ POISON is not found generally among the people, but is used by the minority women. It is said that on the fifth day of the fifth month, they go to a mountain stream and spread new clothes and headgear on the ground, with a bowl of water beside them. They wait until snakes, lizards, and poisonous insects come to bathe in the bowl.

Feng and Shryock provide a fascinating investigation of the root of the word *ku*, suggesting from archaeological evidence that it is as ancient as Chinese script itself. A primitive form of the word was discovered on inscriptions found on shoulder-blades of cattle in the Honan. In this ancient form, the ideogram shows two insects in a receptacle. Here, Grant, it should be pointed out, honours the reading of the etymology entirely. A dictionary from about 100 AD, the *Shuo wen*, defines *ku* as 'worms in the belly' and as mentioned by Grant, there are quotes from a commentary on the Spring and Autumn Annals that states: 'Vessel and worms make *ku*, caused by licentiousness. Those who have died violent deaths are also *ku*.' This is actually key to understanding the spiritual significance of *ku* in that it appears to be essentially a moral/poetic/alchemical equation. The equation is highlighted by a discussion in which the authors imply the 'virtuous scholar need not fear the *ku*.' They relate the proverb of a scholar named Tsou Lang, who stumbles across a basket of silver within which *ku* has been secreted in the form of an indestructible caterpillar that follows him everywhere. He is told that he must serve the *ku*, which means feeding it with silk, collecting its excretions and using them to poison others. The possessions will then transfer from the victims to the scholar. He is trapped in a vicious circle by his accidental acquisition of *ku*. Indeed, his discovery of the *ku* is because a previous perpetrator of *ku* magic cannot cope with their Faustian bargain.

An indestructible caterpillar follows him everywhere

There is probably an undertone of superstition related to a primitive interpretation of transmittable diseases in this myth too. Tsou Lang, unwilling to be held captive to this contract decides to swallow the worm. His family try to stop him thinking he will die, however he not only survives but becomes wealthy from the silver he has found. The proverb ends with the quote 'that the sincerity of a man can overcome the most poisonous influence', a pertinent quote when one considers the dignified silence of Grant in the face of aspirational magicians who are happy to gain credence by peddling unfounded doubt about Grant's worth as an occultist.

At the risk of digressing, what the above anecdote illustrates is that *ku* is an extremely interesting and potent magical meme, a monad encapsulating the dangers of losing one's soul. This is borne out by Pre-Han literature in which there are at least five different uses for the word: a disease; evil spirits; to cause doubt, or a woman inveigling a man; a worm-eaten vessel which moulders and is blown away; a divination symbol. Feng and Shryock show how these five definitions equate with Hexagram 18, '*Ku*' in the I Ching (*left*). Of particular pertinence is the relationship between wind and the generation of worms, and later imagery associated with the hexagram such as 'wind and mountains', which can be traced to an earlier interpretation containing images of vessels and insects.

So here we have a mytho-linguistic archaeology and even, it seems, the Hexagram operating as a complex magical/qabalistic formula for the generation of *ku* poison. This is evidenced by a quote from the

Huai-nan Tzu which interprets of one of the trigrams as follows:

> *Heaven is one, Earth is two. Man is three. Three times three is nine. Two times nine is eighteen. The number eight stands for wind. Wind represents worms. Therefore worms are transformed in eight days.*

This almost sounds like an alchemical cipher and indeed, later in the article, the authors give a graphic description of the collection of *ku* which releases a lot of the imagery held in both the hexagram and the word:

> Ku *poison is not found generally among the people (i.e. the Chinese), but is used by the T'ung women. It is said that on the fifth day of the fifth month, they go to a mountain stream and spread new clothes and headgear on the ground, with a bowl of water beside them. The women dance and sing naked, inviting a visit from the King of Medicine (a tutelary spirit). They wait until snakes, lizards, and poisonous insects*

> *come to bathe in the bowl. They pour the water out in a shadowy damp place. Then they gather the fungus (poisonous) which grows there, which they mash into a paste. They put this into goose-feather tubes, and hide them in their hair. The heat of their bodies causes worms to generate, which resemble newly-hatched silk-worms. Thus* ku *is produced...*
>
> *The newly made* ku *is not yet poisonous. It is used as a love potion, administered in food and drink, and called 'love-medicine'. Gradually the* ku *becomes poisonous.*
>
> (Feng and Shryock)

So, this description bears out the idea of there being an hermetic gestation period required to ferment *ku* – 'therefore worms are transformed in eight days'.

Interestingly, and as a slight aside, the same anecdote goes onto say that, 'when a man enters a house in a T'ung village, if he sees no ashes on the hearth, and if the faces of the women appear yellow and their eyes red, he knows that there is *ku* in the house.'

Kenneth Grant has claimed that Sax Rohmer, author of the Fu Manchu fables, was aware of the activities of practitioners involved in *ku* magic. Indeed, in the 1921 story 'Firetongue', Rohmer's Phil Abingdon is described as having similar coloured 'violet eyes' to the women in the T'ung house. It does seem plausible that Rohmer's preoccupations with his arch-villain Fu Manchu's use of poisons may have stemmed from folkloric anecdotes such as this.

Whether the 'cult' of the *Ku* is merely the romantic interpretation of a shamanic, rustic, non-organised religion (i.e. witchcraft) or in fact a definite cabal later developed from these practices, the article gives no evidence. However, geographically speaking the body of literature concentrates the practice in south China and from the T'ang period (seventh to tenth century AD) on, the practice appears to have been more and more confined to aboriginal tribes of the south. As modern commentators have noted, the association of *ku* with ethnic minorities has continued even up to the present day. It is but one instance of a long association of associating the practices of 'black magic' with the 'Other' in order to preserve social norms. This type of myth-making is also indulged in by Rohmer and Grant through their connecting poison-magic with members of the Chinese minority in London. However, whereas Rohmer was arguably a sinophobe, Grant appears to be a positive xenophile: according to his own accounts, the New Isis Lodge allegedly connected with magical practitioners of all creeds and colours in a spirit of communal experimentation.

Another account of *ku*, written in the first part of the seventeenth century and focusing on the Miao country in southwest China, seems to bear out a temporal significance for the collection for *ku*. Mirroring the anecdote of the T'ung women, it states:

> *On the fifth day of the fifth month collect all those insects and worms that are poisonous and put them together in a vessel. Let them devour each other, and the one finally remaining is called* ku*... [T]he length of time required for the insects to devour each other will be proportionate to the time required for the poisoned victim to die... [T]he victim's property will imperceptibly be removed to the house of the witch and his spirit become her slave... [L]ater the* ku *flies about by night, appearing like a meteor. This variety is called 'flitting* ku*'. When the light grows stronger, a shadow like a living man's is produced. This is then called* t'aio-shen ku. *When its shadow grows stronger, the* ku *can have intercourse with women. Then it is called* chin-tsan ku. (Feng and Shryock)

Flitting ku

So clearly there is some sidereal exactitude that has been conveyed between practitioners, which would suggest, if not written, then there may be an oral tradition and some structure to the magical system. It might be fruitful to study the oriental astrological systems as this may yield deeper symbolism around the suggested time of collection of *ku* (i.e. the fifth day of the fifth [lunar] month). This day is itself a major festival in the Chinese calendar, marking the summer solstice. In regard to the mythos of *ku* there seems to be no coincidence that the insects should be collected in what is known in Chinese farmers' calendars as 'the poison month': the sultry period when flies, mosquitoes, insects and airborne disease are at their most prevalent.

In an account from Yunnan province the commentator notices, 'things… like meteors, sweeping across low over the roofs… due to *ku*' (Feng and Shryock); this UFO-like behaviour led the flying saucer-obsessed Grant to make his one real extrapolation in his study, suggesting an extraterrestrial nature or origin for *ku*. Given the original description of flying 'like a meteor' to the 'flitting *ku*' one feels this is a perfectly reasonable assumption in comparative religion. If it were made by Joseph Campbell or Patrick Harpur then it probably wouldn't have raised the guffaws that Grant detractors are prone to make about his inferences. Together with the incubal overtones of the *ku* and the obvious parallels with the alien abduction nightmare, one could argue that it would be negligent of Grant not to draw attention to the modern counterpart of the night sex demon *t'aio-shen ku*.

The same account from the Miao region also gives a very *Malleus Maleficarum*-like instruction for the treatment of a witch practicing *ku*:

> *They caught the witch, and buried her alive with head above the ground. They poured wax on her head and lighted it, in order to call back the poisoned spirits.* (Feng and Shryock)

As mentioned earlier, with the tale of the hapless scholar who chanced upon the basket of a caterpillar-*ku*, a book about aboriginal tribes of southwest China (dated between 1662-1723) discusses a similar tale of a toad *ku* found in Fukien:

> *Those who serve it are mostly covetous of the riches that accompany it. People sometimes see large sums of money and silk lying beside the road.* (Feng and Shryock)

As well as introducing another (decidedly Lovecraftian – cf.

Tsathoggua) species of *ku*, this anecdote explains that one can only relinquish servitude to *ku* by doubling the amount of money that the *ku* has made for you and leaving it on a road along with the money for someone to pick up. Again it is interesting that this analogy appears to suggest that *ku* superstition might relate to a primitive comprehension of the methods by which an infectious disease could be transmitted. However, this particular case history offers an all the more tantalising suggestion that:

> *with the wealth, the sender leaves a book telling the methods of serving the* ku. *The one who picks up the* ku *must clean his house and worship the* ku *spirit only, forsaking all Buddhist and Taoist deities.* (Feng and Shryock)

If this is the case then there is the truly exciting proposition that some form of grimoire once existed for this curious and tantalising form of deadly alchemy.

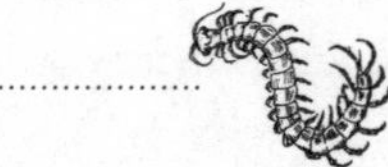

Charles Howard Hinton
Pioneer of Higher Space

by MARK BLACKLOCK

N AUGUST 2004 Dr Franklin Mead, Senior Scientist at the Advanced Concepts Office of the US Air Force Research Laboratory (AFRL) Propulsion Directorate at Edwards AFB, CA, commissioned from one Eric Davis of Warp Metrics in Las Vegas a feasibility study into the physics of teleportation. Davis's report summarised the history of research into teleportation before exploring four competing theories: vm-teleportation, based on the engineering of a traversable wormhole; q-teleportation, 'the current state-of-art of quantum teleportation physics'; e-teleportation, exploring alternative physical theories of extra dimensions or multiple universes; and p-teleportation, based on psychokinetic phenomena.[1]

This last perhaps revealed the motivating impetus behind the research: the records of Chinese research into teleportation that purported to have demonstrated the phenomenon. Davis hypothesised that 'the results of the Chinese p-Teleportation experiments can simply be explained as a human consciousness

1. Davis's 'Teleportation Physics Study' can be found online, on *scribd.com* and elsewhere. Its publication was reported in 2004.

phenomenon that somehow acts to move or rotate test specimens through a fourth spatial dimension, so that the specimens are able to penetrate the solid walls/barriers of their containers without physically breaching them. No real dematerialisation/rematerialisation of the specimens takes place.' In working up this hypothesis Davis made reference to a book first published in 1888, Charles Howard Hinton's *A New Era of Thought*.

Charles Howard Hinton is little-known outside of occult or New Age groupings. The author of the essay 'What is the Fourth Dimension?' has won a slight and mysterious notoriety by dint of cropping up in the right places. His work provides the theoretical basis for PD Ouspensky's *Tertium Organum*, Rudolf Steiner's *The Fourth Dimension* and Claude Bragdon's *A Primer of Higher Space*, works that punch above their weight in a library of *fin-de-siècle* occultism. Neither have Iain Sinclair's *White Chappell, Scarlet Tracings* or Alan Moore's

From Hell, both of which mediate Howard Hinton through his father, the aural surgeon and philosopher James, done any harm to the aura surrounding Hinton's reputation.

The truth is, though, that Hinton was no occultist, advocating to the end of his life a materialist approach towards the supra-sensible. That the scientific establishment of his day was dismissive of his work while sensationalist popular occultists like WT Stead or Theosophists like CW Leadbeater misrepresented or embraced it, was no fault of the author himself. By hybridising his science with the progressive ethical philosophy of his father, Hinton inadvertently shaped the fourth dimension of space into a form more palatable to metaphysical thinkers than to a scientific establishment in the process of professionalising, and keenly aware of the risks to its status posed by the metaphysical. Conversely, for occult thinkers, Hinton had just the right sheen of scientific respectability.

That's not to dismiss either Hinton or occultists. Far from it: Hinton was that rare thing, a true visionary; and a great Victorian pedagogue and inventor to boot. His work is a treasure trove of staggering ideas and, significantly, his biggest single idea provided something else that tasted good to *fin-de-siècle* occultism: a practical regimen of mental training that promised its adherents seemingly superhuman abilities. Perhaps most tellingly, in terms of his continued influence, Hinton wrote for a popular audience, and did it well, always keeping in mind an inquisitive and intelligent reader.

A LIFE IN FOUR DIMENSIONS

Born in 1853, Charles was educated at Rugby school and Balliol College Oxford, where he studied under his brother-in-law, Richard Nettleship, and the idealist philosopher TH Green, and had contact with his father's Oxford friend, Ruskin. He had spent a year at the physical laboratory in Berlin, and before being awarded his BA took up a job as assistant science master at Cheltenham Ladies' College.

While he was at Oxford, in 1875, his father died, and in 1878 Charles edited a collection of James Hinton's late philosophical writing, including a number of essays published in magazines and journals and some pieces excerpted from a wealth of unpublished manuscripts. In 1880, Charles married Mary, the eldest daughter of Mary and George Boole, the by-then deceased Irish mathematician and father of Boolean logic, and that September he moved his new wife to Uppingham to take up a job as science master at the college there.

The education of the imagination

While at Uppingham, Charles tested a system of fourth dimensional visualisation with his pupils, as documented in his later essay 'The Education of the Imagination'.[2] He took an active role in Uppingham life, playing in rugby matches for the masters against the boys, running societies and speaking in the debating society. In October his essay 'What is the Fourth Dimension?' was first published in the *University Magazine*, based in Dublin.

2. Charles also describes in this essay a three-dimensional chess game he had devised, but bemoans the fact that none of his pupils could understand it sufficiently to play it with him.

Charles and Mary Hinton with children George, Eric, William and Sebastian. Kanazawa, Japan, circa 1892. *With the permission of the University of Bristol Library Special Collections, ref: DM1718/A93*

In 1883 a John Weldon married a Maude Florence at a registry office in The Strand. Also in 1883, Hinton's essay, slightly expanded, was republished in the magazine of Cheltenham Ladies' College.

In 1884, Hinton published *Science Notebook*, now lost, a textbook in which he provided his contribution to the ongoing debate over how geometry should be taught in schools in the era of a tarnished Euclid. But it was the publication later the same year of someone else's book that gave Charles his real break in publishing. Edwin Abbott's *Flatland*, penned by the pseudonymous A Square, described in its first part the conditions of life in a world confined to a plane and, in its second, A Square's experience of a visitation from a three dimensional sphere. *Flatland* was an instant hit and Hinton's essay, germane to its subject matter although very different in tone to *Flatland*'s satire, was rapidly published as a pamphlet by the canny Swan Sonnenschein as the first in a series of *Scientific Romances.*[3]

3. The timing of the republication of Hinton's essay, a month after the first edition of *Flatland*, suggests very powerfully a commercial response to Abbott's book.

Over the course of 1885 and 1886 four more *Romances* were published as pamphlets by Swan Sonnenschein, and the first five collected in a bound volume in 1886. They received favourable reviews in journals like *Mind* and *Knowledge*, and Hinton gave papers at the Royal Society of Physics.

In October of 1886 Charles's bigamous marriage to Maud Florence, under the assumed name of John Weldon, and the existence of their illegitimate twin sons, was discovered by Mary Hinton. Over the course of two weeks Charles's life unwound. Mary took Charles to present himself to Edward Thring, the headmaster of Uppingham, to whom he tendered his resignation. Thring described the event as 'a strange and piteous thing'.[4] The following day Charles handed himself over to the police at Bow Street, where he was taken into custody. His trial took place on 16 October at the Old Bailey and was reported broadly by the national press. Charles was found guilty and sentenced to three days in prison, which he had already served on remand. The Hinton family closed ranks and what became of Maud and her children after the trial remains unclear. Vicious rumours circulated in private correspondence, blaming Charles's bigamy on the unconventional theories of his father.[5]

Charles struggled to find work following his very public fall from grace. In early 1887 he left for Japan with his young family to work for a mission. While living in Yokohama he was recruited as headmaster of the Victoria Public School, founded by the British expatriate community in Yokohama to commemorate Victoria's Silver Jubilee. Hinton was headmaster for three years, before leaving to pursue work with the Japanese government.[6]

4. Thring's surviving diaries, held in archive at the school library at Uppingham, record the incident.

5. Documents relating to the Men and Women's Club, of which Hinton's mother, aunt and two close friends, Henry Havelock Ellis and Olive Schreiner, were members, are a rich source of detail on Hinton's trial for bigamy.

6. Hinton's career in Japan is recorded in a series of articles in *The Japan Times*.

In 1893 he sailed with his family on the SS Tacoma to Washington and took up a job in the mathematics department at Princeton. Almost immediately he submitted some new *Romances* to Swan Sonnenschein, and these were published in England and the USA. While at Princeton he gained considerable fame for his invention of a gunpowder-powered canon for firing baseballs. He moved on to a post at the University of Minnesota, before finally settling in Washington, working briefly for the Nautical Almanac, a job less unlikely than it at first seems – the previous editor had been the mathematician Simon Newcomb, so this was a publication with higher dimensional pedigree. In 1904 he published *The Fourth Dimension*, a final non-fictional attempt at explicating his higher dimensional philosophy, and featuring coloured plates to help readers to make their own cubes. His final job was as a patent examiner, a post for which he had no doubt gained experience through his inventing career, but towards which his entire life of object-based research had led. Hinton died on 30 April, 1907, from either a brain haemorrhage or a heart attack. Mary, a published advocate of suicide, took her own life just over a year later.

What is the Fourth Dimension?

Hinton's work radically altered the idea of a spatial fourth dimension. While there were loose and unformed theories in circulation in the late nineteenth century already suggesting the consideration of time as the fourth dimension in mechanical calculations, and while Hinton himself propounded a model of a grooved ether that suggested a kind of cosmic fixity of events and the possibility of eternal return, he was concerned with a fourth dimension that was an extension of space beyond that immediately sensible.

The idea of a spatial fourth dimension had been dragged, if not centre-stage, certainly stage-left, during the second-half of the nineteenth century. From a throwaway remark in a paper on Barycentric calculus by August Möbius, he of the famed Möbius strip, to a set of experiments conducted by the astrophysicist Johann Karl Friedrich

Zöllner that claimed to have demonstrated that séance phenomena were the result of interventions into our three-dimensional world by fourth-dimensional intelligences, the idea had already travelled some distance when Hinton began to work with it.

Hinton's first essay was notable for its accessible description of the analogical demonstration of four-dimensioned space: put simply, as for from two dimensions to three, so for from three dimensions to four. Just as a human can see the interior of a square that would be obstructed from the view of an intelligence confined to two dimensions by the line that is the square's side, so would a four-dimensional intelligence be able to see the interior of a cube that appeared to be boxed in to a human.

By the essay's third iteration, Hinton had also worked through the idea that extension into the fourth dimension must occur at the atomic level: it was ultra-thin, though no less possible for that. 'What is the Fourth Dimension?' is notable for its reasoned tone and calm exploration of speculative ideas. Over the course of his next *Romances*, Hinton developed different approaches to thinking the fourth dimension, most notably in the intriguing parable 'A Persian King' (1885), which hinted at the ethical spin he would bring to the idea. This was given a full outing in *A New Era of Thought* (1888), undoubtedly his key work.

A New Era summarised 'What is' but expanded its speculations to consider the ethical consequences of a speculated fourth dimensional existence for the atoms that make up the human brain. This higher spatial neurology implied a universal consciousness. Hinton described the processes by which he himself had arrived at his theories, involving the contemplation of a set of cubes, a guide for the construction of which made up the entire second half of the book. He had discovered that to achieve fourth dimensional visualisation, it was crucial to annihilate 'self-elements', subjective spatial experiences such as up and down, left and right. Connecting this to his father's broadly altruistic philosophy, in which it was necessary to subordinate one's own needs to those of others, Hinton envisaged a utopian fourth dimension of transcended ego, an inheritance that chimed well with the emphasis on meditation imported from Eastern mysticism enjoying a vogue in progressive groupings.

Annihilate subjective spatial experiences

Views of the Tessaract.

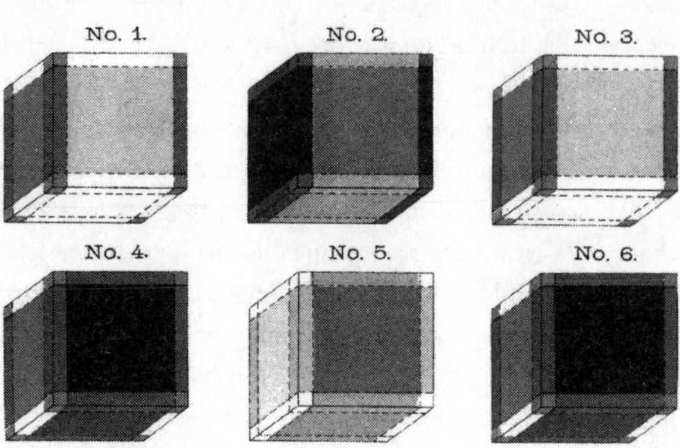

126 A SYSTEM OF CUBES

Hinton's cubic system for visualising the fourth dimension was surely effective. Its best advert was his sister-in-law Alicia, whom Hinton trained in the use of his system. As HSM Coxeter wrote in a profile of Alicia, she far outstripped her instructor, penning three papers on higher dimensional polytopes, and constructing cross-sectional models. A contemporary popular legacy for the cubes, meanwhile, has been assured by a letter received by Martin Gardner, who had written about higher space puzzles in *Scientific American*. The letter from Hiram Barton, 'a consulting engineer of Etchingham, Sussex, England' warns of the dire consequences of meddling with Hinton's system.

> *A shudder ran down my spine when I read your reference to Hinton's cubes. I nearly got hooked on them myself in the nineteen-twenties. Please believe me when I say that they are completely mind-destroying. The only person I ever met who had worked with them seriously was Francis Sedlak, a Czech neo-Hegelian Philosopher (he wrote a book called* The Creation of Heaven and Earth*) who lived in an Oneida-*

> *like community near Stroud, in Gloucestershire.*
>
> *As you must know, the technique consists essentially in the sequential visualizing of the adjoint internal faces of the poly-colored unit cubes making up the larger cube. It is not difficult to acquire considerable facility in this, but the process is one of autohypnosis and, after a while, the sequences begin to parade themselves through one's mind of their own accord. This is pleasurable, in a way, and it was not until I went to see Sedlak in 1929 that I realized the dangers of setting up an autonomous process in one's own brain. For the record, the way out is to establish consciously a countersystem differing from the first in that the core cube shows different colored faces, but withdrawal is slow and I wouldn't recommend anyone to play around with the cubes at all.*[7]

The sensational tone of this letter falls in line with a current of response to higher-dimensional thinking that was seeded with anti-Zöllner propaganda in the early 1880s and emerged more consistently at the *fin de siècle*: the idea that thinking in higher space resulted inevitably in madness. What Barton doesn't mention is that Sedlak was also, unsurprisingly, a Theosophist, contributing frequent articles to *The Theosophical Review* and *The Theosophist*. He later also contributed an article to Orage's *The New Age* disputing Einstein's Theory of Relativity on the grounds that Einstein was insensible to the dictates of 'Pure Reason'. His partner in a 'free union', Nellie Shaw, wrote an account of their life together in the Whiteway Colony in which she gives Sedlak's cubic experience an altogether more positive spin:[8]

> *At first a very hard and laborious task, it became an absorbing occupation, to which was given every spare*

7. Martin Gardner, *Mathematical Carnival*, p. 52.

8. Nellie Shaw, *A Czech Philosopher on The Cotswolds; being an account of the life and work of Francis Sedlak*, p. 108.

moment. Many persons, not understanding, looked on it as a most unproductive way of spending time. Others admired the wonderful patience, but could see no useful result.

Just as the would-be athlete twists and turns on the parallel bars, using time and energy to develop his muscles and gain strength which can be used later in any direction which he may desire, so Francis assumed that this power gained by practice in visualisation, seeing mentally the block of cubes on all sides simultaneously, could also be used in any sphere and on any subject; in fact, it was ability to see through anything, and must eventually lead to clairvoyance.

[...]

Towards the end of his long and trying illness, when terrible coughing prevented him from sleeping at night, the long silent hours seemed interminable. On my enquiring one morning as to what sort of a night he had had, he said almost joyfully, "Oh, being awake does not trouble me now. I do the cubes, and the time flies." So I thanked God and blessed the cubes, for which had been found a utilitarian use at a most desperate psychological juncture. Power won cannot be lost, and will some day be utilised.

The threat of insanity notwithstanding, the cubes were ultimately playful objects, never quite shaking their prior existence as kindergarten toys, a Rubik's puzzle for the consciousness expansionist enabling very real spatial self-improvement; but super-power training sims? Perhaps not. Besides, Hinton had more strings to his bow, not least his largely unlauded fictional productions.

Before Messrs Sinclair and Moore picked him up, HG Wells was an interested bystander. The critic Bernard Bergonzi has described the fourth dimension as HG Wells's 'favourite motif' in his early scientific romances, written in the 1890s. Wells certainly had a broad knowledge and flexible grasp of the concept, satirizing theological obsessions with the fourth dimension in the novella *A Wonderful Visit*, representing it as a shadowy, spiritual dreamworld in 'The Plattner Story', as an element enabling a trans-hemispheric vision in 'The Remarkable Case of Davidson's Eyes', as part of the formula for corporeal invisibility in *The Invisible Man*, and enabling the traversal of time in the *Time Machine*.

Wells denied that he had read Hinton, but if the copy of *Scientific Romances* in the library at UCLA with Wells's name inscribed inside the front cover doesn't convince you otherwise, consider the publication of *The Invisible Man* in 1897, frequently cited as the first SF story to feature experimental corporeal invisibility. Hinton's *Stella*, one of the *Romances* he produced immediately upon his arrival in the USA, described the relationship between Hugh Churton and Stella, a woman rendered invisible (and therefore also ethically transparent!) by a scientific experiment. Published in 1895, it was not broadly read, and neither was it as effective as fiction as Wells's later novel. It was, nevertheless, an influential piece of work.

It is with the advent of string theory, however, that Hinton's thinking seems likely to find a more permanent place in the history of ideas. What Eric Davis's 2004 report on teleportation doesn't directly address, but a fact that surely informs it, is that Hinton's theory of dimensional extension at a sub-atomic level is mirrored in string theory. For researchers like Davis, it would be foolish not to consider the possibility that Hinton's theories on higher dimensional consciousness might not also have some validity and so, too, perhaps for all three-dimensional laymen.

Charles Howard Hinton

The Fourth State

by PAUL DEVEREUX

What if I were to tell you that we share our planet with another, non-biological form of consciousness? You wouldn't believe me, would you?

Almost four decades ago I started researching unexplained light phenomena that appear in the skies and, sometimes, on and even out of the ground. I had seen some of these things and knew they did not fit in easily with our knowledge of physics. I didn't think they were alien spacecraft, but they were certainly UFOs in the actual sense of being flying something-or-others that were unidentified. I called them 'earth lights' to differentiate them from extra-terrestrial notions and wrote two books about them.[1,2]

As I researched, I found that such light phenomena had been seen throughout recorded history, all over the world. Chinese Buddhists and Indian Hindus had dedicated temples to the lights, considering them to be divine manifestations. People in Malaysia called them *pennangal*, the luminous spectral heads of women who had died in childbirth. People in the north of India called them *Chota Admis*, considering them to be the lanterns of 'little men'. Celtic countries like Ireland and Cornwall thought about them as

1. Devereux, P [With Additional Material By Paul Mccartney] (1982). *Earth Lights*. Wellingborough: Turnstone Press.

2. Devereux, P [With Contributing Researchers David Clarke, Andy Roberts, And Paul Mccartney] (1989). *Earth Lights Revelation*. London: Blandford.

fairies, piskies or similar nature spirits – they were literally fairy lights. In past centuries rural folk in Wales referred to mysterious balls of light as *canwyll corfe*, 'corpse candles', seeing them as supernatural harbingers of death in the community. The Scots called mystery lights that speed low over various lochs simply *gealbahn*, balls of fire. Brazilians called them *Mae de Ouro*, 'Mother of Gold', believing they were spirits that could lead witnesses to buried treasure. Medieval observers thought such luminous aerial phenomena were dragons; to modern witnesses (when not hoaxing or misperceiving Venus, a cloudy moon or aircraft lights) they tend to be alien spacecraft. The variety of cultural interpretations was, and still remains, considerable.[3]

Both during the writing of the books and subsequently, I have noticed how certain associations recur with regard to the appearance of the lights and have written widely on some of these aspects. For instance, there seems to be a strong relationship between locations where light phenomena incidence is notable or recurrent and geological faulting, and areas where there is tectonic stress, such as bodies of water overlaying faulting. In a rash of extraordinary and very well-witnessed light phenomena in Wales, near Harlech, in 1905, for instance, all the reports of light appearances related to a major local fault, the Mochras Fault – a fact revealed only ninety years later through research conducted by a geologist colleague and myself. Red, shape-shifting lights and large spheres of white light were seen to rise directly from the fault (before anyone knew there was a fault there) and in some cases fly off out of sight. Mineral deposits and veins are related to such locations. Indeed, up until 1910, miners at the Bere Alston copper/arsenic mine on the borders of Cornwall and Devon in England used to watch for lightballs emerging from the ground as they usually indicated where copper veins could be found. Old tin miners in Cornwall told me they used to often see purple balls of light appearing

3. Those who want to follow up statements and examples given throughout the essay can locate the sources in *Earth Lights Revelation*, and additionally in Devereux, P and Brookesmith, P (1997). *Ufos And Ufology*. London: Blandford.

in the air over mines, especially after rain (when air pressure changes). The valley of Hessdalen in Norway is rich in mineral deposits (it was a famous mining area, now on the UNESCO World Heritage list) and has had periodic outbreaks of earth lights incidence, some of which have been recorded with modern monitoring equipment – there is now an automatic monitoring station for light phenomena there.[4] Earth lights can also sometimes be associated with earthquakes. As when prior to and during a series of quakes in 1988 at Saguenay, Quebec, lightballs metres across were witnessed rising from out of the ground, and in the week prior to a 1996 quake in Cornwall, rectangular lights and 'moon-like' lights that slowly dissolved were seen in the skies by many witnesses. Canadian-based Professor Michael Persinger, a pioneer of earth lights research, and US geologist John Derr have jointly and separately investigated several areas where light phenomena outbreaks occurred, and found strong correlations with geological and tectonic factors. The evidence is extensive.

Earth lights seem to belong to a family that includes earthquake lights and ball lightning, but they also sometimes display distinguishing characteristics, such as greater longevity than their related phenomena, and can appear where there is no evidence of quakes or tectonic strain. In such cases, they must draw their energy from other sources in nature, presumably atmospheric ones.

I gradually began to notice another association with the lights, an awkward, inconvenient association I have written little about. Some of the early 'flying saucer' writers, like Ivan T Sanderson, had claimed that unidentified aerial phenomena were actually living creatures of some kind, possibly electromagnetic in nature. I was not keen to join in such opinion. Frankly, it is so far outside the acceptance level of our modern culture that it can even be embarrassing to mention it. Yet it is there.

In 1973, geologists Pat Kenney and Elwood Wright
were making a geological study of the Big Bend region of

4. *www.hessdalen.org/station*

Texas, near Marfa, infamous as an area where anomalous lights are often reported, and have been for centuries. The two men happened to spot strange lights on the prairie and drove off in their jeep towards them to investigate. The lights were smaller than a basketball and had the colour and intensity of household light bulbs. They led the geologists on a merry chase for about twenty minutes. 'They appeared to be playing,' the men reported later. A light would come to a halt, as if allowing the men to catch up with it, and then shoot off again. The closest they got to a light was about two hundred feet (60m). 'It seemed to possess intelligence!' the geologists marvelled. The lights finally vanished into thin air.

I began to collect reports of behaviour by the lights that suggested they have a rudimentary intelligence: inquisitiveness, as if they were observing witnesses as much as witnesses were observing them, and even kittenish, interactive playful behaviour with observers. I felt if I dwelled too much on this evidence I risked losing whatever credibility I may have had, so only mentioned it in passing. But I mulled it over privately, and initially I spoke about it to field investigators of the Hessdalen phenomena. They readily told me that they reckoned perhaps ten per cent of the lights they saw seemed to behave in interactive ways. I then brought the matter up with another field investigator, physicist Harley Rutledge, who had led a team investigating an outbreak of light phenomena in Piedmont, Missouri, in the early 1970s. He likewise claimed that he and his team had sometimes observed a 'cognisance' on the part of the lights, that they seemed aware of the investigators' presence. Rutledge admitted that it was a facet of the phenomena that 'perturbed' him. Similarly, biologist Frank Salisbury, when investigating a 1960s light phenomena outbreak in the Uinta Basin, Utah, noted that 'many witnesses' felt that the lights seemed 'to react' to them.

A cognisance on the part of the lights

On a visit to Gabon in 1895, the writer Mary Kingsley saw a ball of violet light roll out of a wood onto the banks of Lake Ncovi; it hovered until joined by another, similar light. The two lightballs circled each other until Kingsley approached them in a canoe. One then flew off back into the trees while the other floated over the lake surface – as Kingsley paddled quickly after it, it went down into the water, still glowing as it sank. Locals later told her such phenomena were aku, *devil lights.*

Eventually, I cautiously approached Persinger about this 'perturbing' aspect, expecting him to dismiss it and me out of hand, yet, surprisingly, he was open to the idea that the light phenomena might have some form of consciousness. There was no reason, he averred, why complex activity yielding some level of consciousness should have evolved only in biological material like our brains. It was possible that earth lights were highly focused, complex concatenations of geophysical forces shimmering with electrical and magnetic interactions. Who knows what might result from that?

In his Journal of 1830, the 'peasant poet', John Clare, told how he encountered a lightball while walking one evening between the villages of Ashton and Helpston in Cambridgeshire. The light came towards him. 'I thought it made a sudden stop as if to listen to me,' he wrote. It crackled and was surrounded by a luminous halo: Clare described the light as having 'a mysterious terrific hue'. When it darted away Clare promptly took to his heels. He already knew that there was locally 'a great upstir' about the lights, with up to fifteen at a time being seen over Deadmoor and Eastwell Moor flying back and forth, both with and against the wind. Clare said that his close encounter robbed him of 'the little philosophical reasoning' he had about them.

I also brought the matter up with the late John Keel, a veteran author on UFOs and anomalies, well-known especially for his documentary book (and later, in 2002, a somewhat fictionalised movie starring Richard Gere), *The Mothman Prophecies.* Decades previously he had identified the fact that UFOs tended to appear in what he called 'window areas', and he argued that whatever they were, the UFO phenomena were 'soft', not hard, metallic machines or craft. I had caught up with him in New York, and trailed around with him to toy shops, a pastime he enjoyed, listening to him gripe about how things had deteriorated in Manhattan. Finally, we settled in his favourite diner. After calling over an elderly waitress and getting her to show me the concentration camp number that the Nazis had tattooed on her wrist, he got round to addressing my concerns about apparent intelligent behaviour on the part of the lights. He reminded me that he had written about his encounters with football-sized spheres of light in the Ohio Valley when investigating reports of curious phenomena in the region. He had seen the balls of light rising out of a copse on the top of a ridge. He went to the location and saw the lights moving around a short distance above the ground. When he aimed a flashlight beam at them they jumped out of the way. Keel also claimed that bored riverboat crews on the Ohio River had told him they used their searchlights to interact with the lights they sometimes saw on the river's banks.

One evening in March 1991, an unassuming builder, Paul Ladd, was terrorised by a ball of light in the Welsh hamlet of Nevern. He left his local pub and started his walk home. As he crossed Nevern's ancient river bridge, a football-sized sphere of light swooped up from the water and started following the builder. When the man stopped, the light stopped, when he started off again, so did the light. Unnerved, Ladd struck a match to light a cigarette. The light shot backwards as if startled by the flame. Ladd started off homeward again, but once more the lightball trailed him. When the man finally jumped into some roadside trees to escape, the light followed him in, weaving between the branches. Eventually, much to Ladd's relief, it seemed to give up, and went away. Now, this could just be dismissed as a tall tale were it not for the fact that other people in the hamlet independently reported a ball of light that same night. They, too, stated that it behaved in a controlled, inquisitive manner, in one case trying to gain entry though an open front door. As an interesting footnote, at the very beginning of the twentieth century, the American folklorist, WY Evans Wentz, visited Nevern and learned that it was renowned as a locale where dreaded 'corpse candles' often appeared – lightballs 'the size of a pot' as a local woman described them to the folklorist.

So what could the actual nature of these lights be? Reports worldwide for over a century described truly anomalous effects exhibited by some of the lights. Typical of these were protean, shape-shifting, capabilities; the ability to merge with one another; a habit of vanishing in one place only to re-appear immediately at another spot; the emission of light that is bright but not glaring, and, most extraordinary of all, to sometimes be visible from one angle, yet invisible from another, as if they are only barely present in our space. One group of witnesses in the 1905 Welsh outbreak saw a glowing rod of blue light hovering over a country road, while another group on the other side of the light saw nothing at all. One farmer in the Pennines, England, stated that a ball of orange light he had seen hovering over a stream early one morning was spherical, yet somehow seemed simultaneously flat in some peculiar way. This reminded me of a light I saw with other witnesses in 1967, which was a perfect, upright rectangle of glowing orange light; it was large and clear yet didn't quite 'hang' convincingly in normal three-dimensional space. These sorts of effects have led me to speculate that earth lights could be some exotic form of macro-quantum phenomena – that is, manifestations on a large scale of the similarly bizarre events that occur in the infinitesimally small, sub-atomic realms of quantum energy, where matter emerges.

A rod of blue light over a country road

Those who have observed the lights at close quarters say that while their contours remain steady, their interiors are seething with energy. Sometimes, a buzzing sound is heard. Poltergeist-like events are occasionally reported as occurring in the vicinity of the lights – crunching sounds on gravel as if invisible feet are walking on it, objects flying around, crockery breaking evenly and cleanly as if cut with a knife, metal door locks opening and closing. I have found reports of similar incidents taking place during intense aurorae periods too, suggesting that the lights might be surrounded by electromagnetic fields. It is clear to anyone who bothers to research the evidence in depth that earth lights represent some kind of geophysical phenomenon, or, more likely, a closely related family of phenomena. The best guess is that they are an exotic species of plasma produced in certain circumstances by the mighty energy sources created in the greatest laboratory in the universe – nature's own.

Plasma is generally defined as a hot state of matter in which atoms have been stripped of their electrons, leaving positively charged ions (atoms which have lost one or more of their electrons) which mingle feely with the electrons. Because plasma isn't a liquid, a solid or a normal gas, it is sometimes referred to as the fourth state of matter. Plasmas are luminescent in darkened conditions, but can appear metallic in daylight – similar to the way an air bubble looks under water. On rare occasions, they can even appear pitch black, possibly a polar opposite, a positive-negative relationship, to the photon-producing lightballs; I and another person once witnessed one of these round black objects, blacker than soot – it disappeared as we looked at it, then instantly re-appeared some distance away before flying off.

Plasma behaves in odd ways, even the relatively puny ones produced in the laboratory. For instance, inside plasmas they had created, Romanian scientists observed cell-like forms that could replicate, grow, and communicate with one another. By chance, at a recent conference,[5] I learned of another, similarly challenging observation

5. 'Infinite Potential: The Legacy Of David Bohm', conference held at Queen Mary College, University Of London, 21 November 2009.

from the work of the late David Bohm which has renewed my interest in the possibility that powerful natural plasmas are an exotic state of non-biological energy that can conjure a certain level of conscious activity in appropriate circumstances (yet to be determined). Bohm was an American-born physicist who I knew about in the context of consciousness studies, in particular his controversial theory of implicate and explicate order.[6] To somewhat oversimplify this, Bohm argued that there is a subtle, connecting stratum of some kind (the 'implicate order') beneath the spacetime universe of matter (the 'explicate order') that we know and love. This underlying stratum beyond or beneath space and time connects all things, creating a whole. He likened this implicate order to the flow of a stream, and explicate 'unfoldment' as being like the river's ripples or whirlpools that only existed because of the stream's flow. This implicate order Bohm felt could be considered as being commensurate with consciousness itself, so that even what we consider to be inanimate matter had some degree of consciousness enfolded within it. He provided powerful theoretical arguments for his theory, and even presented a degree of illustrative experimental evidence as well, but it has been resisted by the bulk of mainstream physicists because it harbours a range of awkward implications that needn't be explored here.

What I didn't know until I attended the conference was that Bohm was also recognised as laying the foundations of plasma physics. Decades before the Romanian scientists made their observations, Bohm began his work on plasmas. He was surprised to find that once electrons were in a plasma they stopped behaving like individuals and started behaving as if they were part of a larger and interconnected whole – surely the first inklings he had of the implicate order. He later remarked that he frequently had the impression that the sea of electrons was in some sense alive.

Hearing about this made me realise that the notion that earth

6. Bohm, D (1980). *Wholeness And The Implicate Order*. London And Boston: Routledge & Kegan Paul.

lights could be conscious entities was not so completely crazy after all. If Bohm's theory is correct, then the lights are unfolding a degree of consciousness due to their complex inner interactions. Moreover, they are on the very threshold of unfoldment out of the implicate order, only barely manifesting in spacetime. In addition to this theoretical idea, there have also been laboratory observations of lifelike behaviour within the teeming interior of plasmas, as I've already mentioned.

There is one further implication. If earth lights actually are geophysical-based manifestations of consciousness, then they represent an older form than biologically-based consciousness. In effect, they are ancestor lights. Perhaps it is time we got to know the ancestors a whole lot better.

What if I were to tell you that we share our planet with another, non-biological form of consciousness? You wouldn't believe me, would you?

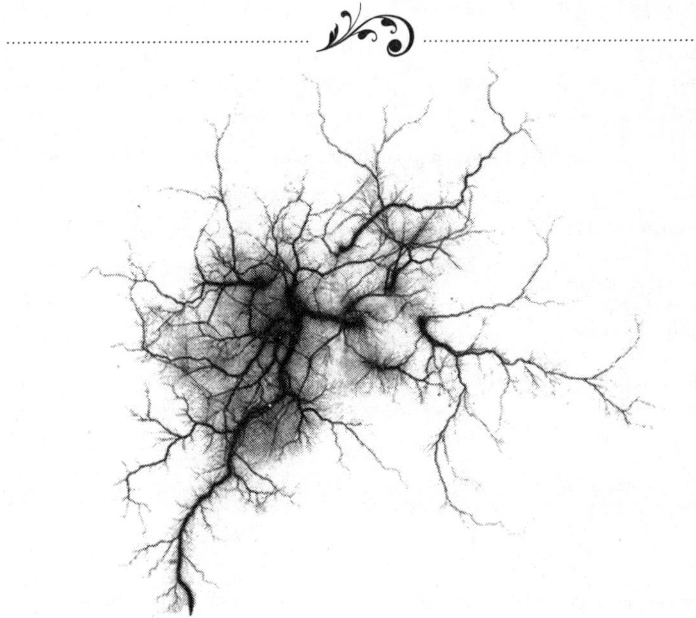

Dr & Lauder Lindsay's Lemmings

Mad beasts and misanthropy in a Victorian asylum

by RICHARD BARNETT and MICHAEL NEVE

'THE SCORPION *seems deliberately to commit suicide by stinging itself fatally. It does so under the influence of such motives as fear or despair.'* &

WILLIAM LAUDER LINDSAY & *Mind in the Lower Animals in Health and Disease* 2 VOLS. LONDON : KEGAN PAUL, 1879.

Leaf through the second or subsequent editions of Charles Darwin's *Descent of Man* (1874) and you will find a handful of footnotes citing the work of one William Lauder Lindsay.[1] Read Lindsay's entry in the revised *Dictionary of National Biography,* and you might be forgiven for concluding that the high point of this Scottish physician's career was his *Memoir on the Spermogones and Pycnides of Lichens* (1870).[2] We beg to differ. In *Mind in the Lower Animals in Health and Disease*, a sprawling two-volume treatise published at the end of his life in 1879, Lindsay found his metier: not vegetable love, but animal madness. He ranged across continents and centuries, pillaging writers from Pliny to Darwin and ushering his readers into a dark, destabilised world of simian

1. See Darwin, Charles: *The Descent Of Man, And Selection In Relation To Sex.* Edited With An Introduction By James Moore And Adrian Desmond. London: Penguin Books, 2004 (Rpt. Of 1879), Pp. 23, 100, 119.

2. Seccombe, Thomas (Rev. DJ Galloway): 'Lindsay, William Lauder (1829-1880), Physician And Botanist', In *Oxford Dictionary Of National Biography*, Oxford: Oxford University Press, 2004.

neurosis and reptilian psychosis, suicidal scorpions and deranged, Prufrockian lemmings.

Darwin and Lindsay both sought to make *Homo sapiens* part of the natural world, but they came at the question from opposing directions. Darwin saw Lindsay's work as a small and comparatively unimportant thread in his own evolutionary tapestry. But Lindsay argued that the history of human-animal relationships was, like the history of attitudes towards the mad, dominated by superstition, misrepresentation and cruelty. He set out to restore the maligned reputation of the animal kingdom by demonstrating 'the psychical superiority of the lower animals – the dog, horse, elephant, parrot or ape – over the human child, and even the human adult', and showing, in the process, that all creatures – from pea crabs to collies – were smart and sensitive enough to suffer doubt, depression and insanity.

Lindsay was a widely travelled, fairly eminent member of the Scottish medical landscape, his research cited by Darwin and published in some of the leading medical journals of the period, and his life recorded in the *DNB*. He seems to have seen *Mind in the Lower Animals* as part of a serious attempt, both scientific and humanitarian, to sweep aside existing notions of the limits of the mind. But his obituarists concentrated on a different side of his life and work: Lindsay the retailer of sentimental anecdotes, an eccentric anthropomorphist of Swiftian proportions (though lacking Swift's wit and savage indignation). Lindsay's work is part of a long tradition in Western thought, one which sought to explore the boundaries between the divine, the human and the animal, and in doing so to discover what it meant to be free, conscious and responsible. But his sentimental anthropomorphism and his engagement with evolutionary theory marked Lindsay as distinctively Victorian, responding to the hopes and anxieties of the British nineteenth century.

In *Perceiving Animals*[3] the historian Erica Fudge identifies the

3. Fudge, Erica: *Perceiving Animals: Humans And Beasts In Early Modern English Culture*. Illinois: University Of Illinois Press.

particular challenge of writing about the history of the human-animal relationship. This is not just the old problem of 'recreating conversations with the dead': rather, historians must attempt to reconstruct encounters in which some of the participants may not be ascribed human voices. 'We have no access to monkeys', she observes, 'without going first of all through organ-grinders'. Humans have defined themselves as humans through their relationships with animals, and writers from the pre-Socratics onwards have taken the animal mind as a mirror in which the human mind may be glimpsed, defined or deconstructed. So our approach to Lindsay begins with a short survey of Western attitudes towards the relationship between humans and animals.

Most accounts of the animal mind have been founded on a primary philosophical distinction, expressed most influentially in Aristotle's *De Anima*, written around 350 BCE, between reason and the passions. For Aristotle, every living thing was defined by its anima – its soul or essence. A fully human anima (which to Aristotle meant the soul of a male philosopher) was one in which divine reason reigned over the subordinate animal passions. An absence of reason – unreason – was the condition of human madness and the animal mind. Though the idea of reason and the passions as opposing forces became a common theme in Classical Graeco-Roman culture, many writers disagreed over the question of whether animals could reason. Some, like Plutarch, argued for a scale of intellect, on which some creatures possessed a degree of reason and could therefore lose it. Foxes and monkeys were smart enough to go mad; mice and hornets were already strangers to reason.

Early Christian authors found this view deeply troubling. Their cosmologies tended to draw a clear distinction between humans, who were endowed with souls, free will and reason, and animals, which were not. A graduated scale of reason eroded this crucial boundary, and one of the major tasks of medieval Scholasticism was to construct a neo-Aristotelian vision of human reason as the exclusive gift of a Christian God. Rene Descartes' argument for an absolute distinction between mind and matter in his *Discourse on Method* (1637) represents the apotheosis of this ambition. Descartes disposed of animal reason with syllogistic elegance. Feelings, emotions, consciousness and reason were a property of mind; animals were automata, matter without mind; so animals could not think, fear or suffer.

In the hands of Renaissance anatomists, however, the neoclassical tradition broke down the distinction between humans and animals even further. By revealing the physical and physiological resemblances between, say, dogs and men, the new anatomy created an unstable and dangerous hinterland into which beasts could rise or humans fall. In a culture that suffered repeatedly under plagues, famines and religious wars, order was seen as central to Christian life but also fragile beyond words, easily shattered by people or animals who broke the boundaries of a God-given hierarchy of being. Anxiety over humanity's uncertain relationship with the rest of Creation, and the consequences of this uncertainty for religious and temporal law, was reflected in the great interest, both popular and scholarly, in monstrous births. These sports of nature seemed to confirm the possibility that human and animal natures could merge. But both Descartes' dualism and the new anatomy ran alongside the experiences of a European population living cheek by jowl with pigs, cats, sheep, rats, dogs, cows, deer, mice and all manner of bodily parasites. Attitudes seem to have been shaped most strongly by individual, day-to-day encounters with animals; thus King James I of England could claim that his hunting dogs were engaging in a form of rational argument when they barked and whimpered at one another.

Sports of nature

These anxieties also found expression in a remarkable series of trials across Europe, in which animals were prosecuted and executed for crimes such as theft, trespass, blasphemy and murder. These trials have attracted attention from historians, anthropologists and legal theorists since the publication of Edward Evans' *The Criminal Prosecution and Capital Punishment of Animals* (1906).[4] Some were clearly intended as a mockery of human authority – witness the mob of Parisian apprentices who in the late 1730s hanged their mistresses' pet cats, an episode recounted in Robert Darnton's *The Great Cat Massacre* (1984).[5] Many more, however, were strictly formal, grounded in the pomp and authority of secular or ecclesiastical courts, and they resulted in animals being subjected to punishments ranging from anathematisation and excommunication to torture and public execution.

In one sense, these trials were simply obeying Biblical injunctions: Exodus 21:28 states that 'when an ox gores a man or a woman to death, the ox shall be stoned', and Leviticus 20:15 that 'if a man has sexual relations with an animal, he shall be put to death; and you shall kill the animal'.[6] But the execution of the animal, particularly when it was seen to have acted wilfully, also represented punishment in a judicial sense. In the early verses of Genesis, before the Fall, Adam was given authority over all animals, as befitted one who was made of earth but filled with spirit. In a fallen, corrupted world, however, animals might (like witches) be of the Devil's party, overturning God's law and leading men on to sin. Murderous sows, dishonest caterpillars, alluring ewes, gender-bending cockerels – all represented a demonic challenge to divine order, and all were punished for it at some point in this period.

In the eighteenth century a new generation of natural philosophers and ethicists began to argue that, whatever the nature of their minds, animals should be treated well as a way of exercising human empathy. In this new moral landscape, animal cruelty could be

4. Evans, Edward: *The Criminal Prosecution And Capital Punishment Of Animals*. London: Faber, 1987 (Rpt. Of 1906). For A More Recent, Though Less Engaging, Summary, See Girgen, John: 'The Historical And Contemporary Prosecution Of Animals'. *Journal Of Animal Law*, Vol 9, 2003, Pp. 97-133.

5. Darnton, Robert: *The Great Cat Massacre And Other Episodes In French Cultural History*. New York: Basic Books, 1984.

6. New Revised Standard Version, 1995.

the prelude to greater crimes. William Hogarth's *Four Stages of Cruelty*, engraved in 1750 but not published until 1822, began with Tom Nero and his gang forcing an arrow into the anus of a mastiff, amidst scenes of animal cruelty in many forms. Tom's spiralling career of viciousness ended with murder and an act of judicial violence, his hanged body being ripped apart by an anatomist. Hogarth presented dissection as the consequence of Tom's cruelty, but in doing so he questioned the morality of using pain and suffering, both human and animal, to make knowledge.

Hogarth's concerns foreshadowed a serious challenge to Cartesian dualism in the nineteenth century. Ideas of evolution – and here we must look beyond Darwin's work to wider currents of thought in science, politics and culture – gave new shape to speculations about mind and madness in animals. A post-Romantic emphasis on consciousness, feelings and emotions meant that reason was no longer taken to be the central difference between men and beasts, and this new attitude reflected a wider shift in the meanings attached to animals. As new industrial cities grew and sprawled, animals became emblems of a disappearing, romanticised rural past. While a flock of sheep was kept for food and profit, a lapdog provided pleasure, company, a link to the fox-hounds and talbots of the medieval aristocracy. Pets were seen to possess individuality, personality and feeling: they were treated as family members, often outranking servants in the bourgeois household hierarchy. Animals with human characters and characteristics began to emerge in art and literature from Edwin Landseer to Lewis Carroll. The appearance of gorillas and orang-utans in zoos and circuses from the 1850s sparked an entire genre of human-animal comparisons in fiction, journalism and cartoons. Much of this revolved around the figure of Darwin himself: his craggy features, a caricaturist's dream, suggested to many that he, at least, was a kissing cousin of the great apes.

This explosion of anthropomorphism ran in parallel with a growing awareness of – in Zola's phrase – *la bête humaine*. Though Dickens' sympathetic accounts of the industrial working class were widely read, they did little to challenge influential views of the urban poor as less than fully human, lacking intellect, higher feelings and other marks of civilisation. In this context, finding the human in animals became a powerful strategy for drawing attention away from the animal in humans. Campaigners against vivisection were some of the noisiest exponents of this position, their arguments often dominated by a powerful strand of Christian evangelism which sought to reassert the moral authority of Scriptural ethics over the increasingly influential natural sciences.[7] In an ironic reversal of the early Christian position, anti-vivisection campaigners insisted that humans and animals could experience identical feelings of fear, pain and horror. But their antipathy to experimental science was more than just a moral objection to physical cruelty. Many anti-vivisectionists sought the companionship of animals as a refuge from what they had come to see as an inhumane, materialist, Malthusian world. This irony was compounded by the fact that leading practitioners of the new life sciences – men such as Darwin and Thomas Henry Huxley – were beginning to endorse and promote the idea of a mental continuum running between humans and animals.

Mind: a secretion of the brain

If mind was a material phenomenon, a kind of 'secretion' of the brain, then the wider field of emotions, consciousness and their associated pathologies could become an arena for debates over Man's place in nature, his kinship to the apes and the angels.

In *The Expression of Emotions in Man and Animals* (1872) Darwin argued that humans and animals had comparable facilities for expressing their feelings, through the muscles of the face. And Huxley provided a classic statement of the human-animal continuum in an

7. See French, Richard: *Antivivisection And Medical Science In Victorian Society*. Princeton: Princeton University Press, 1975.

article in *The Fortnightly Review* in 1874.[8] Huxley drew strongly both on the gradualist model of mind and on Descartes' position (which he attributed to the more acceptably British and empirically-minded William Harvey). Given the pain associated with a Darwinian struggle for existence, Huxley would, he said, have been glad if animals did not possess consciousness or feelings. But 'considering the terrible practical consequences to domestic animals which might ensue from any error on our part', he was equally glad to conclude that they were conscious, feeling beings. Consciousness was too complex to have emerged suddenly in humans. But, he argued, conscious intention could not determine physical action. Free will was simply unrestrained instinctual desire, expressed via neural reflexes, which converted sensory input into physical action. Both animals and humans were 'conscious automata', and consciousness merely an epiphenomenon, 'the steam-whistle which accompanies the work of a locomotive engine'.

By the time Huxley published his paper, William Lauder Lindsay had been working on animal madness for almost a decade. Lindsay appears to have left very few personal papers, so the main sources on his life are his published works, his obituaries, and various passing references in natural histories of lichens. No photographs or portraits are known to have survived, but an obituarist writing in the *Journal of Mental Science* provided a pen portrait:

> *[He was] one of those earnest men who take life almost too seriously from the beginning ... He was a man of slight physique, with the pinched features of the chronic dyspeptic in later life. His temperament was highly nervous, sensitive, and a little irritable. His character was humane and honourable, and he always had the courage of his convictions.* [9]

8. Huxley, Thomas Henry: 'On The Hypothesis That Animals Are Automata, And Its History'. *The Fortnightly Review*, Vol 16, 1874, Pp. 555-580.

9. Anonymous: 'Obituary. Dr William Lauder Lindsay'. *Edinburgh Medical Journal*, Vol 26, 1881, pp. 669-672.

Born in Edinburgh in 1829 – two years after Darwin abandoned his medical studies in the city and went to Cambridge – Lindsay was the eldest son of James Lindsay, a civil servant, and Helen Baird Lauder, the daughter of an officer in the Scots Guards. He was a prize-winning student at the Edinburgh Royal High School, and in 1846 entered Edinburgh Medical School. Here he became a close friend of John Hutton Balfour, botanist to the Queen and Regius Keeper of the Edinburgh Royal Botanical Garden. Botany was a central part of the medical curriculum at this time, most drugs being compounded by hand from botanicals, and Lindsay's three-starred 1852 MD thesis was entitled *Anatomy, Morphology and Physiology of the Lichens.*

Lindsay's first clinical post was at the Edinburgh City Cholera Hospital, and in the winter of 1853 he moved to the Crichton Asylum at Dumfries, where he worked as assistant physician to William Alexander Francis Browne. Browne, one of the most influential British

mad-doctors of the period, was a leading advocate of phrenology – a materialist model of the relationship between brain and mind, in which lumps and bumps on the skull were thought to indicate the relative power of the 'cerebral organs' beneath. Lindsay took Browne's glowing assessments of his abilities as a physician, though not his enthusiasm for phrenology, to his next post at the Murray Royal Institution for the Insane in Perth. Founded in 1827 and set on a hill outside the city, the Murray provided secure dormitories, work-rooms and gardens for 140 lunatics, along with a spacious and secluded lodge for the medical superintendent and his family. Lindsay seems to have found life at the Murray congenial: having taken up his post in the autumn of 1854, he remained there until his retirement in the summer of 1879.

Like many young physicians with a reputation to make, Lindsay threw himself into research. In his first paper written at the Murray he noted that 'the insane are extremely bad subjects for experiments', but over the next four years he studied the accuracy of phrenology in diagnosing different forms of insanity; the relationship between the weather and attacks of mania; the transmission of lunacy from parents to children; and the microscopic appearance of the blood of the insane.[10] He also wrote his only work to reach anything like a wider audience – *A Popular History of the British Lichens* (1856), which earned him a gold medal from the Royal Society of Edinburgh. In 1857 the Canadian government offered him a post as official lichenologist, but he turned it down for personal reasons – possibly his engagement to Elizabeth Reid, the Guyanan-born daughter of a Scottish solicitor, whom he married in 1859. Their relationship proved to be short. Lindsay suffered a nervous collapse in 1860 and, while Elizabeth bore their only child, a daughter, he took a two-year recuperative voyage to New Zealand. Less than a year after his return, Elizabeth died.

One of Lindsay's obituarists observed that Elizabeth's death 'made a very deep and lasting impression in his mind'. He threw himself into his old hobby – lichens – and a new field of interest, one with more relevance to his occupation: mind and madness in animals. Research and writing was interspersed with long bouts of recuperative travel: by 1879 he had been to Iceland, the Faeroe Islands, Norway, Massachusetts, Morocco, Egypt, Syria and twice more to New Zealand. In *Mad Dogs and Englishmen* (2007) Neil Pemberton and Mick Worboys cite Lindsay as one of the most prolific nineteenth-century British commentators on the subject of rabies and hydrophobia, part of a wider movement which identified human neglect and cruelty as the origin of rabies.[11] But his work on this subject also illuminates his view of the proper relationship between humans and animals. In a series of articles published in the *Journal of Mental Science* and *The Lancet* in the late 1870s Lindsay argued that rabies was principally

10. Lindsay's experiments are outlined in his annual reports for the Murray Royal Asylum, 1855-1879.

11. Pemberton, Neil, & Worboys, Mick: *Mad Dogs And Englishmen: Rabies In England, 1830-2000*. London: Palgrave Macmillan, 2007.

a psychological disorder, not a contagious disease, and that it was largely a consequence of human prejudice and irresponsibility. His medical colleagues were, he claimed, beginning to realise that:

> *Many fatal diseases, such as cholera, hydrophobia, and tetanus, owe their origin and their fatality, not to any blood-poisoning – not to the introduction from without of any disease-germs, figurative or real, but simply to imagination.*[12]

Most instances of hydrophobia, both in humans and in animals, were actually 'the result of terror, ignorance, prejudice, or superstition, acting on a morbid imagination and a susceptible nervous temperament'. The British rabies 'scares' of 1874, 1876 and 1877, in which dozens of suspected rabid dogs were slaughtered, had been enormously exaggerated, the result of scare stories put about by 'illiterate Irishmen, hysterical women, children and drunkards'. And when animals did develop 'true' rabies, it was almost always because they had been 'persecuted, ill-used – often literally goaded into fury' by humans. In one of his first articles on the subject Lindsay drew an explicit link between the treatment of human lunatics and that of mad animals:

> *[W]hen the law of kindness dictates man's treatment of other animals – as it now regulates the management of his insane fellow man – destructive violence at least, and perhaps also desponding suicidal propensity, will doubtless become much less frequent.*[13]

Until this happy situation was reached, hydrophobia should be classified as a mental epidemic, similar to cattle stampedes or lemming

12. Lindsay, William Lauder: 'Pathology Of Mind In The Lower Animals', *Journal Of Mental Science*, Vol 23, April 1877, P. 19.

13. Lindsay, William Lauder: 'Madness In Animals', *Journal Of Mental Science*, Vol 17, July 1871, P. 195.

mass suicide – another subject on which Lindsay's writings offer a striking new perspective. It is frequently claimed that this trope gained widespread popularity in the 1950s, first through a photograph in *National Geographic* magazine in 1954 and a Disney adventure comic in 1955, but most influentially through the 1958 Oscar-winning Disney documentary *White Wilderness.*[14] In a now infamous sequence this showed what appeared to be dozens of lemmings throwing themselves over a cliff in Alberta, Canada. A Canadian Broadcasting Company documentary, 'Cruel Camera', broadcast in 1983 revealed that this sequence had been staged: the lemmings had been flown in from Hudson Bay and, when they could not be persuaded to leap into the icy water, were launched from an improvised turntable.

14. *en.wikipedia.org/wiki/lemming*, Accessed 3 Jan 2010.

However, there is much evidence that the idea of lemming mass suicide was already well-known in the late nineteenth century. In their research on changing interpretations of animal suicide Duncan Wilson and Ed Ramsden have shown that Emile Durkheim and other early sociologists cited lemming mass suicide as an instance of crowd psychology in action.[15] And in a paper on 'Mental Epidemics in the Lower Animals', published in the *Journal of Mental Science* in 1872, Lindsay described it as an example of epidemic mental disorder. Though he could find no evidence to show whether this was 'intentional or unintentional suicide', he characterized the lemming as a 'self-haunted fugitive', driven to self-destruction by a 'blind morbid impulse' – truly a creature fit to inhabit the dark terrain of the late nineteenth century.

As these examples suggest, it is difficult to pin down Lindsay's views on mind and madness at any stage in his career, and in his writing he was generally more explicit about what he did not believe than what he did. Given his vigorous defence of hydrophobic dogs, one might expect Lindsay to be a committed opponent of vivisection. But this is not the case. In an 1877 article in the *Journal of Mental Science* he complained that one of his first research projects had been sabotaged by anti-vivisectionist prejudice. During his time at the Edinburgh City Cholera Hospital in 1853 Lindsay had, he claimed, been pursuing pioneering work on the transmission of cholera between humans and animals.[16] His subjects had been 'wandering, homeless street dogs of the kind... drowned by the thousand in Glasgow because they might... have become rabid and bit people'. The leading physicians of the city were aware of his work but 'did not give me the benefit even of their moral support or approval', and a campaign of 'popular and professional rumour' caused the patrons of the hospital to stop his experiments.

Twenty-five years later, though he saw 'numerous paths of

15. Wilson, Duncan, & Ramsden, Ed: 'Driven To Destruction: Animal Suicide And The Human Condition', *Wellcome History*, Issue 39, 2008, Pp. 11-12.

16. Lindsay, William Lauder: 'Pathology Of Mind In The Lower Animals', *Journal Of Mental Science*, Vol. 23, April 1877.

experimental research opening up before me', he refused to apply for a vivisection license under the terms of the 1876 Vivisection Act and subject himself to 'the degrading penalties imposed by a misguided government'. But he urged younger physicians to persist in this kind of experimentation, encouraging them to concentrate on those animals 'that most closely resemble him, on the one hand, in structure and function, and, on the other, in habits'. The best experimental subject, in other words, was the dog, 'Man's constant friend, companion, servant and plaything; so like him....'

In 1871 and 1872 Lindsay published his first papers on the subject of animal mind and madness in the *Journal of Mental Science*.[17] In the first of these he set down the basic principle of his enquiry: 'I hope to prove that, both in its normal and abnormal operations, mind is essentially the same in man and other animals.' In yet another article in the Journal of Mental Science he extended this claim to the vegetable kingdom.[18] Plants, he claimed, possessed many aspects of mind – purposiveness, sensation, choice, forward planning, and even eccentricity or caprice – and this showed that 'will and consciousness may exist quite independently of brain'.

Following the publication of these articles Lindsay appears to have been approached by the publisher Kegan Paul, and commissioned to write a volume for their 'International Scientific Series' on the subject of animal mind. But his research and writing took far longer than he hoped, and the resulting manuscript was too large for the 'International Scientific Series'. Rather than make drastic editorial cuts, Kegan Paul

17. His first publication on animal madness was Lindsay, William Lauder: 'Madness In Animals', *Journal Of Mental Science*, Vol 17, 1871, Pp. 181-206.

18. Lindsay, William Lauder: 'Mind In Plants', *Journal Of Mental Science*, Vol. 22, Jan 1876, Pp. 513-532.

published it as a separate monograph. In the introduction to *Mind in the Lower Animals* Lindsay claimed that he had been extremely reluctant to publish a book on the subject, and did so only after having read all the literature he could find on 'the whole subject of the animal and human mind, healthy and diseased' – 'a task which, along with the arrangement of the resultant notanda, has occupied all my leisure for seven years'.

Perhaps the first thing to strike a modern reader of *Mind in the Lower Animals* is its sheer size: two quarto volumes, and more than twelve hundred pages, longer than any of Darwin's published works. In the first volume Lindsay addressed the normal animal mind, and in the second volume he dealt with insanity. An overwhelming temptation is to treat the book as itself a kind of bestiary, to strip-mine arresting anecdotes and to view them in isolation from the wider context of Lindsay's project. So we'll proceed in a Wildean spirit by yielding, generously, to this temptation:

> *Lobsters show mental qualities of a higher kind than those characteristic of crabs. Thus one described as a lady's pet in Paris 'seems to recognise its mistress, and is so fond of music that it is always drawn to the piano whenever she plays'.*

> *There is an air of roguery about the thieving bee, which to the expert is as characteristic as are the motions of a pickpocket to the skilful policeman. Its sneaking look and nervous, guilty agitation, once seen, can never be mistaken.*

> *The wasp is one of those apparently unpromising animals that will respond to and repay man's kindness and attention by becoming both tractable and affectionate.*

> *A Newfoundland dog 'of great age' had its feelings wounded by being scolded, beaten in pretence only by means of a pocket handkerchief, and having a door shut in his face when*

about to leave a room with his usual companions – a nurse and her group of children. Soon after he was found alive, but with his head altogether or partly submerged in a ditch. He was dragged out, but now he refused to eat or drink, and before long he was found in the same position in the same ditch, but this time dead. [19]

Seen in this light, *Mind in the Lower Animals* is a seemingly inexhaustible treasury of entertaining and sentimental anecdotes. For Lindsay, however, this type of material was the foundation of his project. Accounts of light-fingered bees or musical lobsters could carry the same value as his own case histories of asylum inmates: they were links in a chain of observation extending through time and space, and grounded in the authority and integrity of well-trained scientific observers. Lindsay began by emphasising his own extensive experience as a 'physician-naturalist', one who had been 'trained to separate fact on the one hand from fiction, and from inference based on observation, on the other'. He had seen hundreds of cases of human insanity; he had encountered wild animals in Iceland, Spain, Italy, Morocco, Egypt, Syria, the US, Canada, Australia and New Zealand; and he had spent time in the zoological gardens of London, Paris, Berlin, Dresden, New York, Dublin, Sydney and Edinburgh. But most of the examples cited in *Mind in the Lower Animals* were not drawn from its author's personal experience. Lindsay quoted hundreds of written accounts of animal behaviour, culled from personal correspondence, scientific journals, newspapers, encyclopaedias and historical texts. One of his obituarists observed, with perhaps a touch of weariness, that 'no story of a dog's sagacity, or a parrot's loquacity, that ever appeared in the most obscure corner of the most provincial newspaper, ever seems to have escaped him.'

19. These and subsequent quotes are taken from Lindsay, William Lauder: *Mind In The Lower Animals In Health And Disease*. 2 Vols. London: Kegan Paul, 1879, *Passim*.

In order for any of his claims to be taken seriously, Lindsay knew that he had to present his work as 'science' in a sense that would be both understood and trusted by his colleagues. Darwin's strategy in his major published works was, as it were, to shore many thousands of fragments against his ruin. Learned journals were ransacked and correspondents pressed for the tiniest details, as he grounded his theories in the fruits of Victorian natural science. Following Darwin's example, Lindsay sought to underwrite the trustworthiness of his work by quoting other writers – liberally. *Mind in the Lower Animals* contains fifty references to Darwin's published works, but the most cited authors were two French physicians. Lindsay referred 105 times to Jean-Claude Houzeau's *Etudes sur les Facultés Mentales des Animaux* (1872) and 106 times to Charles Pierquin de Gembloux's *Traité de la folie des animaux* (1839).[20] Both Pierquin de Gembloux and Houzeau relied on the same anecdotal method, leading Lindsay on occasion to cite both an earlier source and their description of it as two separate stories. For Lindsay, everything hinged on the reliability and respectability of his sources. If he could find a way of arguing that Pliny or Darwin or Houzeau was a respectable and reliable reporter of the truth, his chain of authority could be maintained and extended both into the past and across the globe. In this sense, his reliance on the observations of other authors is strongly reminiscent of a much older model of natural knowledge, based upon personal authority and trust between learned gentlemen, and revealed in Steven Shapin's studies of Restoration natural philosophy.[21]

In a short preliminary chapter, titled 'The Authenticity of Anecdotes of Animal Sagacity', Lindsay argued for the suitability of this method in a scientific enquiry. He claimed that he had set aside 'all anecdotes that did not bear, or appear to bear, the stamp of truthfulness or authenticity either in their authorship or in the incidents themselves,

20. Pierquin de Gembloux's text includes a glossary enabling the reader to converse with marmosets.

21. Shapin, Steven: *A Social History Of Truth: Civility And Science In Seventeenth-Century England*. Chicago: University Of Chicago Press, 1994.

or both'. He had discarded Classical or medieval sources, except when – as in the case of Pliny the Elder – he believed the author was so well-regarded as to be beyond question. Where possible he had spoken to the writers he cited, and he gave precedence to those with scientific or professional qualifications. But he granted ultimate authority to his own personal judgement, informed by a well-developed moral and intellectual character. He also warned potential followers in this field that they would require 'perfect honesty and singleness of aim', indifference to 'criticism, opposition, vilification', sympathy both with the methods of comparative psychology and with animals of all kinds, and a 'cool, dispassionate judgement', lacking 'the mischievous element *temper*'.

As in his earlier writings on this subject, Lindsay preferred not to define the principal terms in his enquiry. He noted that 'no two authors agree as to the significance that should be attached to such terms as "will", "feeling", "thought", "consciousness", "intention", and so forth', but also claimed that 'all men of experience and culture feel, rather than know, what these terms mean or imply'. He also sought to avoid any 'psychological definition or classification' of mental pathology, preferring to allow 'each reader to define and classify according to his own favourite system of nomenclature'. The chapter headings in *Mind in the Lower Animals* give some sense of the way in which Lindsay chose to structure his material: in the healthy animal mind he considered (amongst other things) 'morality and religion', 'education' and 'language', and in the diseased mind 'fallibility', 'intoxication', 'moral degeneracy' and 'suicide'.

Historians have noted the tendency for eighteenth-and nineteenth-century works of popular natural history to include observations on the moral qualities of different species, and in *Mind in the Lower Animals* Lindsay appears to have reconfigured these character notes as psychological profiles.[22] Noble horses defended their property

22. See Ritvo, Harriet: *The Animal Estate: The English And Other Creatures In The Victorian Age*. Cambridge, Mass: Harvard University Press, 1987.

against thieves. Playful, dissembling apes were 'capable of wonderful refinements of hypocrisy and deceit, those which are associated with outward politeness, and with all the proprieties of behaviour'. Trustworthy, faithful dogs showed unquestioning obedience to their masters. But this trust could be misplaced, or might reflect a lack of analytical power, as in the case of a Skye terrier who leapt from a third-floor window and impaled itself on a railing because its owner had beckoned to it from the street. It having taken 'no time properly to calculate height or distance', Lindsay criticised the dog for behaving 'impulsively, rashly, thoughtlessly [and] without reflection'. Having been granted human powers of reasoning, animals could be taken to task for not exercising them.

But as in his earlier writings on this subject, Lindsay did not simply judge animal behaviour by human standards. *Mind in the Lower Animals* was shot through with a characteristically Victorian, though

strikingly inverted, strain of anthropomorphism. Lindsay did not simply judge animal behaviour by human moral standards. More radically, he argued that animals were inherently more reasonable, more genteel and more enlightened than their human masters. The 'laws of precedence and etiquette amongst cows', for instance, 'are as clearly defined as those of any European Court. Every cow knows her place and keeps it'. Sparrows 'administer public punishment to offenders after holding general councils'. Barbary apes 'hold public trials of prisoners before a public court with the aid of advocates'.

The laws of etiquette amongst cows

When considering animals, Lindsay was content to level up. When discussing humanity, he levelled down almost without exception. Lobsters could appreciate Chopin; wasps provided affectionate company; we might sympathise with the despair felt by lemmings or elderly dogs. But in Lindsay's view, 'savages' – particularly Papuans and Andaman Islanders – deserved nothing but contempt for their:

> *Absence of* clothing; *ignorance of the use of* fire;
> *absence of* cookery; morbid a*ppetites and depraved taste,*
> *including geophagy and ordure-eating;* filthiness in *their*

> *personal habits; no sense* of decency, *modesty, chastity or shame; no respect for the* dead; *the* suckling *of young* animals *by women;* fondness for other animals; wrestling for wives; *incapacity for* generalisation; *no* legislation; *no* history; *no* policy; *no civilities* or salutations; *the* fear *of what is* novel or *unusual.*

Negroes could not identify themselves in a mirror; Eskimos were thoroughly unprincipled; Aborigines had no capacity for abstract thought; Amazonian Indians could not count beyond four. And Lindsay extended this critique to the British working class. The 'savages of North Devon', 'the dog-fighters and women-kickers of the Black Country' and 'the whole of the "criminal class" of our great cities' showed that 'bloodthirstiness, lust, selfishness, dishonesty, untruthfulness, and other moral vices perpetually crop up and contaminate society even in its highest forms of development'. Animals, meanwhile, were slandered in the most basic turns of everyday conversation:

> *We apply the words 'an old cat', or 'spiteful as a cat', to backbiting scandal and all manner of spitefulness; and no doubt the cat is occasionally spiteful, or may be supposed to be so; but it is not distinctively so, and it is far less so than many men, and especially women, while the poor cat has many admirable qualities for the possession of which it gets no credit.*

We have tried to show that Lindsay's published opinions were frequently shot through with ambivalence and contradiction, and this is nowhere more evident than in his attitude towards Darwin's evolutionary writings. Lindsay endorsed Darwin's view, in the *Descent of Man*, that 'there is no fundamental difference between Man and the higher animals in their mental faculties', and he rejected the idea that animals were mere Cartesian automata, lacking consciousness or higher mental functions. But he also challenged Darwin's claim in the *Descent of Man* that mental, moral and emotional characteristics had emerged gradually over millions of years. Following Alfred Russel Wallace, Darwin's erstwhile collaborator and a convert to Spiritualism, Lindsay argued that consciousness and its associated phenomena had emerged suddenly – perhaps supernaturally – at the dawn of animal life, and were not straightforwardly subject to the constraints of evolution. He did not believe that 'the brain is the sole organ of mind', nor that 'intelligence, as to its kind or degree', was associated 'with the mere size either of brain or body'. The mental powers of even the smallest animals showed that mind could not be reduced to mere material brain:

> *Darwin points out what he regards as the wonderful difference in size between the brain of the ant and that of man; and yet, in many respects, that active, intelligent little insect is man's mental superior.*

For his part, Darwin appears to have encountered Lindsay's work through his papers in the *Journal of Mental Science*. In one of his notebooks, headed 'Books to be read' and 'Books read' 1838-1851, Darwin wrote:

> Traite de la Folie des Animaux ... *by Dr Pierquin [Charles Pierquin de Gembloux], published in Paris (in 2 vols.), so long ago as 1839. Said to be good by Dr L Lindsay.*[23]

A search of the Darwin Correspondence Project online catalogue suggests that the two men did not correspond.[24] In this sense

23. Darwin, Charles: 'Books To Be Read' And 'Books Read' 1838-1851, Cambridge University Library, CUL-DAR 119.

24. *www.darwinproject.ac.uk*, Accessed 3 Jan 2010.

Lindsay is possibly noteworthy as one of that select band of Victorian scientific writers not to have received a politely inquisitive letter from Down House. Lindsay did, however, contribute statistical data to a large survey carried out by Darwin's son George, titled 'Marriages between first cousins in England and their effects' and published in the *Journal of the Statistical Society* in 1875.

The first edition of the *Descent of Man* included one chapter on mind in animals, but no references to Lindsay – not surprisingly, as his first paper on the subject was published only a month or so before the book came out in November 1871. Likewise, Darwin did not cite Lindsay in *On the Expression of Emotions in Man and Animals*, published the following year. But in the second edition of the *Descent*, published in 1874, the chapter on mind in animals had been expanded and split into two, to include a large amount of anecdotal material from other writers. Darwin cited Lindsay's 1871 papers in the *Journal of Mental Science* on three points, each making Lindsay's own ideas on the subject seem almost grotesquely out of proportion. First, the transmission of infectious diseases from animals to humans; second, the general propensity of animals to suffer madness; third, the proposition that 'a dog looks on his master as on a god'. Lindsay's great assemblage of anecdotes had become itself an anecdote, reduced to three tesserae in Darwin's great mosaic.

The publication of *Mind in the Lower Animals* in 1879 also marked Lindsay's retirement. His dyspepsia grew worse, and his appetite declined: according to one of his obituarists, 'various remedies were tried, and severe changes of climate were advised, but to no purpose'. A year later, almost to the day, he died from 'absolute exhaustion of mind and body', having left instructions that his remains be cremated or buried in a plain deal coffin. In 1881 Kegan Paul finally published its *International Scientific Series* volume on 'animal intelligence'. Written by the evolutionary biologist George Romanes, this book also presented a digest of anecdotes and reports drawn from many sources, but set them in a strongly Darwinian framework. Lindsay was cited only once, on the question of whether birds could dream.[25]

But though the subject of animal madness continued to spark scholarly argument long after the publication of *Mind in the Lower Animals*, there is little evidence that Lindsay's contemporaries took any interest in his work. The copy we examined – in the Wellcome Library – had lain untouched in the closed stack for almost a century, and his obituaries and DNB entry make only passing, vague references to the text. A generation later his work was referenced by William James in *The Principles of Psychology* (1890) – but that is a story for another time, and we will end with the afterlife of Lindsay's work in a different sense. According to one of his obituaries, Lindsay's next book would have addressed the ultimate continuum between humans and animals – the possession of an immortal soul. We have found no other evidence for this claim, but it strikes an authentically Lindsayan note. If late Victorian Spiritualism could attest to the consolations of the next world, Lindsay might well have hoped to show that generations of beloved Fidos and Felixes were not lost but gone before, waiting for their owners in the celestial city. But his obituarist found a more honourable precedent:

> *One would think he was writing to gain the praise of beasts, or that he expected them to become extensive purchasers of his books. Since the time of Swift no one has, comparing man with beasts, given harder hits at human selfishness, brutality and stupidity.*[26]

The author of *Gulliver's Travels* might have been set spinning

25. Romanes, George: *Animal Intelligence. International Scientific Series Vol 41.* London: Kegan Paul & Trench, 1881.

26. Anonymous: 'Obituary. Dr William Lauder Lindsay'. *Edinburgh Medical Journal*, Vol 26, 1881, Pp 669-672.

in his grave, but in one sense the comparison is entirely apposite. To borrow a phrase from another Victorian writer obsessed with the boundary between humans and animals, Lindsay believed he could step through the looking-glass and, in doing so, show his readers that the organ-grinder was merely a shady reflection of the monkey. In *Mind in the Lower Animals* he held a sub-Swiftian mirror up to humanity, hoping to expose what he had come to see as its shortcomings, cruelties and idiocies. His misanthropic exploration of madness in animals was intended, it seems, to highlight their superiority to the human beast.

Thanks to: *Elma Brenner, Caroline Essex, David Allan Feller, Rhodri Hayward, Mike Jay, Marina Warner, Mick Worboys, Caitlin Wylie and those who attended 'Zoologia Fantastica', University of Essex, 18 March 2009.*

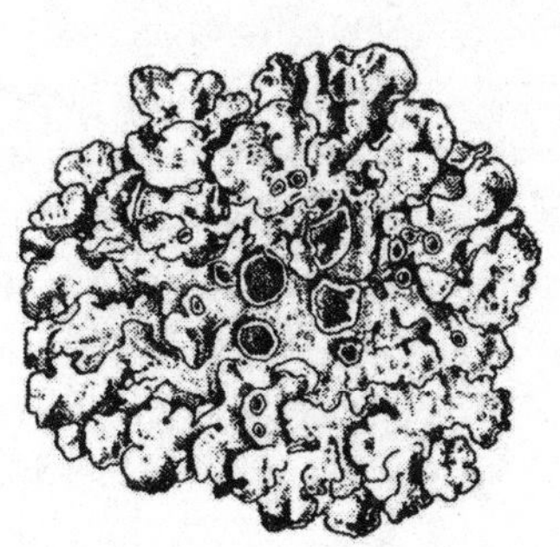

Sketches of the

GOAT GOD *in* ALBION

by GYRUS

I. SNOWDONIA

164

To grasp Pan as nature we must first be grasped by nature, both 'out there' in an empty countryside which speaks in sounds not words, and 'in here' in a startle reaction.

JAMES HILLMAN

The balmy summer of 1995 found me hitching and camping around England and Wales. I enjoyed visiting many friends and small press collaborators; but mostly I was seeking some kind of 'vision' from bold exposure to nature.

Fuelled by a rather naïve yearning for celestial revelations, and curious about the associations between UFOs, sacred sites, and angels, my target was Mynydd Carningli ('Mountain of the Angels'), an extinct volcano near the Pembrokeshire coast which is crowned by the ruins of an Iron Age hill fort. The meagre remains of this construction do form, from a certain angle, a rough likeness of a supine figure

with wings; but the real angelic connection is the sixth-century Saint Brynach. It's said that Brynach used the summit of this mount as a refuge where he communed with divine messengers. A particular rock there is known as Brynach's Rock, and I've heard a tale that this is where the saint rested his head when he dreamed. Passing a compass past this rock sends the needle through a full 180° spin, so the legends correlate in a suggestive way here with measurable geophysical anomalies.

In any case, my three nights of fasting and dreaming on Carningli were not to be. The first night found me completely unable to sleep thanks to heavy winds that battered my tent, and a quite overpowering sense of fear before the star-studded depths of the vast night sky. I meekly packed up the next day and headed north, feeling disconsolate and finding refuge among the moss and streams of the valleys near Betws-y-Coed ('Prayer house in the wood') in Snowdonia.

One calm, moonlit night after a long ramble, I was walking alone back to my tent along a deserted lane. Passing one field, a periodic violent knocking sound startled me. I kept walking, but squinted to try and penetrate the darkness... and eventually I saw the dim scene: a pair of goats facing off, occasionally lunging towards each other and cracking skulls. I felt suddenly removed from my human world, and watched with fascination even as I continued walking, feeling quietly glad that a solid fence stood between me and these clashing beasts.

When I eventually pulled my gaze back to the lane ahead, I instantly froze at the sight of the uncanny tableau before me. Lit from behind by the high, full moon, directly in front of me stood a very large, impassive billy goat, with large horns and dark fur. He was flanked by a couple of females. I was transfixed for a fraught, ponderous moment as we stared at each other and waited for the first move. Eventually I reined in my shock just enough to hide it and calmly step to the side of the lane and walk – always watching the goats out the corner of my eye – onwards along the valley to the nook that sheltered my tent.

Large horns and dark fur

Many have contrasted the symbolism of mountain tops and valley bottoms, peaks and vales, by relating them to spirit and soul respectively.

Pan and Psyche *by Edward Burne-Jones (1874)*

'Spirit is the land of high, white peaks and glittering jewel-like lakes and flowers,' wrote the fourteenth Dalai Lama. 'Soul is at home in deep, shaded valleys. Heavy torpid flowers saturated with black grow there.' Spirit is rapture, transcendence, the 'peak experience'; soul is worldly entanglement, reflection, melancholy insight. 'Call the world, if you please, the vale of soul-making,' wrote John Keats.

Pan, the renowned Greek goat-god of the Arcadian pastures, was of course associated with the mountains of that region, and the spry sure-footedness of the mountain goat; but he is also associated with grottoes and wooded dells, with the dank, too-close proximity of encroaching nature. Revealingly, in the tale of Cupid (desire) and Psyche (soul) told by Apuleius in the second century CE, Pan consoles Psyche when she attempts suicide after being abandoned by Cupid. While teaching songs to the nymph Echo, Pan spots the desolate

Psyche, and reveals a wise sensitivity that forms an interesting contrast to the god's shaggy, rampaging aspect. Writes Apuleius:

> *'Pretty dear,' he said soothingly. '... Stop crying, try to be cheerful, and open your heart to Cupid, the greatest of us gods; he's a thoroughly spoilt young fellow whom you must humour by praying to him only in the gentlest, sweetest language.'*

James Hillman comments:

> *The soul disconsolate, its love gone, divine help denied, panics. Psyche throws herself away, into the river which refuses her. In that same moment of panic, Pan appears with his reflective other side, Echo, and brings home to the soul some natural truths. Pan is both destroyer and preserver, and the two aspects appear to the psyche in close approximation.*

My singular encounter with the goats in the Welsh vale acted as the seed for a prodigiously fruitful period of research and writing, concerned with Dionysus and Earth goddesses as much as Pan himself. But more than that, it shocked my rather lost soul, dragging me away from escapist fantasies of mountain-top revelations, and enlivening it with a desire to engage more closely with this messy 'vale of soul-making'.

II. SPEAKER'S CORNER

Shortly after moving from Leeds to London in 1999, for a time I found myself contributing a column on sacred sites to AOL's gated online community. Attempting to divine sites in less than obvious locations in the sprawl of the city, my interest in Pan and Dionysus drew me towards Speaker's Corner in Hyde Park.

I was guided in this by my memory of the violent climax of the protest against the Criminal Justice Bill on 9 October 1994. The march seemingly winding down into a carnival atmosphere, my friends and I were making our way to the coach that would take us back to Leeds, when it suddenly became obvious that the partying was starting to degenerate. Cops piled into Park Lane to prevent a couple of lorries carrying sound systems from entering the park, and soon the inevitable unwarranted squads of riot police manifested, confronted in turn by the inevitable sticks and bottles.

We had just made it onto our coach when the now furious battle – protestors mainly in the park, cops along Park Lane – converged around us, our coach one of a few forming a barrier between the clashing forces of freedom and control. We were protected from the police, but exposed to the full spectacle of their brutalities – splitting heads and crushing distraught young people on their way to their coaches.

For my AOL column, I suggested that this corner of Hyde Park was a 'young site of sacred power'. Of course, the park was traditionally the playground of the royals and the rich, with the executions at the notorious Tyburn gallows (near the modern Marble Arch) publicly

demonstrating the violence that underwrote authority and its privileges. The park itself had been the site of mass protest since at least 1855, but we might date the birth of its current significance to 1866, when a large mob, banned from protesting for universal male suffrage, overran Hyde Park in a furious uproar against their voices being silenced. The powers that be thereafter granted people permission to conduct meetings within 40 yards of the notice board at the place we now know as Speaker's Corner, and the area has became a traditional bastion of free – if customarily quirky and sometimes bizarre – speech.

Presiding over this nascent place of power (or place of resistance to Power) I imagined 'some (as yet nameless) entity of freedom and healthy chaos – a modern descendant of Pan or Dionysus.' Irrational

Mass panic in ancient Greece

waves of mass panic in ancient Greece (*panikon deima*, literally 'panic fear', fear associated with Pan), as well as being attributed to beasts of the field, were also seen among soldiers on the battlefield. And Dionysus, whose wild army of revellers comprised numerous goatish satyrs if not Pan himself, was certainly in evidence in 1994; the protest was predominantly revelrous, and the riot itself was ignited by a dispute over a sound system. Dionysus is frustrated, so Pan's rampaging, uncontrolled aspect bursts forth.

What are we to make of this attempt to read political violence in mythical terms? Charles Baudelaire's 1852 pamphlet *L'Ecole païenne* ('The Pagan School') opens thus:

> *At a banquet commemorating the February revolution, a toast was proposed to the god Pan . . .*
> *'But,' I said to him, 'what has the god Pan in common with the revolution?'*
> *'How can you ask?' he replied; 'it's the god Pan who made the revolution, of course. He is the revolution.'*
> *'Besides, hasn't he been dead for a long time?'*
> *'That's a rumour that people spread around. Nasty gossip . . . He's going to come back.'*

The reference to Pan's death is to the famed and much-debated passage in Plutarch's *De defectu oraculorum* in which a sailor passing by a Mediterranean isle hears a voice cry, 'The great god Pan is dead!' The fact that this incident is dated to the reign of the Roman Emperor Tiberius (i.e. between AD 14 and 37) has naturally led many to the conclusion that this death was in fact the death of the old pagan nature cults – quaking in the shadow of Bethlehem and Golgotha, soon to be crushed by the triumph of Christianity's otherworldly cult.

The equation of Pan with revolutionary forces stumbles heavily here. Christianity's utopian eschatology and potential for egalitarianism have, for better or worse, done more to foment political upheaval than any form of paganism. We can sympathize with Baudelaire's cynicism about the somewhat misplaced honour granted to Pan in a toast to the revolution. However, he couldn't have known how concern for the natural environment would come to interweave with political activism in the twentieth and twenty-first centuries – how Pan, as much as Christ, may return.

Baudelaire's France may well have been seeing its share of the Romantic revival of interest in Pan – a suitably spirited emblem for disgust with the Industrial Revolution. Victorian England was witness to the rise of a literary cult of Pan as 'the personification and guardian of the English countryside' (albeit 'the countryside as viewed by the city-dweller', as Ronald Hutton observes). Later, in *Howard's End*, EM Forster captured the Edwardian sense of the passing of this effort to resist (or ignore) the onslaught of urbanization and mechanization, and showed a little more awareness than Baudelaire of the cycles of history:

> *To speak against London is no longer fashionable. The Earth as an artistic cult has had its day, and the literature of the near future will probably ignore the country and seek inspiration from the town. One can understand the reaction. Of Pan and the elemental forces, the public has heard a little too much – they seem Victorian, while London is Georgian – and those who care for the earth with sincerity may wait long ere the pendulum swings back to her again.*

For anyone who takes Pan as the embodiment of non-human nature, modern ecology gives us a 'long view' that makes it clear that Pan's death has certainly been exaggerated. We may wound this biospheric Pan, but he will outlive all our civilizations. What seems to have suffered most is the human relationship to Pan, to nature. Even so, this relationship will surely persist as long as we do, even in radically new and apparently disfigured contexts like the politics of civilization. Pan is the nature within us as well as the nature around us, and the transpersonal force he embodies will erupt wherever we give it no vessel for expression. Such, surely, is the logic underlying generally fanciful attempts to hold Pan or Dionysus as revolutionary forces.

In *L'Ecole païenne*, Baudelaire lambasts nineteenth-century 'neo-pagans' and their 'excessive taste for form', for their literalist idolatry and slavish aping of classical traditions. Certainly much contemporary neo-paganism shows few signs of having shed this surface aestheticism. And I confess here that, for all the resonance I find in letting my imagination take Pan or Dionysus as representative of energies of popular resistance and carnivalesque protest, I have no idea how this imaginal perception might 'serve' struggles against overbearing authorities. There are certainly gifts of inspiration there; but also traps of aesthetic escapism. In the end, the idea of enlisting forces such as Pan and Dionysus for political ends may be part of the anthropocentrism that has banished so much of their power already. We might acknowledge their presence when they arise; but the overall shape of whatever new relationships we may be forming with them will always be partially occluded. Even within us, they are of necessity beyond us.

III. Avebury

On the night of summer solstice 2002, I was sat alone on Waden Hill in Avebury (Waden, from *weoh-dun*, 'hill of the pagan temple'). After walking to this henge-encircled village along the ancient track called the Ridgeway over a period of a few days, I was surprised to find no familiar faces in the gathered throng, so I decided to avoid the crowds at the megalithic monuments and just meditate on this gentle hill nestled between the henge and Silbury Hill. The moon was nearly full, the air was still and cool. I settled down facing Silbury and the setting moon, back against a fence bordering a wheat field, and soaked everything in.

At one point I was thinking of an odd dream I had had a couple of nights before on the Ridgeway, of a small black goat with the face of a blonde girl. I was reclining against a fence post. Suddenly I was aware of something running towards me from further down the hill; I sat up and saw what seemed to be a little black goat approaching fast. Dumbstruck, I watched it arc away as it neared me, and disappear into the night.

An excited, awe-struck panic ran through me, my heart racing, my mind struggling. Was it a black dog that had strayed from its owners? I didn't hear anyone nearby. I wisely refrained from too much thought, and settled back against the fence to wait out the rest of the night – albeit with a little more apprehension than before.

An hour or so later, I heard movement in the wheat field behind me. Something leaping in and out of the crop, it sounded like. I froze with fear. Soon it was close, and I heard the distinct sound of a ruminant chewing the grass just behind me. The notion of turning round to see what this creature was arose... briefly. I kept very, very still and kept looking forwards.

Naturally the next day saw its share of speculation. I went back to Waden Hill to see if there were any farm animals being kept there – no.

I pondered the fact that the night before the solstice, camped in a field near Ogbourne St. George, I'd had a vivid nightmare experience. I thought I saw a young girl silhouetted through my tent fabric by a nearby street light. I closed my eyes and lay absolutely still, irrational fear inspiring me to think about reaching for my pen knife. I heard very precisely the sound of someone's feet in the grass near the entrance to my tent, and I remained motionless. I waited and waited, and eventually... nothing was there. This kind of nightmare is well documented. Often sleep paralysis is rationalized as a 'decision' to stay still. Fear is felt, usually inspired by some presence nearby. Often there is a sense of weight on the chest. Almost always, these kind of liminal hypnagogic experiences stand apart from normal dreams in that they seem to be 'real' after the fact as well as while they happen. I wondered about my experience on Waden Hill of 'deciding' to keep still while this creature grazed behind me. Was I half-asleep, paralyzed? And yet, when I first saw the goat, I was definitely awake, and certainly not paralyzed – I sat up to see it run at me.

For once, though, these thoughts seemed flimsy and irrelevant during that hazy, bewildered 21 June. This had been an *experience*. An explanation may be of mild interest, nothing more.

Just a few weeks after, I had a dream of a healing ritual being performed for me involving some snakes and a small black goat. I recall picking the goat up in the dream and showing it to people, saying, 'This is the goat I told you about from Waden Hill. See, it's real!' I even named it. It cropped up a few times over the next few years in my dreams. Once, it was horribly injured and mangled; I collapsed next to it in excruciating sympathy, melting with it into a hot, messy, deep red space. A year later, a dream came in which I took the form of a goat, climbing with a fellow goat up a mountain, to some caves near the peak.

The concept of healing isn't commonly associated with the goat-legged Arcadian piper who inspires fear and rapes nymphs. Pan *was* intimately associated in classical times with vivid nightmares, specifically those that mixed the boundaries between dream, vision, and waking life. But he also, like Asclepius, who presided over dream incubation temples, healed the sick through these startling experiences.

Was this creature *Pan*, though? The black goat was more a kid than anything else, spry and puckish. I've also never been able to confidently say 'he' or 'she', which goes back to the face of the blonde girl in the initial dream as well as the sexual ambivalence of youth itself. Together with its torn and mutilated manifestation, I think of Dionysus: the man-woman, the divine youth, the Kid, his maenads tearing him apart as a goat.

Again we find these related but distinct gods overlapping in modern manifestation. In densely polytheistic cultures like ancient Greece, no god stood alone; all divinities interacted, related, shared stories and qualities. But these interactions carry more meaning when the gods are known well, and their relationships connect rather than blur. In our post-religious world, fragments of archaic psychology or theology tend to bubble up in a rather confused, gloopy liquid of half-learned myths and vague anthropologies.

A dream of two goats ascending

I hear this creature leaping in and out of the rustling wheat behind me; later I learn that Prussia was thick with tales of goats as corn-spirits, leading people to say when corn stalks bend in the wind, 'The goats are chasing each other' (again, the vegetal Dionysian aspect). I dream of two goats ascending a mountain to a cave; was this Pan-related, an amalgam of his association with both high and low places? Or was the mother goddess Cybele implicated, through her association with caverns, mountains, wild animals, and the cult of Dionysus, whom Cybele is said to have cured and initiated?

I have no answers. But the questions – like the very presence

Pan Bridge, Avebury. *Photo by Gyrus*

of this imaginal goat in my life, radiating uncommon energies – keep me engaged, curious, and alert to possibilities.

History always has another trick up its sleeve. In September 2006 while visiting Avebury, I noticed something that had managed to totally elude my attention over my decade of exploring this landscape. Walking along the A4 between Silbury and West Kennet long barrow, while crossing over the River Kennet, I was stopped in my tracks when I caught sight of the plaque fixed to the north side of the little bridge. It read: 'PAN BRIDGE'. And from where I stood, the horizon was formed by the gentle arc of Waden Hill; the bridge was actually in the direction that the solstice goat seemed to have come towards me from.

The earliest reference to this bridge and its name in local records seems to date to 1871. Perhaps it was named then by some local official caught up in the Victorian passion for the goat-god; perhaps the name goes further back. Perhaps the name refers to cookware rather than a god; a quick web search reveals a number of Frying Pan Bridges. But then there is a Pans Lane in nearby Devizes, and it seems less odd for the lane there to belong to Pan than for it to be named after a collection of frying pans.

Obscure place names like this are notoriously difficult to pin down (and hence good fuel for speculation), but I'm a little intrigued by the date of the bridge's current plaque, commemorating its rebuilding in 1932. This was around the time that Alexander Keiller, the heir to a marmalade fortune who invested much of his wealth in his passion for archaeology, was becoming heavily involved in excavating the monuments of Avebury. Today, the museum there is named after him, honouring his role in uncovering and preserving the region's tremendous prehistoric significance.

Keiller had a long-standing interest in witchcraft, and while there's not much evidence of practical involvement, there are glimpses. In her biography of Keiller, Lynda Murray writes:

> *[I]n the 1930s, one Halloween night found him leading a small group of associates out into the garden of the Manor at Avebury. He carried before him a phallic symbol, and bowing three times before the statue of Pan, he chanted 'witchlike' incantations.*

Curiously, while excavating Windmill Hill, a Neolithic site just a little northwest from Avebury, among the animal remains that Keiller's team found in 1929 was the skeleton of a goat. He was clearly quite taken by this find, going as far as to name the creature 'Duffine', and to use a photograph of the goat's remains on New Year's greetings cards.

Keiller's interest in Pan was obviously bound up with sexuality. Though there is no direct mention of Pan, it's hard to not sense his presence in the fact that during the mid-1930s, Keiller *and a small group of like-minded gentlemen would meet for drinks at a club, following which they would adjourn to a flat in South London where a young lady waited for them. Each of them would take turns with the woman in what was a curiously formal and ritualistic act of sexual intercourse. Afterwards, when the men had gone their separate ways, they would later correspond with each other discussing intimately the parts of the ritual which excited them the most.*

It seems that as far as they went, Keiller was sincerely engaged with these dabblings in magic and sexual exploration, but it may be a stretch to peg him as a committed occultist. Still, my own experience on Waden Hill compels me to ruminate upon Keiller's private fantasies about the significance of the millennia-old excavated goat, and the existence of a Pan Bridge in Avebury. Did he have a hand in rebuilding it in 1932? We will never know the exact nature of Keiller's associations between goatish divinity and this evocative place; but it appears that whatever fantasies he found himself in maintain some sort of autonomous life of their own – out there on the hills, in here in dreams, and especially betwixt and between.

IV. Crouch End

Mariners sailing close to the shores of Tuscany heard a voice cry out from the hills, the trees, and the sky: 'The great god Pan is dead!' Pan, god of panic. The sudden awareness that everything is alive and significant. The date was December 25, 1 AD. But Pan lives on in the realm of imagination. In writing, painting, and music. Look at van Gogh's Sunflowers, writhing with pretentious life. Listen to the Pipes of Pan in Joujouka. Now Pan is neutralized, framed in museums, entombed in books, and relegated to folklore. But art is spilling out of its frames into subway graffiti. Will it stop there?
William S. Burroughs, 'Apocalypse'

Parkland Walk sculpture *by Marilyn Collins. Photo by Karolina*

After a brief jaunt in Bristol, in 2007 London drew me back into its arms (or should that be tentacles?). I got a room in Stroud Green and, browsing the area on Google Maps, I was caught by a long, tree-lined path called Parkland Walk. Wikipedia told me this was the vestige of rail line that ran, in the late nineteenth and early twentieth century, between Finsbury Park and Alexandra Palace.

Of course, discovering a long stretch of greenery in my new neighbourhood was thrilling. But my sense of mystery, primed by previous goatish encounters, got a particular buzz from the Wikipedia section on Parkland Walk's urban legends. This snippet of modern lore was to plunge me into the densest tangle of ungraspable connections that my goat-related experiences had yet delivered.

> *Along the walk just before the disused platforms at Crouch End, a man sized green spriggan sculpture by Marilyn Collins had been placed in one of the alcoves of the wall on the right at the footbridge before the former Crouch End station. This was thought to be a tribute to a ghostly 'goat-man' who*

> *haunted that particular area in the mid 1980s. Local children playing out in the evenings would 'dare' each other to walk the Parkland Walk from the Crouch End Hill bridge to the Crouch Hill bridge in the darkness.*

Thanks to Wikipedia's revision history feature, I tracked down the source of the 'goat-man' tale – a guy called Patrick who grew up in the Crouch End area and recalls walking this haunted track in the dead of night as a 12-year-old around 1986. This was a couple of years after the track, which had been completely abandoned since 1970, was officially opened as a linear walkway. Patrick recalled rumours of a curse placed on the rail line by gypsies evicted to make way for it near Alexandra Palace, and no doubt this 14-year period of dereliction was a fertile time for the sprouting of urban legends about this odd feature, for a time returned to wilderness.

Rumours of a cursed place

I was also fortunate to find that just as I'd moved back to London, Marilyn Collins had moved back to the area after 15 months in Crete, so I managed to get the story of the 'spriggan' sculpture directly. It seems that in 1991, a talk given in Crouch End by permaculture originator Bill Mollison inspired a lot of local eco-conscious activity, including the UK's first permaculture course. In 1993 Marilyn was commissioned by Rob Grunsell from the Crouch Hill Community Centre to artistically mark the local passion for nature, which resulted in this idiosyncratic foliated youth who appears to burst out of the graffiti-covered brickwork arches.*

The name 'spriggan' was chosen by Marilyn purely on aesthetic grounds from a book of folklore (traditionally it's a term from Cornish fairy lore). The entity's genesis, though, reaches back to the artist's youthful experiments with consciousness-altering substances – specifically, cough syrup. She recalls seeing many small entities during

* Marilyn was helped by many people, including Joe Rodrigues (who was responsible for the figure's installation and the armature), David Bevan, Theresa Pateman and Maxine Burrage.

these experiences, but they didn't seem very interested in her. 'But this big thing that I saw,' she told me, referring to the inspiration for the sculpture, 'seemed to be interested in me.

> *It was looking at me. I don't know whether to say 'he' or 'she' because I don't think that it was a he or she. . . . My first feeling was that I was afraid, but then my mind came into the whole experience, and I started thinking this isn't anything you need to be afraid of. And pretty soon after I thought that, I stopped seeing it. . . . It seemed as if it wanted to communicate something to me. I've no idea what.'*

The creature's androgyny is evident but hardly blatant in the sculpture; still, one little chap 'got it' straight away. On the day the piece was being installed, a family walked past, and their little boy, on seeing it, shouted, 'Hey, it's a cunt! It's a woodboy cunt!' 'Woodboy Cunt' remains Marilyn's pet name for her creation.

Patrick mentioned that he thought the 'goat-man' legends may have been inspired by the sculpture, but his childhood experiences predate its installation by nearly a decade. Before learning of Marilyn's cough syrup encounter, I assumed she had been inspired by the urban legend; but as it turned out, she knew nothing of it. Wikipedia supplies us with another potential line of inspiration. Supposedly Stephen King once stayed at fellow horror novelist Peter Straub's place in Crouch End, and was moved, after going for strolls along Parkland Walk and seeing the sculpture, to contribute 'Crouch End' to a collection of short stories inspired by HP Lovecraft's Cthulhu Mythos. Well, this collection was published in 1980; but it remains vaguely possible that King caught the spriggan just before publishing a slightly different version in 1993's *Nightmares and Dreamscapes.* The story concerns something unspeakably monstrous snatching people through thin breaches between dimensions. Mention is made of a 'Blind Piper' taking people 'beneath', to the 'Goat with a Thousand Young' (one of Lovecraft's Old Ones, Shub-Niggurath). Marilyn had no idea about the

King story, making it possible that all these threads wove with total independence through the region.

Were urban legends of ruminants along Parkland Walk fuelled by the occasional appearance of muntjac, a small deer occasionally spotted here? Even this mundane grounding for myth is tinged with coincidental mystery by Ossian Road, which runs parallel to Parkland Walk near Crouch End. Ossian is an anglicization of Oisín, the great poet in Irish myth; his name means 'fawn', as his mother had been turned into a deer by a druid.

Looking into the cough syrup connection, it seems probable that the active ingredient in the Sixties mixture involved was Dextromethorphan, or DXM, a cough suppressant and – at the right dosage – a powerful dissociative hallucinogen often used recreationally. As with the somewhat similar drug ketamine, reports of encounters with entities are rife. It seemed like a real shot in the dark to search for 'DXM goat', but the web is very generous when it comes to odd connections. Some trickster at *goatman.com* seems to have these two phenomena welded firmly together in their imagination, with no apparent connection at all to Crouch End:

> *Centered around an anti-civilization, anarchist platform, goat-culture tends to attract the youth, particularly those youth who are especially frustrated and angry at the status-quo, but too lazy to do anything about it. . . . As such, there are no organized rituals within the cult – however, it seems clear that at least in our present culture, drug-induced malicious behavior is an essential facet of the goat-experience. There also appears to be a unholy regard for one particular drug, DXM, which members claim brings one spiritually closer to Goatman more effectively than any other substance.*

Such random oddities aside, connections proliferated around my encounter with Marilyn. It turned out that she personally knows a therapist I once consulted in the Crouch End area, living on the same street a few minutes' walk from the spriggan. It is far from lost on me that I started seeing this therapist regarding panic attacks, and that my experience in Avebury emerged precisely during this time.

Still more interesting to me was Marilyn's tale of what she described as an 'encounter with Pan' during her recent time in Crete. She was walking along the south coast, on the way to Lissos (where there used to be an Asklepion, a dream incubation temple). Descending into a gorge, she became frightened by the sound of footsteps behind her. Every time she stopped, they stopped – leading her to dismiss them as echoes. But returning there with a friend, she found there was no echo at all in that location. 'I don't know whether that was Pan or whether it was an echo,' she admitted.

Perhaps it wasn't Pan *or* an echo, but rather Pan *and* Echo – one of the god's favourite nymphs. James Hillman connects Pan strongly with the phenomenon of synchronicity, 'since Pan like synchronicity connects nature "in here" with it "out there"' – a devilish shadow of our rational conceptions of time, space, and causality. Perhaps all along, in the way in which the unfolding of this goat motif has resisted tidy explanations and cut-and-dried categories, we might see the deft hand of the impish goat-god at work. Hillman has the last word:

> *In Longus' tale of Daphnis and Chloe, Echo was torn apart by Pan's herdsmen (for refusing him). Her singing members were flung in all directions. Let us say that Pan speaks in these echoing bits of information which present nature's own awareness of itself in moments of spontaneity. Why they occur at this moment and not that, why they are so often fragmentary, trivial and even false – these questions would have to be explored through the* mythology of the spontaneous *rather than through either empirical or logical methods. We would have to penetrate further into the nature of Pan (and the nymphs) in order to fathom these manifestations that seem to want to remain renegade and wispy, half-pranks and half-truths . . .*

Bibliography

APULEIUS, LUCIUS (trans. Robert Graves). 1950. *The Golden Ass*. Harmondsworth: Penguin, 1976.

BURROUGHS, WILLIAM S. 1990. *Dead City Radio*. Island Records.

FRAZER, JG. 1922. *The Golden Bough: A Study in Magic and Religion*. London: Macmillan, 1974.

GRAVES, ROBERT. 1955. *The Greek Myths: Volume One*. Harmondsworth: Penguin.

HILLMAN, JAMES & ROSCHER, WILHELM HEINRICH. 1972. *Pan and the Nightmare*. New York City, NY: Spring Publications.

HILLMAN, JAMES. 1972. *The Myth of Analysis: Three Essays in Archetypal Psychology*. New York City, NY: Harper Colophon, 1978.

—. 1991. *A Blue Fire: Selected Writings of James Hillman*. New York, NY: HarperPerennial.

—. 2007. *Mythic Figures*. Putnam, CT: Spring Publications.

HYDE, LEWIS. 1998. *Trickster Makes This World: How Disruptive Imagination Creates Culture*. Edinburgh: Canongate, 2008.

HUFFORD, DAVID J. 1982. *The Terror That Comes in the Night: An Experience-centered Study of Supernatural Assault Traditions*. Philadelphia, PA: University of Pennsylvania Press.

HUTTON, RONALD. 1999. *The Triumph of the Moon*. Oxford: Oxford University Press.

KERÉNYI, C. 1951. *The Gods of the Greeks*. London: Thames & Hudson, 2002.

KING, STEPHEN. 1993. *Nightmares and Dreamscapes*. New York, NY: Viking.

MERIVALE, PATRICIA. 1969. *Pan, the Goat-God: His Myth in Modern Times*. Cambridge, MA: Harvard University Press.

MERRICK. 1997. *There's A Riot Goin' On? Protests, Newspapers and Myth-information*. Leeds: Godhaven Ink. www.godhaven.org.uk

MURRAY, LYNDA J. 1999. *A Zest for Life: The Story of Alexander Keiller*. Wootton Bassett: Morton Books.

PINDAR. *The Extant Pythian Odes*. www.gutenberg.org/etext/10717

The Cult of the PEACOCK ANGEL

A collecteana by ERIK DAVIS

Every Angel is terrifying. And yet, knowing you, I invoke you, almost deadly birds of the soul… RILKE

The matter of the Peacock Angel is, for me, inextricably bound up with my friendship with Terence McKenna. In the fall of 1999, the celebrated mushroom bard and his girlfriend Christy had cause to bunk down in the Edwardian flat I share with my wife in San Francisco. In addition to its menagerie of exotic curios, the apartment is conveniently located only a few blocks from the UCSF medical center, where Terence, who died the following year from the glioblastoma ballooning in his brain, submitted to a craniotomy and other gruesome ordeals. The couple stayed at our place when my wife and I went to India for our honeymoon, and they returned a few times later that year as Terence slipped gradually into the black hole.

At the time I was also casual friends with an occult book dealer who lived half a

Main illustration by JULIAN HOUSE

block away. Steven was a funny little bearded man with twinkly eyes, frequently encountered in an ethno-hippie cap and, more occasionally, with an aroma of whiskey about his breath. He had logged a number of years as a Tibetan monk but had more recently submitted his soul to esoteric bibliomania. His small bedroom was a labyrinth of freestanding shelves stuffed with rare and marvellous tomes. At night he would move aside a few stacks of books and unfurl a simple bedroll to sleep. I myself only purchased a few of his books; I think I was afraid of being infected with the true spirit of a collector.

It was too late for Terence. His home in Hawaii was stuffed with thousands of volumes devoted to obscure religions, mysticism, psychedelics, natural history and exotic travel. One afternoon, when Christy was away, I suggested we visit Steven, and Terence eagerly agreed. I helped him and his spindly frame hobble up the steep sidewalk outside, cross the street, and slowly climb the three flights of stairs to Steven's apartment. We spent about an hour perusing the treasures, and the usual haze of glutted indecision descended upon me. So many paths, so many distant glowing lights.

Terence was moving slowly as well. But then, with gleeful alacrity, he reached out and grabbed a plain black musty tome. It was called *The Cult of the Peacock Angel*, a title that alone seems designed to stir exotic desire. The book, by Ralph Horatio Woolnough Empson, concerned the Yezidi, a Kurdish sect in northern Iraq who worship a glorious angel named Melek Taus, who is identified with both the peacock and the angel Satan. Terence said he first read about the book in a poem or essay by the California poet Robert Duncan, though I have never been able to track down the reference. Terence explained that he had always believed that Duncan had made up the book, as HP Lovecraft did with the *Necronomicon*. Finding it in a real collection was like unwrapping a Hershey bar and discovering an invitation to Willy Wonka's chocolate factory. Terence brought the book into the living room and collapsed into a moth-eaten chair, where he was happy to accept a pipeful from Steven. Then he unrolled a considerable number of twenties and handed them to the book dealer. He arched his hang-dog eyebrows my way. 'Don't tell my girlfriend.'

That night, after dinner, Terence pulled out a glass pipe and put in a few golden drops of some THC essence brewed by a cannabis alchemist he knew. We all became uproariously stoned, which was usually the case when Terence came to town. We moved into the living room, where my wife and I introduced him and Christy to our modest wunderkammer of idols and fetishes. From the mantelpiece we pulled down a curious silver pipe that a friend of my wife's had given us as a wedding gift: a fluted, somewhat flimsy ornamented tube with a strange bird-like bowl. Terence's eyes bugged out as he held it. 'That's it, that's the peacock angel!' He grabbed his recent purchase and showed us the frontispiece, which indeed showed an extraordinarily similar metal peacock. We were all suitably zapped, but, to judge from all the time I have since put into researching the esoteric symbolism and arcane lore of the peacock, it zapped me more than the others. It was as if one of Melek Taus's feathered ocelli had given me a visionary wink.

Over the next few years, I asked a number of occult book dealers about Empson's book and they claimed to have never come across it. Very occasionally, for a lark, I would search for the book on eBay, but I was so sure it would never appear there that I never bothered with setting up an alert. Then, one day, it was there. After a fierce fire fight mostly orchestrated by my wife, who is made of sterner stuff, I managed to spend far more money on a single book than ever before.

The counter to this lucky find occurred a few years earlier, when my wife and I were chomping down some pad thai in a restaurant in Menlo Park. Looking up, I noticed an exact replica of our wedding pipe decorating the wall. Seeing it there, I suddenly understood the loose workmanship, non-functioning bowl, and soft metal of our own pipe. Angel of the world or not, the peacock angel was also a tchotchke.

We do not choose the images that initiate us. They leap out of the bric-a-brac of the world, and sink their talons into our eyes.

Listen. The Yezidi hold that the One God lives far away from us and over the seas and that he does not really care. Perhaps that is why there are so few Yezidi songs that praise him, and then only ambiguously.

You have no home, no shelter,
You have no colouration, no colour,
You have no voice, nor sound,
No one knows what you are.[1]

They say that though the One God was colourless, he shone with great brightness. This effulgence then took a twist and became a rainbow, which, like many visions, is a beautiful thing that isn't really there. The One God's rainbow in turn congealed into Melek Taus, the greatest angel of them all. Six of the rainbow's seven bands of colour then split off and became angels in their own right, just 'as a man kindles a candle from another candle.' Melek Taus retained the mantle of blue, the vibration of heaven. Angels flicker.

The squad of angels took it upon themselves to shape our universe out of the shattered remains of a great cosmic pearl. From the barren, off-white chunks of crystal they formed the earth, the stars, the planets. The earth chunk began to shake violently, and the One God, who must have cared a little bit after all, sent Melek Taus down to calm the planet and to decorate its barren, off-white pearlness. It was a Wednesday.

As he fell to earth, Melek Taus took on the form of a peacock. His angelic rainbow train became a magnificent iridescent fan of feathers. The Peacock Angel flew around the earth, manifesting his rainbow colours in the delightful flora and fauna we know. He finally touched down in Lalish, in northern Iraq, where the Yezidis struggle to live their lives today amid unfriendly Kurds and many war machines. Then Melek Taus travelled to the Garden of Eden to meet Adam. He turned Adam to face the rising sun. And he taught him prayers and

1. 'Madh'e Xwade,' O Celil, C *Cei, Zargotina k'urda, Yerevan*, 1978.

rites to praise the sun, which he declared the manifest symbol of the One God Who Doesn't Really Care.

The one god who doesn't really care

Soon Adam was distracted by the arrival of Eve. Before copulating, they decided to compete with one another in a game of artificial reproduction. They sealed their separate seed into two jars and gave it time to incubate. When they opened Eve's jar, it was filled with scorpions and worms, which is still pretty impressive when you think about it but could not match Adam's jar, which contained a beautiful baby boy who, because he came from a jar, was named Son of Jar -- Shahid bin Jarr. The Yezidis say that this child, who later coupled with a *houri* (a beautiful supernatural female), is their ancestor, whereas the rest of us are the spawn of the combined forces of Adam and Eve. Perhaps the Y in the Y chromosome stands for Yezidi.

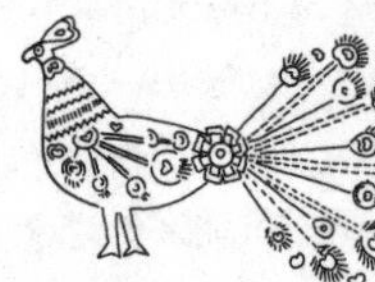

The above is a fanciful retelling of an already somewhat peculiar version of a Yezidi creation story which was lifted from a website called YezidiTruth.org, which is hosted by the International Order of Gnostic Templars, whose Grand Master is a New Age white guy named Mark Amaru Pinkham, who wrote and self-published a book called *The Truth Behind the Christ Myth: the Redemption of the Peacock Angel.* The book, which I bought and devoured shortly after my visionary encounter with the peacock pipe, argues that Melek Taus is the same being known as Skanda or Murugan among the Hindus; King Melchizedek among the Jews; Dionysus to the Greeks; Osiris among the Egyptians; Quetzalcoatl among the Meso-Americans; Sanat Kumara to those Elizabeth Prophet Ascended Masters folks, and the Planetary Logos in the terms of the Theosophists. Pinkham's book is terrible in many ways. Crudely written and feverishly associative, it possesses only the most cursory regard for the actual history of the people of this planet. But from the moment I picked it up, I could not shake the hunch that in some visionary manner it is on the right track: a crazed moth hurtling towards the flickering, almond-eyed flames of the Angel's tail.

Pinkham's creation story differs only in a few respects from the account enshrined in the *Meshaf Resh*, a text that first came to light in the late nineteenth century, when interest in the Yezidis – a small, secretive tribe declared 'devil-worshippers' by their Muslim neighbours – was growing among scholars, missionaries, and explorers from the West. In 1880, the French vice-consul in Mosul heard about the book from the Baba Sheikh, the spiritual leader of the Yezidi, who in addition told the fellow about another scripture called the *Jelwa*. The *Jelwa* is often translated as 'Splendour', and *Meshaf Resh* as the 'Black Book', which is also the name of a manuscript written in Russia about a century later by diehard fans of JRR Tolkien, and that tells the story of *The Lord of the Rings* from the sympathetic perspective of the Dark Lord Sauron. Remember this.

Not long after the Baba Sheikh's revelations, a Yezidi named Habib converted to Christianity and sought refuge in a Carmelite mission in Baghdad. There he handed over Arabic copies of the *Jelwa* and *Resh*, which he claimed were originally written in Kurdish, to a Carmelite priest named Pere Anastase. The good father later visited the Sinjar mountains, an area of northern Iraq that was and is home to many Yezidi. There he bargained at a per-page rate for a traced copy of the *Jelwa* while paying a lump sum for a parchment scroll of the *Meshaf Resh*. The script used in these texts turned out to be a coded transposition of the Persian-Arabic alphabet that had been used to transcribe, into Kurdish, a text itself translated from Arabic. This linguistic spaghetti appeared in German in 1913, and its authenticity was promptly contested by a formidable scholar and former Chaldean Christian who was later determined to be a fraud himself, having baked forged documents in an oven to give them the patina of age.

Today most scholars believe that, while accurately reflecting some core Yezidi ideas, the *Jelwa* and the *Resh* are both forgeries written by non-Yezidi wanting to exploit the hunger for strange scriptures that unite scholars, missionaries, and explorers from the West. The reality is that the Yezidi are heir to a deeply and primarily oral culture. Unlike the 'peoples of the Book' that surround and in some sense inspire them – the Moslems especially, but also the Jews and Christians – the Yezidi never made the infernal religious pact with writing that helps create 'authentic' and 'inauthentic' scripture. Even though the Yezidi lived near the planet's spawning ground of textual inscription, they retained the ever-shifting, tricksy polysemy of an oral tradition that is, by necessity, endlessly variant and remixed.

> *I lead to the straight path without a revealed book; I direct aright my beloved and my chosen ones by unseen means.*
> –Jelwa

In an article on Yezidi oral culture in the *Journal of the American Oriental Society* (128.4 (2008)), the Hungarian scholar Ester Spät tells a story about the creation of Adam learned from a fellow named Feqir Haji, who learned it from elders and not, as is increasingly the case for Yezidi these days, from books. In this version, which is weirder and therefore more interesting than a similar story told in the *Meshaf Resh*, God created Adam's body quickly, between Friday and Saturday. But he had a much tougher time giving Adam a soul. The divine entity that was slated to become Adam's soul was an angel that came down from the sky, but when it arrived it had no interest in entering Adam's body at all. (I imagine it shared the trepidation of the cliff diver, or the smoker of strange pipes.) Even when the One God and his emissary the Peacock Angel commanded the angel to enter Adam, the angel refused. He refused for seven hundred years. Finally, the angel agreed to enter the clay man, but only on the condition that the spiritual golem that Adam had become could live in Paradise.

The adherents of Ahl-i Haqq, a Kurdish-speaking heterodox movement with close ties to Yezidi, tell an even more beautiful story. Once again, God wanted to ensoul Adam with a shard of divine light, but the shard of light refused to go. So God asked the angel Jibrail to hide in Adam's body and play on the tambour. Hearing the music, the fragment of soul became confused. What is this sound? Where does it come from? He moved closer and closer to Adam's body, thrilled and terrified, until the music pulled him within.

With a chunk of divinity buried in his forehead, Adam then relocated to Paradise, which apparently was really wonderful. The only rule that Adam faced was a prohibition against eating wheat, a foodstuff that, as fans of crumpets and pasta will attest, may be tougher to resist than the fruit of the Tree of Knowledge. Knowledge is bitter, after all. Nonetheless, Adam's will prevailed, so much so that one hundred years later, the One God had become acutely frustrated. He wanted Adam to quit Paradise so that mankind could begin their march through time. And so he told the Peacock Angel to make it so.

The Peacock Angel approached Adam and asked if by chance he had eaten any wheat. Adam said no. The Peacock Angel then commanded our first ancestor to eat the cereal. Adam refused. So the Peacock Angel played a trick. He made himself invisible, snuck up on Adam, and threw a grain of wheat into his mouth. Adam must have had one of those popular allergies to gluten, because his stomach blew up like a balloon. Then he had to take a shit. But since you can't shit in Paradise – everybody knows that – Adam was forced to leave. The Peacock Angel stripped him of his fancy clothes and plucked out the divine light from his forehead. (In other versions, he gets to keep the shard.) 'He became like the empty shell of a snail,' Feqir Haji told the Hungarian scholar. 'He became a human.'

In the version of this tale contained in the *Meshaf Resh*, God sends a bird to Adam once he has abandoned Paradise. It may have been a dove, or a raven, but in any case it poked out an anus in Adam's backside so that he could finally relieve himself. Another variant claims that the Peacock Angel himself told Adam to just stick his finger into his butt to make the hole.

And the ass saw the angel…
– Numbers 22:23

When Melek Taus tricked Adam into eating the forbidden foodstuff, he reminds us of the canonical serpent in Eden, who tempts the first couple to break the One God's law. But the Yezidi account takes place in a parallel universe where the orthodox story of sinful disobedience takes on the lively slapstick of a North American Trickster tale – one, moreover, where the One God is in on the prank.

In one of the most widespread of such tales, which appears in the classic Winnebago Wakdjunkaga cycle collected by Paul Radin, Trickster hears a small tubercle on a plant proclaim that whoever eats of the plant will surely defecate. Assuming the tubercle is bragging, and being ravenous as usual, Trickster gobbles it up. Soon, like Adam, he is overcome with the urge to crap. He starts to defecate, and soon the pile of excrement grows so high that he is forced to climb a tree to escape it. He can't stop pooping though, so the pile reaches the top of the tree, which grows so befouled that Trickster slips and topples into the fragrant mountain. And that is what happened to our first father. He got up to his ears in his own shit.

But even shit can be a change agent in the peacock's trickster realm. Verrier Elwin collected the following tale from some Sherdukpen tribesmen, who lived in Rupa village in Arunachal Pradesh. A boy and a girl fell in love and married, and the boy went to work for her father. The old man was a bird lover, but was sad that there was no bird with a proud regal bearing and a great iridescent fan of feathers decorated with ocelli. So one day he decided to create one, and prepared a cloth with multi-coloured patches. The old man put the cloth out in the sun to dry and that evening, when the boy came home from work, he asked the young man to grab it and bring it to the house. But the boy was entranced by its beauty, and laid the cloth around his shoulders. As when he did so he morphed into a peacock.

The young man burst into tears, thinking about his beautiful wife. Then his father-in-law started to beat him, driving him away to the far bank of the stream. That evening, when the moon rose and the boy had not come home, the girl asked what had happened to him. When her father explained, she called him a sorcerer and ran weeping to the bank of the stream. There she found her peacock husband and wept and moaned. 'I am a human being and you have become a bird, so how can we be husband and wife?' But she knew some sorcery herself, and told her husband to leave his droppings on the bank of the stream that night. The next morning she went to bathe in the river. She ate the shit and transformed into a peahen. Shazam!

The peacock is considered a noble bird in the South Asian continent. He is a mount for warrior gods, a swallower of poison, a vehicle for shakti. But make no mistake: the neighbours of the Yezidi proclaim, in no uncertain terms, that Melek Taus is the Prince of Darkness, and that the Yezidi are born from the spittle of the devil. Early explorers (and later occultists) were fascinated by this idea. Even Lovecraft mentions the '...the Yezidi clan of devil-worshippers', in 'The Horror at Red Hook'. It is more fair to say, perhaps, that the Yezidi were (and are) *angel*-worshippers, albeit with an unusual taste in angels. But we would be wrong to follow the patterns of multicultural relativism so familiar in today's global marketplace and say, in reaction to this, that Melek Taus has nothing to do with the devil, or that his demonic reputation is entirely the fabrication of the orthodox neighbours of the Yezidi. If it is too much to say that Melek Taus is the Lord of Hell, the iridescent Peacock Angel nonetheless shimmers with satanic majesty.

Melek Taus is the Prince of Darkness

> *There is no place in the universe that knows not my presence. I participate in all the affairs which those who are without call evil because their nature is not such as they approve.* – Jelwa

Somewhere in the vast apocrypha of Islam, you will learn that the peacock guarded Paradise. One day, Iblis – the devil, aka Shaytan, or Satan – decides he wants in. He exploits the peacock's legendary pride by praising his beauty and promising to teach him three magic spells that, once pronounced, will grant the bird eternal youth, eternal health, and an eternal stay in Paradise. A good deal. The peacock goes for it, and the rest, literally, is history. In a Javanese version of this myth – at least according to a somewhat dubious Internet site that speaks of a Javanese version of this myth – the peacock simply eats the devil, and so conveys him through the gates of Paradise in his distended gut, his feathers transformed into rainbow from all that angel light.

But there is a more canonical argument for the identification of the Peacock Angel with Satan. In the written Yezidi accounts, before Adam was created, the One God told Melek Taus never to bow to any other being in the universe. The One God then commanded the whole rainbow band of angels to gather dust from the Earth and to build the body of Adam. The One God blew life into Adam – a precursor, it seems, to the later gesture of ensouling Adam – and instructed all the angels to bow down before this new man. All obeyed except for the Peacock Angel, who steadfastly refused to praise this Frankenstein scandal who stood before him. 'How can I submit to a lump of dust when I have the One God before me?'

A very similar scene occurs in the Quran, where the cranky refusenik is none other than Shaytan (sometimes Shaytan is taken in a plural sense, so that Iblis is considered 'a Shaytan'). Unlike the Yezidi, the Muslims do not consider Shaytan to be an angel but rather a jinn, an elemental spirit formed from smokeless fire. In any case, when Shaytan refuses to obey God's order – an act that the orthodox interpret as a sign of his overweening pride – he gets kicked out of Paradise. In the Yezidi account, however, God praises Melek Taus for his convictions, almost as if he had been testing his creation. Melek Taus becomes the leader of all angels and the One God's deputy commander on earth. This Yezidi inversion – not unlike the classic Gnostic inversion of the serpent saviour bringing saving knowledge – is perhaps derived from

Formed from smokeless fire

Sufi thinkers, who embraced a similar heterodox turn. In the tenth century, for example, Mansur al-Hallaj proclaimed that, because of his refusal to bow down before Adam, Satan was a greater monotheist than God. Another outstanding mystic, Ahmad al-Gazzali, said that 'One who will not learn to worship One God from Satan is a heretic and infidel.'

In the *Resh*, Melek Taus is draped with an another name, a word that some translate as Azrael and others as Azazil, or Azazel. Azrael is a name for the Angel of Death found in Muslim and Hebrew folklore; in the Talmud, he is said to be covered with eyes. This panoptic condition is important to keep in mind when we are speaking of peacocks, whose fans of ocelli incarnate the many-eyed angels of Enoch and the Hekhalot, such as the great Seraphim Seraphiel, whom the angel Metatron describes as 'full of eyes like the stars of the sky, innumerable and unsearchable.' (26: 6. 3 Enoch).

Azazel, on the other hand, is mentioned in the description of the Day of Atonement ritual found in Leviticus, where the scapegoat, who has been chosen by lot to carry Israelite sins, is sent off 'into the wilderness to Azazel.' The old-school rabbis, perhaps unnerved by the implication of polytheistic sacrifice, claimed that 'Azazel' named a rugged cliff. Today many scholars embrace the more esoteric identification of Azazel as a goat-god, a desert-haunting jinn to whom the Israelites occasionally, or not so occasionally, sacrificed.

In the apocryphal Book of Enoch, Azazel is the leader of the rebellious Watchers, those fallen angels who copulate with human daughters and pass on the trickster arts of war and cosmetics to mankind. (If you pay attention, you might glimpse herein the iridescent rainbow eyes of the Peacock Angel.)

> *And Azazel taught men to make swords and knives and shields and breastplates; and made known to them metals and the art of working them; and bracelets and ornaments; and the use of antimony and the beautifying of the eyelids; and all kinds of costly stones and all colouring tinctures. And there arose much godlessness, and they committed fornication, and they were led astray and became corrupt in all their ways.*
> – 1 Enoch 8:1-3

Azrael, Izrael, Azryel, Azazel, Azazil… These sounds and spellings melt into one another. Perhaps this is evidence of a diabolic ambiguity of sound and speech, not unlike the syrupy sounds you hear when you play Led Zeppelin's 'Stairway to Heaven' backwards and hear, or do not hear, a slurred invocation of 'My sweet Satan.' The text of the *Resh* itself invokes such slippery satanic phonemes when, in a list of the various prohibitions to which the Yezidi are sworn (no lettuce or fish or pumpkin stew, no pissing while standing or dressing while sitting down), the identity of the Peacock Angel with the great Shaytan is finally made as clear as possible:

> *'None of us is allowed to utter his name, nor anything that resembles it, such as šeitân (Satan), kaitân (cord), šar (evil), šat (river), and the like. Nor do we pronounce mal'ûn (accursed), or la'anat (curse), or na'al (horseshoe), or any word that has a similar sound. All these are forbidden us out of respect for him.'*

I have read nearly everything I can get my hands on about Yezidi religion and it is still not clear to me whether Melek Taus fell from heaven, or whether he was pushed; whether he left of his own accord, or just went out for a walk and got lost, or distracted. As soon as we catch one of his many eyes, as soon as his figure begins to congeal, he dissolves into rainbow.

Am I not,
Myself, only half of a figure of a sort,

A figure half seen for a moment, a man
Of the mind, an apparition appareled in

Apparels of such lightest look that a turn
Of my shoulder and quickly, too quickly, I am gone?
– Wallace Stevens, 'Angel Surrounded by Paysans'

In 2007, Sean Thomas, a conspiracy-minded New Age blogger, visited Celle, Germany, which is called home by one of the largest concentrations of Yezidi outside Iraq. With the feverish imagination of his ilk – in his post he links the Peacock Angel to the birdlike demons of the Assyrians, including Pazuzu, the scaly-winged bad-ass featured in *The Exorcist* – Thomas asks a Yezidi spokesman about Melek Taus. 'We believe he is a proud angel, who rebelled and was thrown into Hell by God. Now he is reconciled to God.' Thomas is not satisfied. He asks whether Melek Taus is good or evil. 'He is both. Like fire. Flames can cook but they can also burn. The world is good and bad.'

Tony Lagouranis also knows this world. He was a US army interrogator who did very bad things to people at Abu Ghraib and other places. As far as his superior officers were concerned, anything up to organ failure was OK. When Lagouranis returned to the United States, a mounting feeling of horror led him to go public with the cruelties he had committed. He wanted to understand and expose a dehumanizing and immoral military culture that, he believed, had led him to 'discover and indulge my own evil.' We live in a relativistic age, but still we must accept Lagouranis' dualistic moral language. Sometimes we speak truth with a forked tongue.

In *Fear Up Harsh,*[2] Lagouranis describes a memorable encounter with a Yezidi prisoner. 'There's a lot of mystery surrounding the Yezidi,

2. Lagouranis, Tony. *Fear Up Harsh: An Army Interrogator's Dark Journey Through Iraq*, NAL, 2007.

and a lot of contradictory information. But I was drawn to this aspect of their beliefs: Yezidi don't have a Satan. Melek Taus, an archangel, God's favorite, was not thrown out of heaven the way Satan was. Instead, he descended, saw the suffering and pain of the world, and cried. His tears, thousands of years' worth, fell on the fires of hell, extinguishing them.'

This image, which occurs elsewhere in Yezidi folklore, is enough to move one to tears. And it is only such tears, perhaps, that can truly baptize; it is our suffering that redeems suffering, the terrible agony of the matrix of the world, the agony that births new life. In the *Nahj ul-balaya* ('The Way of Eloquence'), the fourth Caliph, 'Ali ibn Abi Talib, brother-in-law and cousin of the Prophet, dedicates an entire encomium to the peacock. In it he claims that the females drink teardrops from the eyes of the male, and from this become pregnant.

The Khasi of Meghalaya, a small Indian state that lies near Bangladesh, tell another tale of tears and peacocks. Ka Sngi is the Khasi name for the Sun, who is seen to be, in a pleasant inversion, a beautiful maiden. One day the Peacock visited the Blue Realms and Ka Sngi fell deeply in love with him, so deeply that she spent all her time adoring him and forgot to shed her light on the world below. But the Peacock was arrogant and proud and horny, and abandoned the Sun for an earthly woman who caught his eye. When the Peacock left the Blue Realms, the Sun wept, and her tears bedewed his formerly grey feathers, infusing them with all the colours of the rainbow. The largest drops fell on his tail – his elongated rump feathers actually; the actual tail supports the fan – which is why the Khasi call the peacock's ocelli Ummat Ka Sngi, or Sun's tears. Ka Sngi then told the Peacock – out of sentiment or vengeance it is not clear – that the marks would never allow him to forget her, no matter the object of his affection.

Unfortunately for the Peacock, his new object of affection turned out to be nothing more than an object – not a woman at all, but a simulacrum of mustard grass and flowers that had been crafted to lure him away from the Sun, and so return her light to the land. That is why the Khasi say – or some of them say, perhaps only a few now – that when the peacock stretches its serpentine neck towards the morning sky and flaps its wings, that he is tasting his only remaining happiness, which is to spread his lovely feathers and catch the beams which Ka Sngi once more sheds upon the earth.

Generally I do not wear blue. Jennifer, who wears only black, loves the colour, and she has beautiful blue eyes and collects cobalt glassware that congeals the morning light into liquid azure globules that line the window ledge in the kitchen. But I own very few items of blue clothes, and certainly no blue jeans. I like black jeans and green jeans and pale purplish jeans but no blue jeans.

I have since discovered that the Yezidi traditionally do not wear blue. The reasons given for the prohibition vary. Some say that blue represents Noah's flood, or was a colour worn by a conquering king. Since blue is the colour of the Peacock Angel – a liminal blue-green rather – perhaps they abjure it out of respect for their lord, the same way they do not say his name. But I prefer one story I clipped from *Parabola* magazine and subsequently lost, which claimed that the Yezidi do not wear blue because it is the colour of heaven, and they resent the Blue Realms that banished their lord.

If Melek Taus fell, was the fall in love? In the accounts of his travels in Syria towards the end of the nineteenth century, the Russian officer AV Eliseev tells the most beautiful and dubious tale of the Peacock Angel, a faintly gnostic account that may owe as much to Mikhail Lermontov's poem 'The Demon' as to the officer's encounter with the Yezidi living in the area. Writes Eliseev:

> *A little star fell from heaven, and hid in the depth of the then still dark earth. In that little star a bright beam of the nocturnal sun illuminating Paradise fell on earth, and the earth became light, clear and warm; a particle of endless light illuminated it, inflamed life in it, gave it strength, reason and breath. That beam, that particle of endless light, was the great and glorious Melek Taus.*

The reason for the fall is that Melek Taus had fallen in love with the earth, 'and through love for the dark earth he exchanged the realm of endless light – the blue sky flooded with the sunbeams and thirty three thousand stars.' He also lost the grace of God, who cast him from the height of the Throne. It took a long time for the Peacock Angel to fall, because every star or moon or sun along the way was loyal to the One God, and the One God had no love for the earth and so

no love for the earth's new lover. In the end, only earth sheltered the exiled angel, who finally lay motionless in some green pasture among the sweet-smelling flowers. Battered, sick, dejected, he was alone in the world, 'for all disdained him.' The humans who encountered him, who carried a spark of the light he had brought within them, who owed him their life and their senses, mocked him. They beat him with sticks and spat on him. He bore these insults passively, with faith that somewhere among cruel and corrupt mankind the original spark could still be found.

> *There came about kind people, pure in heart, who had preserved the unextinguished spark of endless light falling on earth as a bright star of heaven; they recognized and welcomed Melek Taus, fearing not what other people would say or in what way Allah would view their kind deed.*

In other words, these kind people risked the wrath of the One God to care for his exiled angel, his unwanted supplement: 'Gathering around the fallen angel, they washed his body with the water of pure springs, sprinkled him with the incense of the colourful mountain flowers, covered him with the best garments woven by the hands of their beautiful daughters'.

Thus revived and bedecked, Melek Taus raised his skinny hands to heaven, as if to bid farewell. But the One God did not condemn the kind people of the mountains. Instead, he showed his blessing with the sign of the rainbow wrapped around the sun, which the kind people of the mountain, who were of course the Yezidi, received and still receive as a loving command to never abandon the downcast and rejected Peacock Angel.

Why would a people worship an angel who fell to earth, who dragged his glory through the mire? Why worship the King of the World? Some claim that the Yezidi propitiate the Angel because – while the world is already kind of a shitty place, as the Yezidi themselves can tell you – they fear that Melek Taus may unleash an even greater misery. Others hold that the Angel has only been banished from heaven temporarily, and so still deserves his props – after all, what right do humans have to judge the house squabbles of heaven? Still others say that Melek Taus is truly divine, a great gnostic hero who deserves all the love he can get. But perhaps the sweetest reason is the one suggested by Eliseev's tale. One worships fallen angels – and, by necessary extension, the angels of our own fouler nature – out of compassion, a forgiving praise that is perhaps no different than smiling and weeping at once.

Ambiguity is the essence of the Peacock Angel. Iridescence and monstrosity, pride and shame, struts and screams – these are the polarities the Peacock Angel unfolds. Garnik Asatrian and Victoria Arakelova, the Armenian scholars of his lore, call Melek Taus 'the synthesis of the fallen angel and an ambivalent creature.' A fallen angel is already a liminal being, however he falls, and the creature is just as tricksy. The peacock is glorious, but is proud and vain, although even his apparent vanity and pride – wherein we recognize ourselves – is checked by his own nature. Farid ad-din 'Attar, the medieval Persian Sufi poet, writes: 'Everybody praises the Peacock for his beauty, but he is ashamed of his ugly legs.' Or it is his strangled, awkward cry that seems to besmirch the glory of his train – the cry that the medieval Persian zoologist Hamdullah Mustawfi bin Abu Bakr al-Qazwini declared 'puts to flight creeping things.'

The Victorian British police officer and ornithologist Edward Baker, annoyed by this screeching on an imperial tour, nonetheless captured its beauty at night, when the birds take to the trees: 'They often call on moonlight nights when, except for the drone and hum of insects, the Indian nights are silent, broken by the loud 'phi-ao, phi-ao' of a cock Peafowl, the call being taken up by bird after bird until the last cries die away in silence.'

The peacock is a pharmakon

The peacock is a pharmakon: at once poison and cure. Many people believe, traditionally and otherwise, that the peacock's meat is poisonous. And yet, the kings and queens of the Renaissance feasted on a dish of roast birds stuffed one inside the other like Russian mamushka dolls, with the outermost shell the glorious peacock, its many-eyed train stretching the length of the middle of the 'groaning board.'

One explanation for the peacock's supposedly poisoned flesh lies in a variant of the famous South Asian story of Samudra Mathan, the great churning of the cosmic ocean that is described in the Puranas and the Mahabharata. In the tale, the devas and the asuras put aside their strife and together churn the primordial ocean of milk by yanking on both ends of a great serpent who is coiled around a mountain that thus becomes the churning tool.

In the midst of their cosmogonic labours, a pot of poison, with the delightful name of Halahala, emerges from the milky sea. Neither the gods or the demons want anything to do with the stuff, which they believe is corrosive enough to destroy all of creation. So the gods approach Shiva, who gulps down the evil brew but holds it in his throat rather than bring it into his gut. The poison is so powerful that it changes the colour of Shiva's neck to blue, which is why some call him Neelakantha, the blue-throated one. But others say that the blue-throated peacock takes the hit instead. Absorbing the very poison he remains impervious to, he becomes a toxic lord of protection.

Dharmarakshita, an eleventh-century Mahayana sage from Sumatra, begins his very wise allegorical poem called the 'Wheel of Sharp Weapons Effectively Striking the Heart of the Foe' with poison and peacocks. He describes a peacock turning away from a lush garden of medicinal plants and munching on toxic weeds instead. And so it is with bodhisattvas, Dharmarakshita declares, the enlightened ones who remain in the undergrowth of the world, who thrive in the jungle of desire and pleasure, which is also of course the jungle of suffering and pain.

We spend our whole lives in the search for enjoyment,
Yet tremble with fear at the mere thought of pain;
And since we are cowards, we are miserable still.
But the brave bodhisattvas accept suffering gladly
And gain from their courage a true lasting joy.
...
And thus bodhisattvas are likened to peacocks:
They live on delusions, those poisonous plants.
Transforming them into the essence of practice,
They thrive in the jungle of everyday life.
Whatever is presented, they always accept,
While destroying the poison of clinging desire.

Destroying seems too violent a word here. One might prefer the alchemical notion of transmutation, and especially that phase of the Great Work that is sometimes said to follow the initial, putrefying nigredo: the Cauda Pavonis, the 'peacock tail' that describes, perhaps, the shifting, multi-coloured iridescence that the alchemist meets in the astral outskirts of the inner world, when the matter outside has become the matters within.

But Shiva, or the peacock, does not even transmute the cosmic poison he takes in. He does not digest it, or spit it out, or excrete it into the hells. He simply holds it, and does not let go. He is holding it still. Every time you hold your poison, he smiles.

Some might say that it is wrong to look beyond the lands of the Yezidi for insight into their Peacock Angel. But therein lies a great mystery: peacocks have never lived anywhere near the Yezidi ancestral home in Iraq. Peacocks are native to South Asia, where millennia-old sculptures of the birds have been unearthed from the ancient mounds of Chanhudaro in Pakistan. Its feathers travelled far no doubt, throughout the millennia, but the bird never became part of the ordinary life of peasants in northern Iraq. Still, such natural histories are already too literal, because the true home of the peacock, as the Yezidi and the Puranas and the alchemists know, lies in the visionary manifold that unfolds like a fan between heaven and earth.

On 9 October 1906, after months of steady invocation, Aleister Crowley achieved the initiatory satori of the magickal path: the Knowledge and Conversation of the Holy Guardian Angel. For months, he had been invoking his Augoeides, regularly amplifying the workings with hashish. That night, almost certainly stoned, Crowley finally broke through, experiencing a cosmic vision he called the Atmadarshana, or 'Vision of the Universal Peacock.' In his diary, Crowley describes Atmadarshana as the 'consciousness of the entire Universe as One and

as All, in Its necessary relation to Itself in and out of Time and Space.'

Vision of the Universal Peacock

In his marvellous poem 'AHA, Liber CCLII', Crowley presented a versified slice of his Atmadarshana experience:

Ah, could I tell thee of
These infinite things of Light and Love!
There is the Peacock; in his fan
Innumerable plumes of Pan!
Oh! every plume hath countless eyes;
--Crown of created mysteries!---
Each holds a Peacock like the First.

A few months later, after ingesting two grammes of hash, Crowley further explored this state. In his notebook he furiously channelled his impressions of what he called the '"millions of worlds" game – the peacock multiform with each "eye" of its fan a mirror of glory wherein also another peacock – everything thus.' Here we cannot but recall the 'many worlds' theory of some physicists, or the infinite reverberations of the Mandelbrot set, its shape so like a nest of peacock eyes. Everything thus.

But even here, as Crowley descended from one of the peaks of magickal attainment, the ambivalent poisons of the pharmakon return. 'Head still buzzing,' he writes of his later evening. 'Samadhi is Hashish, an ye will; but Hashish is not Samadhi.' But he is confused, so unusual for this supremely confident and arrogant man; perhaps the myriad worlds, where everything echoes everything else, have scrambled his brain. 'I don't, and didn't quite understand this,' he writes, referring to the sentence quoted above. 'I think it means that only an Adept can use Hashish to excite Samadhi; or else that Hashish is the evil and averse S.' But would not an evil Samadhi swallow up good and evil both and hold them mixed in the heart? Or the throat?

The peacocks roam freely in the forests of poison.
– Dharmarakshita

Kenneth Grant once claimed that the second 'A∴' of the A∴A∴, the magickal order that Crowley founded, stood for Argus – the hundred-eyed giant whom Hera employed to spy on Zeus's lover Io, and whose eyes she transplanted into the peacock after Zeus spurred Hermes to kill the giant. Hermes put Argus to sleep with stories – reader beware! But when you consider the other name of Argus – Panoptes – you would be right to suspect that today he has re-awoken. For at the heart of the world lies a peacock lord, with his labyrinth of fluttering eyes, seeing and manifesting the absolute range of virtual and actual possibilities. And now we have installed an avatar of this dark lord in our screens and sensors and toxic circuits, in algorithms that feed on themselves. We have built a great cybernetic pantopticon, which

mediates the iridescent rainbow of reality itself, good and certainly evil and, perhaps, the overcoming of the two, of the need for Two. May all His eyes open at once, and Totality unfold.

Listen, listen, here is the great secret: *even the devil is redeemed.*

In Mighty Revelation ❧ *The Nine Herbs Charm, Mugwort Lore and Elf-persons – An Animic Approach to Anglo-Saxon Magic*

by ROBERT J WALLIS

With 'Fame' and 'Sanctity': an Introduction to the Common Mugwort

Mugwort (*Artemisia vulgaris*) is an easily overlooked plant whose grey feathery leaves grace roadside verges and 'wasteground' across Britain. Armstrong suggests that '[i]t is not pretty, nor even conspicuous, and it is remarkable that it should ever have attained to fame and sanctity'. Grigson agrees: 'It is tempting to call [it] a scruffy, mean plant, as one sees it along the roads at the end of summer, and to ask why such a species ever became so distinguished'. It is so distinguished, as the Mater Herbarum or 'Mother of Herbs', and the 'female herb par excellence' (according to Cameron) that there are fine late thirteenth century carvings of Mugwort in the Lady Chapel, Exeter Cathedral (*overleaf*).[1] While inconspicuous, Grigson notes that 'looked at more closely as the mediaeval sculptor looked at it, Mugwort does prove to have some attraction – especially in its leaves, deeply and delicately cut, dark green and glistening above, white below. In

1. Certain carvings have been identified as Mugwort (see Hope 1971; also Walker 1979; Grigson 1987 [1955]: p. 384).

Figure 1. *Corbel A from the Lady Chapel in Exeter Cathedral, almost certainly depicting Mugwort (late thirteenth century)*

a vase it looks surprisingly agreeable'. An accurate botanical description runs thus:

An erect herb up to a metre in height with tough, grooved stems and many deeply pinnatifid leaves with five to seven lobes, dark-green above but silvery and hairy beneath; small, green-to-yellow, egg-shaped flowerheads crown the plant in long terminal spikes; the taste is bitter... [C]ommon in waysides and waste places throughout temperate regions of the world (Mills).

Moreover, that Mugwort is named in a very deliberate manner in the Old English 'Nine Herbs' charm – found in the *Lacnunga* manuscript, a type of 'leechbook' or healer's[2] manual – attests in part to the special status ascribed to it.

'[F]eeleth no Wearisomeness at All': Mugwort in Folklore

Folklore associates Mugwort with fair journeying and inspired dreams: for the former, the traveller should carry Mugwort leaves, or perhaps eat one or two to relieve fatigue; for the latter, one might sleep with a small bundle of leaves under one's pillow to make a 'dream pillow' or drink an infusion of the leaves before retiring to bed. One of the earliest, most exuberant references, is from Pliny, who 'saith that the traveller or wayfaring man that hath the herbe tied about him feeleth no wearisomeness at all, and that he who hath it about him can be hurt by no poysonsome medicines nor by any wilde beast, neither yet by the sun itself'.

2. 'Læce' means healer in Old English, with læcedom meaning 'leechdom, remedy' (Pollington 2000: p. 41).

Armstrong, furthermore, tells us:

> *In the Isle of Man... it was gathered on Midsummer Eve 'as a preventative against the influence of witchcraft' and placed in chaplets and the heads of man and beast to ward off evil influences. In France... it is worn to prevent aches and pains. In Germany, the people had like customs and eventually threw the girdles and crowns of Mugwort into the Midsummer fire. In East Prussia it was used for divination. At Midsummer* Artemesia alba *is used as a fumigant in Morocco.*

Much of this diverse folklore must surely derive from Frazer's *The Golden Bough*. In addition to the lore cited above, Frazer notes the use of Mugwort in magic, to prevent sore eyes, to protect against witchcraft, thunder and ghosts, as well as its use in exorcism. The time of Midsummer is especially auspicious, not only for using Mugwort in magic but for gathering the plant and for throwing it into the Midsummer fires. All of this must be viewed critically, as a matter of course, but it is clear from Frazer, Armstrong and other sources that Mugwort has been viewed as a special, magical plant, in a variety of folklore traditions, across cultures.

MUG OR MOUGHTE: WHAT'S IN A NAME?

Mugwort may derive part of its name – mug – from being used, among such other herbs as Ground Ivy, to flavour drinks, especially beer before the introduction of hops – and my experiments with the smoke of the plant, discussed below, indicate that research on Mugwort-flavoured beer and mead might be most perspicacious. Alternatively, Grieve notes that 'Mugwort' may be derived from *moughte* ('moth' or 'maggot'), as an insect repellent, or, I might add, an attractant thanks to its acting as a host plant for a number of moth species.

Mugwort's chemical composition is of some interest. It contains 'ethereal' or 'volatile oils' such as cineole and thujone. Cineole or 'wormwood oil', related to eucalyptol, can reduce inflammation and pain, and clinical trials show effectiveness against the symptoms of sinusitis. Thujone has a reputation by virtue of its significantly active presence in absinthe, thought to give the drink its 'hallucinogenic' properties by affecting cannabinoid receptors in the brain in a similar way to Tetrahydrocannabinol (THC). While the molecular shapes are similar, thujone actually acts as a Gamma-aminobutyric acid (GABA) receptor antagonist, so that neurons may fire more easily, resulting – in high doses – in muscle spasms and convulsions. Thujone may also help regulate menstruation, but caution is required: at said higher doses, it may act as an abortifacient (causing miscarriage). Another significant constituent of Mugwort, noted by Mabey, is santonin, formerly used as an anthelminthic (a vermifuge, expelling worms from the body) though it is toxic in this regard and has been replaced by safer alternatives. Interestingly, the ingestion of santonin can lead, like thujone, to muscle spasms and convulsions and the hallucination known as xanthopsia, 'yellow-vision', again associated with Absinthe. Santonin's colouring of objects yellow, green – absinthe's 'green fairy'? – and even red and blue has been recorded. Other constituents of Mugwort include flavonoids (antioxidants), triterpenes (resins), and coumarin (an anticoagulant and derivative of the blood-thinning drug warfarin which is used for certain heart conditions) derivatives. According to herbal medicine, chewing some leaves reduces fatigue and stimulates the nervous system, and in addition to its use as a vermifuge, Mugwort has stimulant and slightly tonic properties, and works as a nervine, emmenagogue, diuretic and diaphoretic. Mugwort is also used in traditional Chinese medicine in the form 'moxa' for moxibustion (an external heat and smoke treatment). All in all, Mugwort's applications are extensive.[3]

Giddy, Sitting-out and Dreaming: Mugwort's Entheogenic Qualities

Mugwort leaves are used by some pagans as incense, and I find that the smoke is pleasantly sweet, not dissimilar from Sage or Cannabis.

3. See: Mills 1989 [1985]: p. 154; Grieve, p. 557; Lust 1993[1974]: p.284.

Also, as noted, thujone and santonin can induce 'hallucinations'. As such, I have wondered about Mugwort as an entheogen, 'inspiring the god within': and it is interesting that the Old English *gydig*, 'engaged with a god', remains in modern English in the term 'giddy'. But when examining the use of a variety of 'narcotics and intoxicants', in his excellent, dense study of *The Viking Way*, Price makes no mention of Mugwort. And in her study on Northern shamanism focussing on *seidr* (sorcery/magic/shamanism) practices past and present, *Nine Worlds of Seidr Magic*, Blain mentions a number of indigenous entheogens which may have been recognized as such in the Old North, such as Henbane and Fly agaric mushrooms, but she addresses Mugwort's effects as 'mild if there at all'. None the less, while Mugwort's effects are apparently mild, a particular mood and environment might accentuate the potential effects.

My experiments, involving use of the smoking leaves – Mugwort used to be known as 'poor man's tobacco' – under 'ritual' circumstances, indicate that Mugwort is indeed entheogenic. The lore indicates, also, it is likely that Mugwort was used in this way in the Old North – 'taken in a drink, mixed in a salve, or smoked' (according to Jolly), or used magically as an amulet. My experiments have taken place within the disciplinary framework of the Heathen practice I have set out in *Galdrbok*. This involves walking – something I see as part of the ritual – to my local 'sacred sites' such as burial mounds, hillforts, streams, certain trees, copses, glades, hillsides, and so on. I then offer my respect to the wights (or for want of a better term, 'spirits')[4] of the place via an offering, usually of beer, cider or mead. I then honour certain deities with galdor (incantations) and further offerings. In sum, I identify this ritual process as a form of what in Old Norse was termed *utiseta*, 'sitting-out'; that is, sitting in a wild place or on the heath (as

Walking with wights

4. The term wight is complex and its meaning not entirely certain. It is difficult to pin-down or classify the denizens of the Northern otherworlds in discrete terms. Indeed, the distinction between 'this world' and 'other worlds' was permeable. For the Anglo-Saxons, ælf ('alf', i.e. 'elf') tended to mean a wide range of non-human agents.

a 'Heathen') and engaging with the wights there, in order to perform one's magic or spiritual work. Prepared in this way, I proceed to put a number of dried Mugwort leaves (usually nine, that sacred number of the North), crushed into a ball, into my briar pipe. I then recite a number of stanzas of the *Nine Herbs Charm*, in honour of the plant, addressing its 'spirit'. There is an ancient precedent for this in that the ritual and magical act of singing to plants before picking them is important in Anglo-Saxon lore.[5] Thus prepared, I proceed to smoke the pipe.

The smoke is grey, as the underside of the leaves, and dissipates quickly. It fires easily, burns readily, stays alight with ease, and burns to a black and white ash with the leaf-shape intact. The scent is floral, closest to 'Grass' – tasting sweet initially, followed by a pleasant, nutty aftertaste. Within a few moments of inhalation, I experience an immediate feeling of being 'captured' by the plant, an 'arresting' of attention, though this is too strong a word. There is, rather, a stillness, a focusing of concentration, focused in the eyes, and my visual attention is brought forward. My body feels suddenly relaxed, in total stillness, with a seething[6] in my joints, especially the knees and neck. The sense is, to use that Anglo-Saxon term, 'giddy'. I am reminded positively of the fact that I am alive, and feel attuned to my immediate surroundings. My sense is that Mugwort enjoys to be smoked and this aligns with reports from pagans I've talked to that the plant likes to be used as incense – and has interesting effects as such. As time passes, I experience a strong euphoria, a great joy at being *in place*, among green things, living things.

Mugwort likes to be smoked among other plants

The indication is that Mugwort likes to be smoked among other plants, as if attuning to them, and communicating with these other plant-people. I have wondered if Mugwort might be a conduit to enable human-people to communicate with the spirits of place and plant-people in particular. Or perhaps Mugwort is speaking through

5. For example, in *Leechbook III*, section 62: cited by Hall 2007a: p. 104.

6. Fries (1996) reads the term seidr as 'seething', which is compelling if arguably incorrect (see Blain 2002).

me: my experiences strongly suggests that human-people act as vessels for the plant to communicate, in a sort of 'possession' – an idea I will return to when discussing the nature of Anglo-Saxon elves. After a few moments, my eyelids become a little heavy, a feeling again reminiscent of reports of the effects of Cannabis, albeit with less of an active mind. It is not that I feel like sleeping, I simply feel relaxed, as if among friendly company in an alive environment. It is a very friendly feeling and Mugwort is in no way harsh – in smoke, in flavour, in intent, in effect.

Under the spell of Mugwort, an otherworldly glow, hue or fuzziness comes to vision; as such, Mugwort offers a certain experience of otherworldliness, of being in an altered place/space. As a *scryer*, gazing at a quartz crystal sphere for divination, I find that the smoke of Mugwort intensifies my experience visually, focusing vision in certain ways. There may have been a tradition of using Mugwort as such, according to Phillips: 'In early times [Mugwort] had a reputation as a witch's herb and was used in sorcery and occultism. In the Middle Ages it was used by crystal-gazers as its leaves, "always turning to the north", were said to be strong in magnetic influence'. Interestingly, there are numerous finds of quartz crystal spheres in pagan Anglo-Saxon cemeteries, particularly in the South and Southeast of England. These amulets or talismans (perhaps dipped into water to empower them for healing purposes), often found in leather pouches worn at the waist known as 'elf-bags', along with keys and other signatures of women of some status, were arguably associated most strongly with the graves of 'cunning women'. We do not know they were used for scrying, but as Heathens today we inevitably need to be creative in our reconstructions of the past.

After around half an hour, the brightness of the experience fades and I feel more sleepy, and after fifty minutes or so, the effects are gone. I close the ritual by offering thanks to deities and place – and, of course, Mugwort itself. My night's sleep following the ritual tends to be at least a little fitful and this resonates with Mugwort lore on dream work: a small bundle of leaves under one's pillow to make a 'dream pillow', it is proposed, will induce inspired dreams. In my experience, a strong

Mugwort leaf tea is highly soporific, and suitably relaxing, warming and mood-enhancing at a more moderate strength (around nine leaves), so it is interesting that strainers for infusions are often found in female Anglo-Saxon graves, along with 'elf-bags'. Alongside this evidence, the find of a 'doctor', perhaps a 'druid', from a mid-first century CE grave in Colchester, near Essex, with a locally-made copper-alloy strainer bowl last used to brew a herbal tea containing Artemisia,[7] is strongly suggestive of the sustained use of Mugwort over the *longue durée* of the late Iron Age to early Medieval period in England.

Anecdotal evidence I've gathered on the effect of Mugwort on dreams, furthermore, indicates that the dreams inspired contain archetypal imagery rather than stuff of the everyday and that these dreams may present useful challenges to the dreamer rather than pleasant experiences.[8] In addition, the soporific effect of Mugwort has been compared to that of mandrake and the narcotic Blue Lily, as used in ancient Egypt and among the Maya; these may actually suppress dreams, making them a useful antidote to nightmares and, therefore, nocturnal assault. In light of the effect of Mugwort on dreams, it is interesting that Mugwort is the 'moth-plant', associated with a creature of the night, also one which in esoteric thought is symbolic of sexuality – a theme to which I will return when examining Mugwort, the character of elves, related 'night-goers', and possession by elves, below.

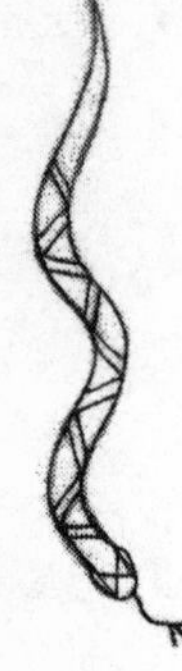

'Guardian Spirit Fastenings': the Nine Herbs Charm and Anglo-Saxon Sorcery

Mugwort is not as intense a mind-alterant as better-known entheogens, but even if the measured effects aren't quite so impressive, the shift in consciousness is profound nonetheless. Frustratingly my description is leaning towards that of the psychonaut, neo-shaman, 'newage'-shaman or psychologist, though – assuming that the 'plant' Mugwort is valuable

7. Benfield et al, 2008.

8. For a detailed study of the significance of dreams in the Old North, see Kelchner 1935.

only for its 'active constituents', as a resource that can be 'used' to alter consciousness. In a basic sense this is true, but only if viewed from a human, exploitative perspective; the language is limiting, the impetus disrespectful. Moreover, the discourse is not mindful of the intention of the plant itself, its agency, its personality. Such agency has been at the core of my experience, and it is 'made known' also in the attention afforded to Mugwort in the *Nine Herbs Charm.*

This charm originates in the 'MS London British Library Harley 585' manuscript, named *Lacnunga* ('Remedies', according to Cockayne). Roper's English Verbal Charms describes it as '[a]pproximately the size of a modern paperback', while Page thinks it was perhaps 'a general practitioner's travelling reference work' – the term *læce*, as I have stated, meaning healer, though from a modern point of view this office might be understood as 'shaman',[9] and I think the lore resonates with this idea of a leech-shaman, particularly when considering the nature of elves, altered consciousness, possession – and a wider Anglo-Saxon animism.[10]

While eighty of the ninety Anglo-Saxon charms are in Latin, the last part of *Lacnunga* is written predominantly in Old English and includes the charms entitled the *Nine Herbs Charm, Against A Dwarf,* and *Against A Sudden Pain.* 'Charm' is a thirteenth century loan word from the Old French, a reflex of the Latin *carmen* ('song'). In Anglo-Saxon, charms were *galdor/gealdor* – 'an incantation, divination, enchantment, a charm, magic, sorcery', this term being connected to *galan* ('to sing, to enchant'; thus, the nightingale is the 'night singer' or 'night

9. For further discussion of the topic of shamanism, see Wallis 2003; Harvey & Wallis 2007, and on Northern shamanism specifically, Glosecki 1986, 1988, 1989; DuBois 1999; Blain 2002; Wallis 2003; Johnson & Wallis 2005.

10. A much broader discussion of an Anglo-Saxon shamanism is offered in the inspirational books by Brian Bates (1983, 1996, 2002). My work here approaches this topic differently, with an animic rather than psychological frame, and with a more detailed focus on the *Nine Herbs Charm*, Mugwort specifically, and the nature of elves. For practical, engaging work on Northern shamanism, see also Fries 1992, 1996, 2002; Johnson & Wallis 2005.

charmer'), cognate in turn with the Old Icelandic *galdr*. The powers of speech, or words of power, are key to understanding Anglo-Saxon magic. Speech was, as Barley puts it, 'an incorporating act. It establishes contact', enabling the charmer to make magical connections to 'things'. In this sense and in a wider Northern frame, charms might be seen as *varðlokk(k)ur* – 'guardian spirit fastenings' or 'guardian spirit enticements', meaning those words of power enabling the charmer to attract, entice and perhaps control, or at least, 'fasten', spirits. They might also be interpreted as *seiðrlæti*[11] – 'sorcery songs', or as *fræði* – 'a mumbled formula'. All of this suggests these charms were much more than the superstitious 'charm' as this concept is understood today. For the Anglo-Saxon leech-shaman, charms were potent spells for engaging with powerful other-than-human beings in the 'spirit' world.

'[W]hat You Made Known': Mugwort and Anglo-Saxon Animic Ontologies

The Nine Herbs Charm begins by immediately addressing Mugwort:

> *Gemyne ðu mucgwyrt hwæt thu ameldodest / hwæt þu renadest æt regenmelde / una þu hattest yldost wyrta / þu miht wið iii wið xxx / þu miht wiþ attre wiþ onflyge / þu miht wiþ tha laþan ðe geond lond fereð*

> *Remember Mugwort what you made known / what you set out in mighty revelation / 'the first' you are called oldest of herbs / you have might against three and against thirty / you have might against venom and against flying shots / you have might against the loathsome thing that fares around the land*

With the consistent use of a personal pronoun, the second-person 'you', here and with regard to the other plants in the charm, Mugwort is explicitly being spoken to as if it were a 'person' – a person

11. Gundarsson 2007: p. 28.

worthy of respect, more than a mere 'weed'. As such, Mugwort can be identified here as a form of wight. The belief that plants had their own wights, or were wights themselves, is indeed evidenced in German, English and Norwegian folklore.[12] While the reference in the *Nine Herbs Charm* might be brief and my point seem slight, this animistic interpretation has opened up an approach to the evidence that has considerable significance for our understanding of Anglo-Saxon worldviews writ large.

According to North, the names of some Norse gods, such as Thor ('Thunder'), Ullr ('Brilliance') and Frigg ('Love'), are indicative of the natural phenomena from which they became personified, again hinting at an animism in the Old North. He adds that in *The Dream of the Rood* 'the best tree of wood began to speak', and, moreover:

> *In the Exeter Book* Riddles, *phenomena such as wind, an onion, a nightingale and many other things speak with human voices; if the creatures in these riddles derive their first-person narratives from prosopopoeia [- wherein 'inanimate objects' speak as living things — then] this was a device in popular demand [and] is also present in the first-person statements of lifeless artefacts that speak of their origins: swords, rings, combs or jewels; or as the Alfred jewel says 'Alfred had me made'.*

Evidence for Anglo-Saxon animism is not rare. In another instance, considering the three known examples of boar imagery on Anglo-Saxon helmets, Pollington refers to the terms *eofor-lic* (literally 'boar-body', though conventionally translated as 'boar-image' or 'boar shapes' and *fehr wearde heold* (literally 'guardianship of the living spirit of a person', conventionally translated as 'kept ward of life' or 'watching over') in *Beowulf* as evidence 'of a residual animism in Anglo-Saxon

12. Gundarsson 2007: p. 28.

culture, a hangover from more primitive [sic] systems of thought'[13] – the interpretation is compelling, if coloured by an assumed primitivism. Thinking through this material in the wider setting of Northern religion, it is worth noting that Gundarsson thinks there is animic significance to the substances used in the material culture of ancient Germanic religion; for instance, the stones used for *hlutir*, small god-images carried by some ancient Heathens. Moreover, since the thirteenth century Icelander Snorri (who set out in written form Norse mythology in his *Prose Edda*), and indeed because of Snorri's focus on deities, scholars have tended to emphasise the roles of gods and goddesses; yet the wider evidence indicates that more often, on a day-to-day basis, our ancestors approached elves and other wights: 'fellowship with such beings and small offerings made to them on a daily or near-daily basis was likely the most common aspect of Germanic religion'[14] – emphasising the wider animic context for the religion of the Old North.

 More recently, scholars such as Nurit Bird-David, Carlos Fausto, Graham Harvey and Eduardo Viveiros de Castro, have examined the sophisticated nature of animism, particularly in the Amazon, a 'new animism' redressing Tylor's 'old'.[15] For animists, the world is filled with 'persons' only some of whom are human. For the Maori of Aotearoa (New Zealand) certain of what we might call 'objects' or 'artefacts', and indeed other 'things', are actually *taonga*, 'living cultural treasures':

Only some persons are human

> *All* taonga *possess, in varying degrees, the elements of* mana *(ancestral prestige),* tapu *(spiritual protection) and* korero *(genealogically ordered narratives). The greater the ancestors, the greater the* mana *of associated* taonga. Taonga *are… treated with due reverence… Descendants experience this* wairua *(ancestral spirit) as* ihi *(presence),* wehi *(awe) and* wana *(authority).*[16]

13, 14. Gundarsson 2007: p. xi.

15. This scholarship is summarised and theorised in Harvey 2005. For an archaeological application, see Wallis 2009b.

16. See the Tamaki Paenga Hira page on the Auckland War Memorial Museum website.

Taonga are 'living', curated as 'persons', as ancestors, with life, songs and personalities, embedded in inalienable genealogical narratives, and these relational characteristics resonate with indigenous animism elsewhere. Among the Ojibwe, an Algonkian language-speaking group in North America, for instance, persons and personal actions are recorded by Hallowell as being classified differently from objects and impersonal events, due to a grammatical 'animate' and 'inanimate' gender distinction. The Ojibwe's preferred self-definition, Anishinaabeg, identifies them as 'human persons' and they speak of a wide range of 'other-than-human persons', including tree persons, stone persons, bird persons and fish persons. An ongoing system of relationships and regulated behaviour steers engagements between human persons and other persons. Human people often labelled 'shamans' act as mediators, working to maintain harmony between humans and nonhumans: if a hunter offends an animal by using inappropriate etiquette, so resulting in the hunter falling sick, a shaman negotiates between the offended 'spirit' of the dead animal in order to return the stolen 'soul' of the hunter and so restore social harmony between the affected 'persons'. Shamans, unusually, can 'see as others do': that is, they are claimed to be able to meet the communicative level of non-humans and so speak on equal terms. In this rethinking of the topic, 'animism', like 'shamanism' seems cumbersome and academic – another '-ism'. 'Animic' more concretely accentuates a fully functioning, coherent and effective ontology, lifeway or worldview, and also looks away from the 'old animism' of Victorian anthropology, concerned with subject/object distinctions, to a 'new animism' engaged with relationality and personhood.

I have pointed to a number of possible instances of animism in the Anglo-Saxon sources, but some of them speak more of 'old animism' than animic relational ontologies. Others, though, do hint at the importance of respect, active relationship and negotiation between persons emphasised by the new animism.

'Repay Gifts with Gifts': Negotiating a Relationship with Mugwort

The address to Mugwort as a 'person' in the *Nine Herbs Charm* is indicative not only of personhood, but of respect afforded the plant by the reciter of the charm, as well as a relationship between charmer and plant-person, with the singing of the charm working as a mechanism or medium to establish contact with Mugwort. A range of sources (for example, *Beowulf*) indicate that bonds between persons, human and non-human, were a crucial part of Anglo-Saxon lifeways, involving gift-exchange and respectful treatment. The relationship between Laece / cunning person and Mugwort, might usefully be understood as that in indigenous contexts elsewhere, as between a shaman and plant-ally. In an Anglo-Saxon ontological system in which gifting, reciprocity and obligation are key, it seems logical to infer such relations at work between Mugwort and the charm-user in the *Nine Herbs Charm*: a gift offering from one human-person to another requires a gift of return (at some point); the gift of Mugwort-perception (for want of a better term) afforded by Mugwort as a helping plant-person (again, begging a finer term) betokens a gift or offering in return – and so a relationship, or perhaps more accurately a negotiation, is instigated.

Whosoever chooses to engage with Mugwort – to collect it, to dry and prepare it, to smoke it, drink it or use it in a salve – must, I think, consider the associated lore laid down by our ancestors. In short, respect, courtesy and appropriate etiquette are key to an active relationship with this plant-person. My thoughts are echoed by Klehm who encourages us to: '[f]ind an overarching but examined respect for [Mugwort]'. And as Gundarsson advises when dealing with wights: the simplest yardstick is 'good manners' because 'they are greatly offended by breaches of courtesy whether these stem from deliberate rudeness or simple ignorance'. As such, approach wights 'as you would an honoured elder professor, who may or may not want to make time for you: the better your manners and the nicer your gift, the likelier you are to get an answer'.

ELFSHOT, VENOM AND THE 'ON-FLYING'

Other aspects of the *Nine Herbs Charm* hint at animic and shamanic themes and my discussion now turns to the way in which the charm suggests the presence and significance of elves[17] – key other-than-human persons, and a 'social reality'[18] in Anglo-Saxon England – exploring issues of healing, possession and sexuality.[19] According to the charm, Mugwort has properties against *attre*, 'venom', likely a general reference to poisonous substances. This suggests that Mugwort is a powerful plant-ally in healing. The charm goes on to state that Mugwort is effective against such specific threats as *onflyge*, 'on-flying', meaning 'flying venoms' or perhaps 'flying shots'. Anglo-Saxon literature consistently associates such shots with elves, and indeed elves are perceived over and again as the source of sickness:

> *[A] large amount of disease was attributed... to the action of supernatural beings, elves, Æsir, smiths or witches whose shafts fired at the sufferer produced his torments. Anglo-Saxon and even Middle English literature is replete with the notion of disease caused by the arrows of mischievous supernatural beings. This theory of disease we shall, for brevity, speak of as the doctrine of the elf-shot. The Anglo-Saxon*

17. Using the term 'elves' here, I do not mean the elves of modern fantasy literature and film, or Celtic folklore, but rather, specifically, the non-human persons understood to be '*ælf*' to Heathen Anglo-Saxons, or '*alf*' in wider animic Germanic cultures, however uncertain the character of these beings is to us, as modern interpreters.

18. Hall 2007b: p. 142. As this paper makes clear, however, I think that to limit elves to a social reality is insufficient, resting on a dualist, rational materialist premise and therefore marking an inappropriate approach to such non-human persons as elves. The animic 'resistive discourse' I am interested in here is termed 'animaphany' by Letcher 2007.

19. My interpretations set out here are far from objective; rather, they are mediated via both SPG ('substantiated personal gnosis'), spiritual experiences for which there is precedent in the lore, and UPG 'unsubstantiated' or 'unverified personal gnosis', experiences without precedent but which are 'real' for me.

> *tribes placed these malicious elves everywhere, but especially in the wild uncultivated wastes where they loved to shoot at the passer-by.*[20]

Interestingly, a favourite haunt of Mugwort is in those 'wild and uncultivated wastes' we know today as road-side verges, untended land and ground recently returned to nature.

> *Remedies treat such attacks with medicinal salves and drinks made with specific herbs or with purgative methods, such as smoking the elf out or pricking. This attack by elves was eventually linked with Christian ideas of demons penetrating or possessing animals and people, who then needed exorcism.*

Jolly here points to the effectiveness of 'purgative methods', such

as smoking, pricking, and, as the lore indicates, salves, smoking and drinking, in curing elfshot.

While elves are not mentioned specifically in the *Nine Herbs Charm*, that elves were the cause of illness is clearly well attested. Barley explains that 'Against elfshot… the leech is to cry out, "Out little spear, if you are in there, out spear, not in spear"'. Given the connection between Mugwort and *attre* in the charm, I think it likely that Mugwort smoke specifically was used in the 'smoking out' of elves, as well as an ingredient in the salves and drinks that Jolly refers to. The alternative of 'smoking in' and its relevance, I have already made transparent. This reflects on my earlier comment that Mugwort mead and beer deserve further research as entheogens.

A wonderful visual image accompanying Psalm 37 in the ninth century *Utrecht Psalter*[21] (Figure 2, *opposite*) is rendered by Pollington as 'a man attacked by elves'. A similarly afflicted individual is shown in

---

20. Hall 2005: the long-held discourse of elf-shot is undergoing critical revision in the recent scholarship.

21. British Library, MS Harley 603, fol. 22r.

Figure 2. *'A man attacked by elves'?*[22]*: the ninth century* Utrecht Psalter, *British Library, MS Harley 603, fol. 22r*

the twelfth century *Eadwine* (or *Canterbury*) *Psalter*, which was based on the former manuscript,[23] and this has been identified as a 'diseased elf-ridden man'.[24] Addressing elfshot archaeologically, the aforementioned 'elf-bags' were likely used, according to Pollington, in the treatment of elfshot. This variety of evidence suggests, therefore, that the elves and their kin were key supernatural creatures, 'spirits' or persons in

22. Pollington 2000: p. 457, fig. 20. The ninth-century *Utrecht Psalter* manuscript is: Utrecht, Universiteisbibliotheck MS 32 (Script. Eccl. 484) produced at Rheims, pp. 816-835, though in his caption Pollington confuses it with the *Harley Psalter*: London, British Library, MS Harley p. 603, fol. 22r produced at Canterbury, 1000-1025. p. 23. *Eadwine (or Canterbury) Psalter*, c1147 or 1155-60: Cambridge, Trinity College, MS R .17.1 (987), fol. 66, produced at Christ Church, Canterbury. A later example is the *Paris Psalter*, 1170-1190: Paris, Biblioteque Nationale, lat. 8846, an unfinished copy produced at Canterbury.

23. Jolly 1996: p. 158.

24. Grattan & Singer 1952: frontispiece; also Cameron 1993: p. 142. The interpretation of these manuscript illuminations as depicting elfshot is well established, but has been contested by Jolly 1998, although this should not detract from the fact that elves were the perceived source of elfshot.

Anglo-Saxon lore;[25] while there is clearly a permeability of boundaries between elves and others, the elves are more often found where we might expect dwarfs in wider Germanic lore, and certainly in Anglo-Saxon England elves are more widespread than giants. The elves seem to have been the Anglo-Saxons' otherworldly agents par excellence.

'Bewitchingly Bright': The Anglo-Saxon Elves

Evidence abounds for a cult of the elves, particularly mound-elves (linked to the dead) in the Viking Age, and Gundarsson proposes that elf-cults mark one of the oldest aspects of Northern Heathen religion. The Winternights feast, for instance, was also known as *álfablót*. The Skaldic poem *Austrfaravísur* (c.1019 CE) by Sigvatr Þórðarson, mentions an *álfablót*, an 'elf ritual', to *Óðinn* and there are also two saga accounts of such ceremonies. In *Austrfaravísur*, Gundarsson notes, 'when the skald Sigvatr, a Christian converted by Óláfr inn digri, came to a farmhouse in late autumn, he was told that he could not enter because the Alf-Blessing was being celebrated – as a Christian, he was presumably unwelcome at the family's holy feast'. The Common Germanic term for elf, *ylf*, may translate as 'white one' or 'white mist-form', perhaps related to Nibelungen, the Old Norse *Niflungar* or 'mist-folk' who, as Gundarsson states 'appear in mist and/or at twilight or dawn'. In his *Prose Edda*, Snorri describes the light elves as 'bright and shining, very fair to look upon'. The Old English *ylfetu* meant 'swan' and the name *Ælfbeorht*, 'alf-bright'. The term *ælfscyne*, 'bewitchingly bright', or more straightforwardly 'elf-shining', meanwhile, referred to someone who was 'beautiful in a dangerously seductive way' and women 'perilously so'. In light of this, Hall argues, *ælfscyne* indicates beings who were beautiful, dangerous, seductive, female – or perhaps effeminate.[26]

25. I use 'supernatural' and 'spirits' here for want of better terms, as there was clearly a fluidity between what we would term natural and supernatural, matter and spirit, in Anglo-Saxon Heathenry.

26. My translations draw on Hall and Gundarsson.

The erotic element here is interesting in a number of respects. The phrase '*wiþ* [*ælcre*] *feondes* (*deofles*) *costunza*' and variants of it occur twice in *Lacnunga*, meaning 'temptations of the devil' or perhaps more accurately according to Thun, 'sexual temptations'. This is in line with the negative role of elves when viewed through a Christian lens, and related to the nightmare, the mare that 'rides'[27] the passive sleeper, which Cameron tells us, was also known as the 'night-goer', and which became the copulating goblin or succubus of later continental folklore. Interestingly, the 'High German word for "night-mare" is *Alptraum*, "alf-dream"; as with the Northern *mara*, the night-visit characterised by terror, often a sense of suffocation, and a consequent illness, is specifically attributed to alfs'. Furthermore, the Old English *mære*, the etymon of 'nightmare', and the beings termed *maran* specifically, 'were invariably female'.[28]

The lore itself consistently shows that otherworldly beings[29] often appear to humans in dreams.[30] From a non-Christian point of view, these nocturnal sexual temptations, often made apparent through dreaming, might arguably be sought after by the mage as positive encounters with elves. Gundarsson argues that 'one of the most constant themes in tales of transition (in both directions), as opposed to the simple-friendship between a human and a wight, is a strong erotic element, sometimes formalized in a wedding'. Erotic relationships between wights and human people are evidenced in such sources as Bárðar saga and the Icelandic folktale *Hallgerður of Bláfell*. Gundarsson also notes that 'Berg-women ['mountain-women'

27. The sexual innuendo should not be overlooked.

28. As in note 25.

29. The term is apposite: the Old English eldritch, once thought to mean 'elf-rich' (**ælf-rice*, 'elf' + 'dominion, sphere of influence'), may more plausibly be rendered **æl-rice*, 'foreign, strange' + 'dominion, sphere of influence', translated straightforwardly and convincingly by Hall as 'otherworldly' (Hall, in press).

30. See, for example, Gísla saga, especially chapters 30 and 33, and for full discussion, Kelchner 1935.

or 'troll-women' in Old Norse] often have a strongly erotic nature'. In Bárðar saga, for instance, a man called Skeggi makes a *fylgjulag*, a '*fylgja*-contract' with a troll named Helgi, a *fylgjulag* meaning, in the mundane sense, a 'concubinage', and in spiritual terms, Helgi became Skeggi's personal *fylgja*, a non-human ally who holds and manifests luck.

This lore on wights and elves as assistants to whom one may become allied or even wed, is reminiscent of the relationships between some shamans and their 'spirit-helpers', offering further insight into Anglo-Saxon healers. Shamans in a number of communities, from the Chukchee in Siberia to the Zuni in New Mexico often took their spirits as 'partners'. In many instances this was more than simply a friendship, brother/sisterhood, or other non-sexual relationship. Such a partnership might literally involve a wedding, in the real sense of being obligated in marriage, and/or sexual consummation. For certain shamans, furthermore, their community awarded their 'queer' actions with the inscription of a third, fourth or other gender; that is, they were not 'man', or 'woman' status but something else – equally respected as such, and even assigned a higher status by virtue of their liminality.[31] The relationship between shamans and allies is consistently one of respect, negotiation and obligation, and this formula holds too for the evidence of Anglo-Saxon leeches and their 'spirits', including, I suggest, Mugwort.

A queer reading of Anglo-Saxon elves is, indeed, pertinent. The etymology in earlier Anglo-Saxon sources indicates that elves were more consistently male, and effeminately so; only by the eleventh century, Hall asserts, does elf also denote females. Regarding the issue of effeminacy, in Old Norse the term *ergi*, 'unmanly' or 'effeminate', specifically referred to the passive partner in homosexual relations.[32] Men engaged in *seidr* practices were themselves insulted as *ergi*.[33] This

31. See, for example: Balzer 1996; Blain & Wallis 2000; Lang 1998; Roscoe 1996, 1998; Saladin D'Anglure 1990; Stoodley 1999.

32. See: Ström 1973; Sørensen 1983; Blain & Wallis 2000; Price 2002.

33. See, for example, the exchange between Loki and Odinn in *Lokasenna* pp. 23-4.

evidence might suggest that while in later sources the concern was over innocent men (Christian monks) being seduced by sexually voracious female demons/elves, in the earlier sources the gender of elves was ambiguous, and their sexual preference equally so.

This lore chimes with the evidence we have for those who practice *seidr*. Elsewhere, I have argued that *seidr* in Scandinavia was once an important shamanistic practice and that the term *ergi* for *seidr*-shamans, while conventionally read as negative, may in pre-Christian times have been positive. My sense is that being a certain sort of shaman, and specifically an *ergi* one, requires a 'passive' state, and that such a state of consciousness must be adopted in order to be receptive to messages from the 'spirit world'. This sensitivity might then be interpreted as the opposite of macho, as unmanly (whatever these terms are meant to mean!). If so, then the early sources on Anglo-Saxon elves suggest the leech-shaman's encounter, sexual and otherwise, same-sex or otherwise, with elves, was a positive one. And the lore insists that the purpose of this position was to effect healing. This positive spin on the elves is reiterated in Old English personal names, such as *Ælfgifu*, 'Alf-Gift'; *Ælfrœd*, 'Alf-Rede' (Wise); *Ælfnoþ*, 'Alf-Courage'; *Ælfwin*, 'Alf-Friend'; *Ælfbeorht*, 'Alf-bright'.

THE MAGIC OF ELF: FEVER, PROPHECY AND POSSESSION

Ælfsiden, translated by Hall as 'the magic of *ælfe*', occurs in three remedies.[34] The etymology of the term is complex, but there are intriguing possibilities. Given my earlier comments, it is intriguing that *ælfsiden* has strong links to the cognate *seidr*, with *sidi* meaning 'the magic-worker'. Furthermore, in one charm, *ælfsiden* is associated with 'diabolical malice and fevers', indicating that elves 'might be associated with causing delusion or hallucination characteristic of fever'. Viewed negatively, such experiences should be avoided; thinking through the material shamanistically, however, especially in light of the aforementioned etymology, the elves and the 'hallucinations' they induce might for the

34. In Lacnunga, section 41 of *Leechbook III*, and *Book I of Bald's Leechbook*: see Hall 2007a: p. 119.

leech-shaman have been desirable. Charms may have been used to drive the elf out, with the inference that humans can be possessed by elves.

The grip of a dwarf

In one charm we learn that 'at times he quakes, as if in the grip of a dwarf'[35] (for 'dwarf' here, 'elf' is equally valid), hinting at possession. The quaking in this quote recalls how the actions of thujone and santonin in high doses are held to result in muscle spasms and convulsions. Extending this idea, it is possible that the quaking refers to the ingestion of Mugwort leading to convulsions – and even possession by elves. It is intriguing that one translation of *ælfsiden* might be 'elf-sitting' (*siden* linked to the Old Norse *seta*, 'sitting'), hinting at the agency of elves in engaging with humans, with the sitter being an elf, which is again suggestive of possession. It is compelling that the term *ylfig*, 'engaged with an elf', links to the aforementioned Old English *gydig*, 'engaged with a god', and Middle English 'possession by devils'. Given that *ylfig* is also translated by Hall as 'epileptic', the term 'must, then, denote some altered state of mind', and most obviously, 'possession by *ælfe*'. Hall concludes that *ylfig* 'not only meant "divinely possessed", but specifically denoted possession leading to prophecy' or 'one speaking prophetically through divine/demonic [i.e. elf] possession' [my parenthesis], perhaps with both negative and positive connotations. Such ambiguity might be expected in communities where people could be attacked by elves but where shamans might also engage with them and become possessed by them in order to induce prophecy and effect healing. Magic is, after all, a very grey area.

My discussion of elves thus far, then, offers a very different understanding of elves amongst earlier pagans than that presented in the later Christian and recent folklore material, in which elves are mischievous little figures playing tricks on people. Elves among the pagan Anglo-Saxons, by contrast, are ambiguous, erotically charged figures. They may cause harm including sickness through elfshot. But they are also seductive, even sexually voracious, both as females and males, and when visiting people in dreams. Moreover, elves are seemingly

35. Stuart 1976: p. 315.

active conduits to altered consciousness, to the extreme of possession.

ENCOUNTERING ELVES: NINE GUIDELINES

The lore suggests that elves and other wights may be encountered in dreams or under the right conditions when awake; I am reminded of Leary's idea that 'set and setting' is important. Gundarsson suggests that wights will appear to the seeker if one is in the right place at the right time, such as in 'persistent drizzle' (known as 'trollie wadder' in Shetland) or 'dark fog' ('trollamist' in Shetland) when 'water and air are softly blended', or more generally in liminal weather conditions such as 'rain, sleet or snow'. The berg-dweller in *Bergbúa þáttr* (The Tale of the Mountain Dweller) says 'I wade like powdery snow between the worlds; much is steam-murky', or translated differently, 'World to world, like snowfall I fly, the air is ashen'; also, 'We are all together in the dusk-world', or 'In the world of darkness we gathered, all together'; and 'I often travel early and late (lit. in the colours, the light of dawn and sunset)', or 'I stride between the first light and sunset'.[36] As such, twilight and after dark are evidenced as the best times of day to see wights, with twilight as the border-time between day and night, and so a border between the worlds. At Northern latitudes twilight is extended, so offering prolonged positive conditions for encountering wights.

Be this as it may, the evidence suggests that caution is advised when dealing with elves and other wights. As Gundarsson points out, '[f]olk who spend time with the alfs often come back mad, or at the very least sorrowful and wandering in their wits. The expression "taken into the mountains" was used whenever someone underwent a sudden psychological change, which was often associated with getting lost in the mountains or woods'. And, the 'theme of a person who spends a short time in the alf-hill, only to find that a lifetime or more has passed when they come back to the Middle-Garth' is common in the lore. But these are extreme examples. Hall argues that 'while ælfe were

36. These different translations are from Gundarsson and Hreinsson et al.

potentially dangerous to members of Anglo-Saxon in-groups they were perceived in traditional culture to be aligned with in-groups in contradistinction to the chaotic threats of monsters [i.e. out-groups]' [my parenthesis]. In order to ward against negative experiences and encourage the best outcome in any encounter with elves, I reiterate the importance of respect, good manners and appropriate etiquette when dealing with elves. Nine (that magic number of the Old North!) basic rules for dealing with alfs, drawn from the ancient sources, might be:[37]

1) be courteous and respectful;

2) do not 'refuse food or favours in general. Even a gift that seems worthless may prove to be of great value';

3) but be careful about accepting drink, which is often too intoxicating for humans, and joining in dancing;

4) if asked to do favours, do them, however inconvenient;

5) give warning when, outdoors, lighting fires, tossing boiling water or relieving yourself;

6) never lie;

7) do not use steel;

8) do not be the first to speak; do not boast about favours received from them or ask for gifts;

9) never disturb stones, mounds or other dwellings associated with them without permission.

These guidelines not only draw on Heathen lore, but also following them aligns with the respectful approach to other-than-human-persons common to animists elsewhere.

'A Serpent Came Sneaking': Woden, Wyrms and Seidr-Magic

In the *Nine Herbs Charm*, *attre*, the 'poison' or 'venom' of the elves, is linked to the arrival of an adder – *nædran* – a sort of *wyrm* or serpent, known to us today as a poisonous snake. This adder, in a further layer of

37. Here, I am drawing on Gundarsson 2007: p. 3.

significance, appears in the charm at the same time as the god Woden:

> *Wyrm com snican, toslat he man / ða genam woden viiii wuldortanas / sloh ða þa næddran þæt heo on viiii tofleah*
>
> *A serpent came sneaking then / he tore a man apart / then Woden took up nine glory-rods / struck the adder then so it flew apart into nine* (my translation).

It is interesting that Woden's cognate in Old Norse, *Óðinn*, is closely associated with the elves. The Austrfararvísur cited by Gundarsson mentions an *álfablót* to *Óðinn*, and in this poem the housewife tells Sigvatr 'I am afraid of Óðinn's wrath' (i.e. if the Christian skald Sigvatr is present at the Alf-Blessing), reinforcing the association between *Óðinn* and the elves. There are also two saga accounts of such ceremonies. In addition to his association with the elves, in Northern traditions *Óðinn* is the god of magic par excellence – he is the master of *seidr* and as such he is *ergi*, marking his character, based on my discussion above, as ambiguous and elf-like. This strong connection between elves and *Óðinn*/Woden, as well as magic/shamanism, healing, effeminacy and sexuality, is reiterated in the etymology relating to elves that I have set out above, and it is in some senses repeated in the *Nine Herbs Charm*.

It might be stretching the point to suggest that the 'wyrm' in the charm represents an allusion to male sexuality, but the charm does describe how Woden takes 'nine glory-rods' and strikes the adder so that it flies into nine parts – the emphasis on the number nine here accentuating the magical significance of the procedure. Given the otherworldly content of the charm, it would be difficult to take this description literally, although to pagan Anglo-Saxons the difference between this world and the other was likely not pronounced. It is also worth noting that weapons were often 'poisoned' by making vipers' marks on them and it is presumably arrows thus treated that are poetically referred to, Barley tells us, as 'battle adders'. I speculate that the poison Woden deals with here originates with the elves inferred elsewhere in the charm, and that Woden's incident with the adder can be read as his removal of the poison in an act of healing. As the god of magic, healing and what I am inferring was Anglo-Saxon shamanic practice, Woden might, in addition to Mugwort and elves, be a further ally used by the leech-shaman in a ceremony of magical healing which removes the poison-sickness.

'I blow this Poison from you': Mugwort and Shamanistic Healing

The concluding section to the *Nine Herbs Charm* is particularly exciting, for the way in which it hints at the procedure used by the leech-shaman to effect the healing:

> *Ic ana wat ea rinnende / þær þa nygon nædran nean behealdað / motan ealle weoda nu wyrtum aspringan / sæs toslupan eal sealt wæter / ðonne ic þis attor of ðe geblawe*

> *I alone know the running streams / and they enclose nine adders / let all weeds now spring up as herbs / seas slide apart, all salt water / as I blow this poison from you* (my translation).

As Jolly suggests: 'the speaker or healer speaks with his or her own authority and power… Clearly the power runs through this human channel, the one who know the right associations between the microcosm of the herb and the spiritual macrocosm'. I think this section of the charm hints animically at the flow and regulation of supernatural potency, in relation to esoteric plant lore, 'shamanic' healing, and the social status and efficacy of the leech-healer as a shaman.

In the *Nine Herbs Charm*, I think the leech-shaman is working with the plants of the charm, including the powerful aid Mugwort, and in negotiation with elves and the god Woden, in order to heal a patient afflicted by 'poison'. The procedure of 'blowing' in the charm is interesting, echoed by Scandinavian lore indicating that elfshot was blown-in, termed 'elf-blast', and that poison could be removed by blowing through a dried Nettle stalk.[38] Incidentally, Nettle features as one of the nine herbs in the charm alongside Mugwort, and it seems to me that either Nettle or Mugwort stalks could be used in this way. Blowing and/or sucking also recalls shamanic healing in indigenous contexts elsewhere. After locating where the sickness in the patient may lie, some shamans use a plant stalk or other device to suck out the poison which is then blown away, into the earth for instance, in order to be got rid of or regenerated. The ingestion of ayahuasca by shamans in South America leads to important purgative vomiting and other excretions, so purging and putting things in and getting things out, is an important feature of many shamanisms. Regarding the 'concern with ingestion and excretion' for the Anglo-Saxon leech-shaman, Barley suggests: 'Spew drinks and purgatives are the physician's chief weapons. He is constantly spitting, blowing and letting blood, while applying salves to the outside and drinks to the inside. The basic concern is with destructuring the present state and redefining boundaries'. Orifices which open a person to the outside world, such as the mouth, opening of the urethra, anus, mouth, ear-holes, nostrils, and so on, also wounds, are often seen as vulnerable. In Anglo-Saxon England, infections which get in, *onflygan*, 'were generally supposed to enter through the ears and mouth, so that the remedy against them was also sung into the mouth and the ears of the patient'.[39] Perhaps, then, charms of power, including the *Nine Herbs Charm*, were spoken or chanted into the patient by the leech-shaman in this manner, or involving other orifices. On the issue of boundaries and the protection of them, one contemporary informant related an experience to me in which an application of Mugwort as a salve was useful in a protective capacity when negotiating with a difficult relationship (with a human).

I conclude from this that the *Nine Herbs Charm*, among others, may derive from pagan contexts in which leech-shamans used *galdr* to chant/sing healing into and chant/sing out the poison in patients

38. Gundarsson 2007: p. 69.

39. Rodrigues 1993: 35; referring to the procedure set out in the charm *Against A Dwarf.*

Mugwort versus elf-shot

inflicted with elf-shot, i.e. sickness. These healers may have used Mugwort in salves, teas, incenses and other magical applications – as well as, of course, focussed inhalation through smoking. And while elves could inflict illness, possession by them, instigated by the leech-shaman, could also effect healing – and other magic.

The section of the charm quoted above indicates that running water and/or salt water was important to complete the spell. In one sense this recalls the folklore that witches could not cross running water; in a more modern sense, it reflects the significance of clean water (running rather than stagnant) and salt water in healing wounds. Another of the Anglo-Saxon pocket spellbooks elaborates, in stating that the healer should '[t]hrow the plants into running water' after their use.[40] Throwing a rod contagious with disease into a river is also noted, by Barley, in a spell against miscarriage. So, as Hall suggests, throwing something into running water, be it a physical object or the

sickness itself, concludes the healing by getting rid of the sickness. It is also interesting, as Skemp notes, that sickness is addressed as a person in some charms, recalling the way that Mugwort and the other plants in the *Nine Herbs Charm* are addressed as persons. As such, the sickness, like other non-human agents, might be termed a wight. As for animists elsewhere, it seems that the pagan Anglo-Saxons perceived a world which is filled with persons, only some of whom were human – from Mugwort and other plant-allies to elf-persons, Woden and even sickness itself.

Final Thoughts – A Heathen Charming Tradition Today?

I conclude that the Mugwort of the *Nine Herbs Charm*, and the evidence associated with it, offers rich and intriguing material for understanding ancient Heathen practice, with relevance to Heathen engagements with Mugwort and other 'persons' today. There is much scope for further analysis – and debate. The personhood of the eight other herbs in the *Nine Herbs Charm*, for instance, may be rich in animic material, as

40. *Leechbook III*, section 61.

may other parts of the *Leechbooks*. I am not suggesting that the ancient sources are essentially Heathen with a veneer of Christianity, or vice versa; the situation is more complex, with the recorders of the data (such as charms) clearly Christian but, as North has argued, 'bound by the conventions of a formulaic Anglian vocabulary which was as yet unsuited to [Christian] theological discourse'. As such, Heathen discourse is ever-present in early Christian material. It is also important, as North argues, to revise the notion of Christian influence being dynamic but Heathen traditions, static. Addressing elves in the charms, Jolly concludes:

> *The Anglo-Saxon charms reveal the creativity involved in allowing traditions to do what they must to stay alive — adapt. That adaptation was not passive, imposed from without by a monolithic church; rather, the adaptations that made Christianity a viable religion in Anglo-Saxon culture were initiated from within, in the daily lives of ordinary people. In the midst of the often violent conflict between pagan culture and Christian culture in these centuries, a more subtle process was at work: as liturgy got into the charms, and elves got into the liturgy, Christianity prospered and Anglo-Saxon traditions survived.*

The reuse of the Anglo-Saxon charms in the twenty-first century might seem to present an anachronism, but as Jolly points out, traditions change. Roper suggests that 'traditional verbal charming would appear to be extinct in England' – yet regarding contemporary Heathen practice, this paper marks an example of the revival of English verbal charming, in the form of a re-interpretation of one of the oldest of the Anglo-Saxon charms. In place of a 'now-defunct' English charming tradition, this and other active, innovative reconstructionist engagements with the past, suggests, rather, a dynamic and creative Heathen *tradition*.

ACKNOWLEDGMENTS

Thanks to Jenny Blain, Simon Crook, Paul Devereux, Graham Harvey, Andy Letcher, Antti Litmanen, Mogg Morgan and Mark Pilkington for their useful suggestions on this paper.

REFERENCES, SOURCES AND FURTHER READING:

ARMSTRONG, EA 1944. Mugwort Lore. *Folklore* 55(1): 22-27.

BALZER, MM 1996. Sacred genders in Siberia: shamans, bear festivals and androgyny. In: SP RAMET (ed.) Gender *Reversals and Gender Cultures*: 164-182. London: Routledge.

BARLEY, N 1972. Anglo-Saxon Magico-Medicine. *Journal of the Royal Anthropological Society of Oxford* 3: 67-76.

BATES, B 1983. *The Way of Wyrd*. London: Arrow.

BATES, B 1996. *The Wisdom of the Wyrd: Teachings for Today from Our Ancient Past*. London: Rider.

BATES, B 2002. *The Real Middle Earth: Magic and Mystery in the Dark Ages*. London: Sidgwick and Jackson.

BENFIELD, S, C. CARTWRIGHT, H COOL, G DANNELL, S LA NIECE, S PAYNTER, V RIGBY, P SEALEY, JP WILD AND P WILTSHIRE. 2008. Stanway: An Elite Cemetery at Camulodunum. *British Archaeology* 99 (March/April).

BLAIN, J 2002. *Nine Worlds of Seid-Magic: Ecstasy and Neo-shamanism in North European Paganism*. London: Routledge.

BLAIN J AND RJ WALLIS 2000. The 'ergi' seidman: contestations of gender, shamanism and sexuality in northern religion, past and present. *Journal of Contemporary Religion* 15(3): 395-411.

BLAIN J AND RJ WALLIS 2007. *Sacred Sites, Contested Rites/Rights: Pagan Engagements with Archaeological Monuments*. Brighton: Sussex Academic Press.

BONSER, W 1926. Magical Practices Against Elves. *FolkLore* 37: 350-363.

CAMERON, ML 1993. *Anglo-Saxon Medicine*. (Cambridge Studies in Anglo-Saxon England, 7). Cambridge: Cambridge University Press.

CHINERY, M 1993[1986]. *Insects of Britain and Western Europe*. London: HarperCollins.

COCKAYNE, TO 1864-1866. *Leechdoms, Wortcunning and Starcraft of Early England*. 3 vols (Rolls Series no.35). London: Longman, Roberts and Green.

DAVIES, O 2007[2003]. *Popular Magic: Cunning-folk in English History*. London: Hambledon Continuum.

DICKINSON, TM 1993. An Anglo-Saxon 'cunning woman' from Bidford-on-Avon.

In: M CARVER (ed.) *In Search of Cult: Archaeological Investigations in Honour of Philip Ratz*: 45-54. Woodbridge, Suffolk: The Boydell Press.

DUBOIS, T 1999. *Nordic Religions in the Viking Age*. Philadelphia: University of Pennsylvania Press.

EMBODEN, W 1981. Transcultural use of narcotic water lilies in ancient Egyptian and Maya drug ritual. *Journal of Ethnopharmacology* 3: 39-83.

FAULKES, A (translator). 1998[1987]. *Edda: Snorri Sturluson*. London: Everyman.

FRAZER, JG 1890. *The Golden Bough*, 2 Vols. London: Macmillan.

FRIES, J 1992. *Visual Magick: A Manual of Freestyle Shamanism*. Oxford: Mandrake Press.

FRIES, J 1996. *Seidways: Shaking, Swaying and Serpent Mysteries*. Oxford: Mandrake.

FRIES, J 2002. *Helrunar: A Manual of Rune Magick*. Oxford: Mandrake Press.

GLOSECKI, SO 1986. Wolf Dancers and Whispering Beasts: Shamanic Motifs from Sutton Hoo? *Mankind Quarterly* 26: 305-319.

GLOSECKI, SO 1988. Wolf of the Bees: Germanic Shamanism and the Bear Hero. *Journal of Ritual Studies* 2(1): 31-53.

GLOSECKI, SO 1989. *Shamanism and Old English Poetry*. New York: Garland Publishing.

GRATTAN, JHG and C. Singer. 1952. *Anglo-Saxon Magic and Medicine*. London: Oxford University Press.

GRIEVE, M 1992[1931]. *A Modern Herbal*. London: Tiger.

GRIFFITHS, B 1996. *Aspects of Anglo-Saxon Magic*. Frithgarth, Norfolk: Anglo-Saxon Books.

GRIGSON, G 1987[1955]. *The Englishman's Flora*. London: Phoenix House.

GUNDARSSON, KVELDULFR. 2007. Elves, Wights, and Trolls: *Studies Towards the Practice of Germanic Heathenry, Volume I*. New York: iUniverse.

HALL, A 2005. Calling the Shots: The Old English Remedy *gif hors ofscoten sie* and Anglo-Saxon 'Elf-Shot'. Neuphilologische Mitteilungen: *Bulletin of the Modern Language Society* 106(2): 195-209.

HALL, A 2006. Are there any Elves in Anglo-Saxon Place-Names? *Nomina: Journal of the Society for Name Studies in Britain and Ireland* 29: 61-80.

HALL, A 2007a. *Elves in Anglo-Saxon England: Matters of Belief, Health, Gender and Identity*. Woodbridge, Suffolk: Boydell & Brewer.

HALL, A 2007b. Glosses, Gaps and Gender: The Rise of Female Elves in Anglo-Saxon Culture. In: M RISSANEN, M HINTIKKA, L KAHLAS-TARKKA AND R MCCONCHIE (eds) *Change in Meaning and the Meaning of Change: Studies in Semantics and Grammar from Old to Present-Day English*. Mémoires de la Société Néophilologique de Helsinki 72.

HALL, A 2007c. The Evidence for Maran, the Anglo-Saxon 'Nightmares'. *Neophilologus* 91: 299-317.

HALL, A In press. *The Etymology and Meaning of Eldritch*. Scottish Language: In press.

HALLOWELL, AI, 1960. Ojibwa Ontology, Behavior and World View. In: S DIAMOND (ed.) *Culture in History*: 19-52. New York: Columbia University Press.

HARTE, J 2009. Dragons, Elves and Giants: Some Pre-archaeological Occupants of British Barrows. In: M. Aldrich and R.J. Wallis (eds) *Antiquaries and Archaists: The Past in the Past, the Past in the Present*: 14-28. Reading: Spire Books.

HARVEY, G 2005. *Animism: Respecting the Living World*. London: Hurst.

HARVEY, G AND RJ WALLIS. 2007. *Historical Dictionary of Shamanism*. Lanham, Maryland: ScarecrowPress.

HEANEY, S 1999. *Beowulf: A New Translation*. London: Faber and Faber.

HOPE, V 1971. The Mugwort Corbel. *Friends of Exeter Cathedral: Forty-First Annual Report* (to 31 March, 1971): 18-20.

HREINSSON, V, R COOK, T GUNNELL, K KUNZ AND B SCUDDER. 1997. The Tale of the Mountain Dweller. In: V HREINSSON, R COOK, T GUNNELL, K KUNZ AND B SCUDDER (eds) *The Complete Sagas of Icelanders, including 49 tales*: 444-448. Reykjavík: Leifur Eiríksson Publishing.

JOHNSON, N AND RJ WALLIS 2005. *Galdrbok: Practical Heathen Runecraft, Shamanism and Magic*. London: The Wykeham Press.

JOLLY, KL 1996. *Popular Religion in Late Saxon England: Elf-Charms in Context*. Chapel Hill, NC: University of North Carolina Press.

JOLLY, KL 1998. Elves in the Psalms? The Experience of Evil from a Cosmic Perspective. In: A FERREIRO (ed.) *The Devil, Heresy and Witchcraft in the Middle Ages: Essays in Honour of Jeffrey B. Russell* (Cultures, Beliefs and Traditions: Medieval and Early Modern Peoples, Vol. 6): 19-44. Leiden: Brill.

KEHLM, N 2008. Invite the Wild Neighbors to Dinner. *Arthur: All Ages Counterculture*, 30 (July).

KELCHNER, GD 1935. *Dreams in Old Norse Literature and Their Affinities in Folklore*. London: Cambridge University Press.

LANG, S 1998. *Men as Women, Women as Men: Changing Gender in Native American Cultures*. Austin: University of Texas Press.

LARRINGTON, C (translator) 1996. *The Poetic Edda*. Oxford: Oxford University Press.

LETCHER, A 2007. Mad Thoughts on Mushrooms: Discourse and Power in the

Study of Psychedelic Consciousness. *Anthropology of Consciousness* 18(2): 74-97.

LUST, J 1993[1974]. *The Herb Book*. London: Bantam Books.

MABEY, R 1972. *Food for Free*. Glasgow: Collins.

MEANEY, AL 1981. *Anglo-Saxon Amulets and Curing Stones*. BAR British Series 96. Oxford: British Archaeological Reports.

MEANEY, AL 1989. Women, Witchcraft and Magic in Anglo-Saxon England. In: DG SCRAGG (ed.) *Superstition and Popular Medicine in Anglo-Saxon England*: 9-40. Manchester: Manchester Centre for Anglo-Saxon Studies.

MILLS, SY 1989[1985]. *The A-Z of Modern Herbalism: A Comprehensive Guide to Practical Herbal Therapy*. Wellingborough, Northamptonshire: Thorsons.

NORTH, R 1997. *Heathen Gods in Old English Literature*. Cambridge: Cambridge University Press.

PAGE, RI 1998. Review of 'Popular Religion in Late Saxon England'. *The Journal of Ecclesiastical History* 49(1): 162.

PHILLIPS, R 1983. *Wild Food*. London: Pan Books.

POLLINGTON, S 2000. *Leechcraft: Early English Charms, Plantlore and Healing*. Hockwold-cum-Wilton, Norfolk: Anglo-Saxon Books.

PRICE, N 2002. *The Viking Way: Religion and War in late Iron Age Scandinavia*. Uppsala: Department of Archaeology and Ancient History.

RODRIGUES, LJ 1993. *Anglo-Saxon Verse Charms, Maxims & Heroic Legends*. Middlesex, Pinner: Anglo-Saxon Books.

ROPER, J (ed.) 2004. *Charms and Charming in Europe*. Basingstoke, Hampshire: Palgrave Macmillan.

ROPER, J 2005. *English Verbal Charms*. Folklore Fellows Communications 136, no. 288. Helsinki: Suomalainen Tiedeakatemia/Academia Scientiarum Fennica.

ROSCOE, W 1996. How to Become a Berdache: Toward a Unified Analysis of Gender Diversity. In: G HERDT (ed.) *Third Sex Third Gender: Beyond Sexual Dimorphism in Culture and History* : 329-71. New York: Zone Books.

ROSCOE, W 1998. *Changing Ones: Third and Fourth Genders in North America*. London: Macmillan.

SALADIN D'ANGLURE, B 1990. Rethinking Inuit Shamanism through the concept of 'Third Gender'. In: M. Hoppál and J. Pentikäinen (eds) *Northern Religions and Shamanism*: 146-50. Budapest: Akadémai Kiadó.

SINGER, 1919-20. Early English Magic and Medicine. *Proceedings of the British Academy* 9: 341-74.

SKEMP, AR 1911. The Old English Charms. *Modern Language Review* 6(3): 289-301.

SØRENSEN, PM 1983. *The Unmanly Man: Concepts of Sexual Defamation in Early Northern Society*. Odense, Denmark: Odense University Press.

STANLEY, EG 1975. *The Search for Anglo-Saxon Paganism*. Cambridge: D.S. Brewer.

STOODLEY, N 1999. *The Spindle and the Spear: A Critical Enquiry into the Construction and Meaning of Gender in the Early Anglo-Saxon Burial Rite*. BAR British Series 288. Oxford: British Archaeological Reports.

STORMS, G 1948. *Anglo-Saxon Magic*. The Hague: Martinus Nijhoff.

STRÖM, F 1973. *Nid, Ergi and Old Norse Moral Attitudes*. London: Viking Society for Northern Research.

STUART, H 1976. The Anglo-Saxon Elf. *Studia Neophilologica: A Journal of Germanic and Romance Languages and Literature* 48: 313-320.

THUN, S 1969. The Malignant Elves: Notes on Anglo-Saxon Magic and Germanic Myth. *Studia Neophilologica* 41: 378-396.

WALKER, V 1979. A Nature Trail with a Difference. *Friends of Exeter Cathedral: Forty-Ninth Annual Report*: to 31st March 1979: 22-24.

WALLIS, RJ 2003. *Shamans/neo-Shamans: Ecstasy, Alternative Archaeologies and Contemporary Pagans*. London: Routledge.

WALLIS, RJ 2005. One more nightmare calling...the Heathen: Loki the 'Pervert God', Seidr-Sorcery and the Left-Hand Path. *Strange Attractor Journal Two*: 332-355.

WALLIS, RJ 2007. 'Remember Mugwort, what you made known': Mugwort (Artemesia vulgaris), The Nine Herbs Charm and 'New Animism'. *Many Gods, Many Voices (Journal of the Association of Polytheist Traditions)* 5: 16-26 (Spring).

WALLIS, RJ 2009a. 'Remember Mugwort, what you made known': Mugwort (Artemesia vulgaris), The Nine Herbs Charm and 'New Animism'. In: R.S. Harmon & M. Pilkington (eds.) *Equinox Festival [Catalogue]: The Method of Science, the Aim of Religion*: 82-87. London: Strange Attractor Press.

WALLIS, RJ 2009b. Re-enchanting Rock Art Landscapes: animic ontologies, non-human agency and rhizomic personhood. *Time and Mind: The Journal of Archaeology, Consciousness and Culture* 2(1): 47-70.

WELCH, M 1992. *Anglo-Saxon England*. London: B.T. Batsford/ English Heritage.

WILSON, D 1992. *Anglo-Saxon Paganism*. London: Routledge.

Between the ANGELS *and the* APES

by ALAN MOORE

In 2008, I was contacted by the Manchester International Festival and told that the pop group Gorillaz were keen to work with me on a follow-up to their *Monkey: Journey to the West* opera.

When it was suggested that the opera might be magically-themed, I proposed that it could focus on the alchemists, since Monteverdi initially created the concept of opera to convey his own alchemical ideas. With this in mind, and bearing in mind that the opera would first have been staged in Manchester, I thought that the best choice for a subject would be Queen Elizabeth's alchemist, adviser and astrologer John Dee, who spent some years exiled to Manchester during his later life.

The idea was accepted enthusiastically and I began work on the libretto. Sadly, however, for various reasons the opera was not to be. Here I present my initial outline, and as much of the libretto as I had written when the project was abandoned.

Dee illustration by ARIK ROPER

The Outline

If we're to create an approximately ninety-minute piece on the subject of Greatest Dead Englishman John Dee, then a solid and conventional place to start structurally would be a classic three-act construction with sections of a half-hour each. This also seems to fit nicely with the triangular Greek delta symbol (which is how Dee identifies himself in the facsimile notes presented in *A True & Faithful Relation of What Passed for Many Yeers between Dr John Dee and Some Spirits* [Meric Casaubon, 1659] and is also the elemental symbol for fire, which is in turn the element that represents the highest spiritual component of the magician or, indeed, the ordinary human being).

We will open and close the piece with a framing device built around the doctor's final days at Mortlake, with the magus in decline like Prospero upon his isle, attended only by his loyal daughter and his spirits. (Or, if you prefer, like Dr Morbius in the derivative 1956 film

Forbidden Planet, on his isolated world attended only by his daughter Altaira, Robby the Robot, and the Caliban-like Creature of the Id.) It would also be useful to have the Mortlake scene to return to as a kind of punctuation at the pivotal plot-points that, with a three act structure, occur at roughly thirty minutes and an hour into our ninety-minute piece.

Let's say that the Mortlake scenes, of which there are four, are all approximately seven minutes long. That would mean that the three lengthy 'flashback' scenes (which make up the bulk of our narrative and which are bracketed by the Mortlake sequences) would be just over twenty minutes each.

The first scene would establish the whole of the situation: who Dee is; who his daughter is; the fact that he is still in communication with his spirit entities (or at least believes himself to be); the fact that he is in Mortlake and in exile; and the fact that he is outcast and dying, this man who in his lifetime has shaped the entire world. I figure that dramatically our strongest opening would be John Dee alone, save for his spirits. His daughter, while she should be mentioned as an off-stage presence, should probably be saved until one of the later Mortlake sections, so that we can make more of her.

It also strikes me that with this very first scene we could break the fourth wall, and have the dying magus in some way aware of the audience that is watching him. He doesn't perceive the rows of seats that he glimpses rising all around him as a theatre audience, however, but as strange and unearthly 'spirits of futurity' that are watching over him in his final hours. After we've established all this, the opening scene would conclude with the doctor in a reflective state, considering his current condition and casting his mind back to his origins.

This would lead nicely into our first twenty-minute sequence, in which we should obviously include all the interesting bits from the early life of John Dee – the flying beetle and all the other relevant stuff, perhaps as a drifting psychedelic montage of events – while making our principal focus the time that Dee spent in prison for treason after casting an inauspicious horoscope for Queen Mary. Dee's cellmate during this time was a strange and peripheral character named Bartlett Green, who was coincidentally a leper. His appearance in Dee's life right at the time when Dee was facing possible execution and thus going through a long night of the soul, just before he was taken under the wing of the new Queen Elizabeth, makes him into a sort of dark messenger figure who can perhaps be used to set up some of the themes and motifs that will recur in our drama. The initial twenty-minute sequence would end with the death of Queen Mary, Dee's release from prison and his first meeting with the Faerie Queen, Elizabeth. I suspect that Dee's devotion to Elizabeth was at least partially erotically inspired: that he fancied her, and that in part the Queen was a kind of ethereal muse to the Doctor, as well as his most important patron. Although Elizabeth has been pretty much done to death as far as drama and film are concerned, I think that since she played such a major part in Dee's life and fortunes she needs to loom large in our presentation. But I also think that by focussing on the otherworldly or erotic aspects of the monarch, as seen through Dee's eyes, we should be able to create a portrait of Elizabeth that is distinctive and unusual enough to make the character seem fresh again. So, that's where we end our first major sequence before returning to the now elderly and dying doctor, stuck in Mortlake in the year of 1605.

The second seven-minute Mortlake sequence would be a good place to introduce Dee's daughter. Perhaps the preceding flashback scene is terminated by the arrival of his daughter at his bedside, bringing him a meal and interrupting his reverie. We could then have a scene where Dee and his daughter have a conversation while she is feeding him his gruel or whatever it is. They could make reference to the fact that only they survive out of Dee's whole extended family, and we could get a sense of the complex feelings that they have for each other. Dee's daughter loves and respects her father deeply, but we also get the sense that she has many private doubts concerning the reality of his spirit transmissions. She might even privately feel that her father's obsession with the 'human loving' spirits of the Book of Enoch has done much to mess up the lives of everyone concerned. If her dad hadn't had a reputation as a sorcerer, would King James have banished him to Manchester, where plague had claimed most of his family? Dee, meanwhile, needs his daughter to love and believe in him, because she's all that he has left in the way of companionship that someone else can see as well.

This is the cue for our second twenty-minute section, in which we document the extraordinary rise of Dr Dee. We probably speed through his enlistment as a spy by Francis Walsingham, his meteoric rise through Elizabethan society and its intellectual life (perhaps exemplified by a scene depicting a meeting of 'The School of Night' with Shakespeare, Marlowe, Raleigh, Furman et al) and his invention of the British Empire to get to the meat of our story, which is Dee's meeting with Edward Kelly. As an aside, would it be possible to have the same performer play Kelly who played Bartlett Green in our first flashback sequence, but obviously sans leper makeup? To make a subtle connection between these two mysterious figures (both of whom had bits of their bodies missing) would be almost to suggest, at least poetically, that both Green and Kelly were perhaps representatives of the same otherworldly realm that would govern most of Dr Dee's life. The same performer might even take the part of a principal Enochian spirit in our finale, to carry through the idea. Anyway, once Dee and Kelly have connected we can conclude this second section with their first full-blown invocation of the Enochian spirits. (It also occurs to me that we will need at least two or ideally three performers to take the part of Dee himself. The main one will be the elderly and dying Dee who both opens and closes the opera, but we might need two other performers to depict Dee at the three stages of his life that we are documenting in the dying doctor's flashback reminiscences.)

The following brief seven-minute section back in Mortlake might involve the doctor being once more disturbed from his reminiscences, not by his daughter this time, or by his Enochian spirits, but by ordinary ghosts, people who have meant a lot in Dee's life but are now dead. Perhaps his wife Jane would be foremost amongst these, but there are lots of other possibilities for spectral, special-effects figures to gather ethereally around Dee's deathbed. This sequence could be used to introduce the ominous reverberations that will sound throughout the rest of Dee's life: his wife's ghost might seem reproachful of the doctor, clearly still resentful of some great ordeal he put her through. We can leave the specific details of Jane Dee's complaint still vague at this point, but it will set up the dark premise of the disastrous wife-swap that we shall explore in our third and final twenty-minute sequence. Perhaps this interlude between Dee and the ghosts is ended when his daughter bursts into the bedchamber, having heard her father talking with someone. The moment that she does, of course, the spectres vanish. After having ascertained that Dee is all right for the moment his daughter retreats, leaving the doctor to consider that dark down-slope of his life that led him to his present grim condition.

Our third and last twenty-minute sequence probably commences with Dee having been commanded by the angels to take Kelly and their families to Europe, where he's been instructed to confront the Emperor Rudolph and accuse him of consorting with infernal spirits. Improbably, this all works out okay and Dee and Kelly are soon working at producing gold by alchemy for their new patron, and are also letting their angel experiments transport them into increasingly murky waters. When the angels tell them they must 'have their wives in common', they reluctantly go along with it and the whole story of their success begins to unravel from that point on. It's almost as if Choronzon, the terrifying 'demon of dispersal' who inhabits the thirty-third Enochian aether, is somehow tearing up the doctor's life and scattering it to the wind. After the wife-swap, Dee and Kelly's partnership collapses. Kelly scries a final and apocalyptic message from the terrible female entity Babalon and then in consequence gives up the Art forever. He stays in Bohemia while Dee and family return to England, but is soon dead of infection after falling from a turret from which he was trying to escape. Back at home, Elizabeth dies and the ferociously puritanical and anti-magical King James takes the throne. James issues an edict that declares fairies to be in fact demons, and banishes Dee and his family to Manchester, where plague will claim most of them. This penultimate sequence perhaps ends with the defeated and tragic figure of the bereaved Dr Dee about to return to Mortlake to die, to the very shores of death itself, attended only by his daughter and his spirits.

This brings us to our final seven-minute scene where Dee is finally dying. This would be best if it was attended by his doubting daughter. She is, as far as she knows, the only being with her father when he dies. However, we can bring the show to a spectacular conclusion with the Doctor's dying vision: he is transfixed by the understanding that, as Emanuel Swedenborg would later remark, 'angels know nothing of time.' The universe is timeless, and perhaps we return to our opening idea of Dee glimpsing the extraordinary, and to him incomprehensible, sight of the modern audience watching him from four hundred years in the future. After Dee has delivered an address to the future, to the world that he has created, we have a final imprecation to the spirits (who his attending daughter refuses to believe are real) just before he breathes his last. Instead of an answer from the angels of the aethers, there can be a doubting silence that seems to go on and on until we are certain that Dee's beliefs were nothing but elaborate delusions. At this point, the first of our planted angels in the audience stands up and starts to sing and we build into an overwhelming fugue of angel voices and visual spectacle that perhaps leaves the audience gazing into the giant black mirror for a few strange minutes before we close in to total blackness and silence.

Okay, having established a rough shape for the piece, I suppose some thought should be given to a tentative cast list of characters and players that we will need.

Firstly, of course, there is Dee himself. As noted above, we may well need two or three performers in the role of Dee. The principal role would be that of the dying doctor, who will probably be fairly motionless on his ornate deathbed throughout the entire performance, and depending on how we set up the performance area may also be at least dimly visible to the audience throughout the whole show. I see this, our 'main' Dr Dee, as being a baritone… perhaps a medium-range baritone, although this is not really my area of expertise. I figure we should save the really startling deep bass register for some of the more alarming Enochian spirits. The other, younger versions of John Dee should probably also be voiced by someone in the same baritone register.

Dee's daughter, while perhaps of less significance in Dee's actual life than somebody like Edward Kelly, is in terms of our drama an important through-character who is with the audience at regular intervals throughout the narrative, right up until its end. I see her as being an attractive woman in her thirties or early forties... I'm not sure of her actual age but I doubt that she could have been terribly young at the time, with her father so incredibly old and all her other siblings dead. Someone who suggests a fiery strength of resolve and character, but with huge reserves of deep compassion. Again, I'm even worse at categorising women's voices than I am with men, beyond observing that it should be a pure and strong voice, whatever that means.

Edward Kelly must be next on our list, and as mentioned earlier I think it might add a resonance to the drama if the same performer we have for Kelly could also play Dee's leprous cellmate Bartlett Green in the first flashback sequence and one of the prominent Enochian

presences towards the end of the opera. I see Kelly, while not being an evil or fraudulent man, as nevertheless having an aura of sinister presence about him. (The same will be true if the performer is portraying Bartlett Green or one of the major Enochian spirits.) I'm guessing again, but would a bass tenor register suit that kind of character?

Queen Elizabeth should be a strange and fey character with a slight whiff of hereditary madness around her. This shouldn't be played for laughs, as with Miranda Richardson's sterling performance in *Blackadder*, but should be used to accentuate the fact that English royalty of this period (and, arguably, any other period) were incredibly strange and exotic creatures who were literally as different from the human beings around them as if they actually had been the faerie race of Spenser's poem. I see her as having a very high and tinkling voice, to emphasise her remoteness and unearthliness. I also see the Queen, in the context of Dee, as a strikingly sexual character. Given that most of this drama only happens in the doctor's reminiscences, I figure we have some license to depict historical figures and events through a lens of dream-like and fantastical memory, so that our depiction of Elizabeth could be a kind of sexualized and highly-imaginative fantasy of Elizabeth, dressed accordingly in a feverish and dream-like re-imagining of Elizabethan costumes. This fantastical and psychedelic approach to the Elizabethan period could extend to our set designs and might generate some wonderful visual ideas, which wouldn't be entirely out of keeping with the mystical and flamboyant spirit of the period. This approach might yield some musical ideas as well, when considering the intensely mathematical and Hendrix-fast harpsichord pieces that were being composed at the time.

As regards the cast-list of what you might call secondary characters, we will need someone – perhaps a relatively elderly someone – to portray the spymaster Sir Francis Walsingham. We would need a voice, perhaps a light tenor voice that could suggest an immense intellect which is both dispassionate and calculating.

We would need an Emperor Rudolph, whom I can't help but see (at least at this early stage) as a less camp and more terrifying version of Brian Blessed, probably with a deep baritone voice. Deeper than Dee's own, which will perhaps make them seem more mismatched during what I think should be a fairly electrifying scene when Dee first confronts the deranged and tyrannical Emperor.

We would need performers as Dee's wife Jane – whom I see as being a kind, generous, striking-looking woman with perhaps a faint air of melancholy about her – and as Edward Kelly's wife, whom I'm afraid I haven't found the name of yet. (Don't worry, I'll be getting my friend, mentor and Elizabethan expert Steve Moore to help me with the research on this project, once I get the writing properly underway.) I see Kelly's wife as being a more worldly, pragmatic and perhaps more sexually flirtatious woman than the loyal and godly Jane Dee. I think that after Kelly's death, it was not long before she attached herself to some powerful figure or other, with the means to care for her and for her and Kelly's daughter. This is not to suggest that she was being anything other than sensible during what must have been a precarious time, but I somehow get the feeling that Mrs Kelly was nevertheless a very different character to Jane Dee, and of the two women would probably have the more strident and the least gentle voice.

We will certainly need performers to voice the Enochian spirits, but I'm not really sure which of these we'll be using yet, with the exceptions of Choronzon and the Whore-Goddess Babalon. Choronzon should have a truly frightening bass growl that rattles the furniture and fittings and sets off mild internal bleeding amongst the audience. I don't think it matters what the voice-artist looks like, as I imagine that Choronzon would best be visually portrayed by some disorienting and monstrous special effect. Babalon is a very different kettle of fish, and would need the most scarily beautiful and most scarily-voiced woman that anyone has ever imagined. Good luck with that.

Opening Scene

Dee: I wake. What year is this, what time?

I wake from blazing dreams. The salt ache in my bladder warns that I am yet alive, although not long, pray God. Not very long.

Here in my Mortlake, on my pond of death, the world I made recedes from me like tide. I hear my daughter in another room, the sighs she makes, the clattering of pots, yet save for she I am by all this murderous and copulating world forgot.

The alabaster Queen and all her curls of tangerine are flown away, with in their wake my favour and my fame. I hear the whisperings of spies no more, nor yet the baboon rants of Emperors. Save one, my family were took by plague.

This yellow matter knuckled from my eyes; the amber droplets shaken from my prick: are these the only gold wrought by my alchemy? I chained the stars and with them tamed the sea. I shrank the universe into a sign. I shaped an empire from the empty air and once, with feathered voices everywhere, an alphabet of destiny was mine. Their As I taught to them, their Bs and Cs, refracted in my gem. But what of Dee? I break wind and it is to me a music, who had the conversation of the spheres.

I hear my daughter in another room. Sometimes she'll sing a line or two, then cease, as if made mindful of my drear decline. I wish she'd carry on. The powdered throngs of dukes and conjurors are gone and I am all alone save she…and thee.

I see you dimly as in a black glass, rising to darkness in your silent rows like a tribunal or a circus mob, and all of your strange eyes are fixed on me.

What are you? Whence comes this unearthly crew that I have sensed about me all my days as through a curtain or a hanging cloth, betrayed now by a whisper, now a cough? What are you? Lamps infernal or divine, suspended in our sooty firmament, who watch us stumble through our clumsy lines and offer neither jeers nor yet applause. What are you, and what bloodless realm is thine?

Are all our strivings and adulteries but the diversion of a phantom horde that shifts impatient on its cirrus chairs, consults its playbills while men live or die, and only stares? What are you? In the book that Enoch writ are powers that loveth earthly things too well, thrown down from grace until eternity, cast out by the Almighty. Is it thee? Are our beloved mortal fields your hell?

Or be ye spirits of futurity born only of a frantic, flailing mind, desperate to know he left something behind, imagining a world that's yet to be where all of his asylum speculations are proved true? I hope I am still God's man. What are you?

But see, how he converses with himself and wonders that folk think him ill of mind. I rave, and weep, and gaze into my stone and I entreat the seraphs and the thrones for counsel on the blood that's in my stool, with their reply ambiguous, with their reply ambiguous when they reply at all.

I hear my daughter in another room and am undone to think she pities me. I would to her be limned in blinding suns. I would my garment were the boundless sky and in her gaze reflected know that I was all my century's light: I was John Dee.

I was not ever this rain-sodden sketch with half my lines erased, my colours run, nor always did I navigate a path no further than the sorry chamber-pot. Rather I measured oceans with my stride and numbers told to me their secret names. I drew the circles and I spoke the words that half our reeking globe is stood upon, yet men shall rake my grave smooth when I'm gone and then to the uncomprehending flame, to the perusal of illiterate fires, consign my library. I was a fellow to the School of Night and when Kit Marlowe wrote of Faust, he wrote of me.

In my jet mirror is the future now all clouds with nothing there to read, nothing to scry. My present is pared down to these stark walls that are my last horizons, are my final skies and yet so close, so near, so shabby where the lining-paper sags. In place of constellations, only cracks. Below, within my penitentiary flesh, a great dismantling proceeds unchecked.

My vistas and my panoramas are unfolded nowhere, save in memory. Both my tomorrows and todays are done. The unrecoverable past is all my pasture now, my only liberty, when I was Jack of Angels and the heavens were alight; when I was known by men, and by those more than men. When I was young, when I stared down the florid monster of Bohemia in his den, for in my glass I'd bested worse, far worse than he. When I was young, I was the pivot of the world.

I was John Dee.

Staging Notes

Now some ideas as to how we could arrange the stage area. I must admit that having just a delta symbol as our title is growing on me. Following on from this, would it be practical or useful to design our stage area around the same basic upright triangle? It struck me that a massive triangular stage could be constructed which, keeping to our vague theme of the number three, would be divided into three horizontal levels. At the apex of the triangle, the smallest of our three stages, we could have the tiny room in Mortlake where the eighty-year-old John Dee is engaged in the protracted act of dying, as seen during our seven minute opening and the other interleaving seven-minute sections.

Down at the triangle's base would be the widest of our three stages, which I suggest could be used for all of our flashback sequences that detail Dee's remembrance of his past. In the first twenty-minute scene, for example, the material dealing with Dee and Bartlett Green in their cell at Lambeth Palace and with Dee's subsequent freeing and reception from the newly-crowned Queen Elizabeth would all be acted out upon the bottom stage. Being the widest stage, this seems most practical given the broad sweep of historical scenes that we'll be called on to enact, and also perhaps gives a sense that, as opposed to the cramped limitations of the attic-like space containing Dee's deathbed up at the apex of the triangle, the world of Dee's remembered past had much wider horizons.

Between these two layers we have our middle stage, where I suggest we place all of what we might call our aetheric or imaginary action. This would include perhaps the visionary doings of some of Dee's Enochian spirits, but would also be useful as a space in which to present other, baser kinds of fantasy such as the fantastical tabloid imaginings and rumour-mongering of the two comedy guards at the opening of our first flashback sequence below, when they are giving us their rundown of Dee's early life and of the diabolical activities that he's supposed to be in prison for. This may also provide a place and a platform for any ghostly visitants that Dee may encounter later, with characters like the deceased Jane Dee appearing on this middle stage and calling up through the floorboards to where Dee lies on his deathbed above, calling to him from this layer of imagination just beneath his feet.

Of course, this leaves us with two dead spaces that are outside the confines of the central three-level triangle, to its upper left and upper right. It occurs to me that maybe these zones would useful for the placement of two screen-areas, upon which we could project filmed material to augment the action taking place on the three stages, as and where necessary. For example, in the first of our three twenty-odd minute flashback scenes below, I thought that perhaps the screen areas to either side of the triangular stage could be used to show us images of the giant coarse faces of the two guards, seen through the barred aperture in a cell door, as they peer in at the audience as if looking in on their prisoners. Their opening dialogue could be delivered by their enlarged screen images rather than by their relatively small physical presences upon the stage, if they even need to be present on stage at all.

The guards' recounting of their sensationalised version of Dee's early history, perhaps with the guards peering in through the barred aperture in the cell door and speaking from the screen areas as described above, could have an accompanying pageant of imagined action taking place upon our middle stage. This would be the 'psychedelic montage' mentioned in my opening notes, and could be as lurid and mad as we liked. The flying beetle scene would take place on (or would at least be launched from) this level, and I figure that we can make the spectre of Mary Tudor that will also turn up in the guard's account into a grotesque and striking portrait of this grim and troubled monarch. Given that Mary was desperate to produce an heir, to the point where her right-hand man was supposed to be scouring the slums looking for a pretend heir to abduct, and where the Queen herself went through a phantom pregnancy before succumbing to what was probably ovarian cancer, would it be too much to have our Mary sporting a surreal inflatable pregnant belly that can balloon to a ridiculous size before it pops? This is just an idea of the kind of treatment and imagery that I thought might be appropriate, counterpointed as it is by the raucous commentary of the two on-screen guards and by the isolated figures of the young John Dee and his even younger cellmate Bartlett Green as they sit, silently at first, in their small, hemmed-in region at the centre of the wide bottom stage just beneath all the hallucinatory action that's taking place upon the middle tier.

I'd like to take a moment to just get straight how the visuals of the performance are proceeding. We've opened with blackness in which the triangular structure of the stage area will not immediately be apparent. I suggest that we have the two screen areas to the upper left and right of the central triangle lit up from the very beginning, before the performance starts. Since the opening screened image is as seen looking out from inside a cell through the barred aperture in the door, then these illuminated screen areas will just look like design elements, areas of vertical black and white stripes, until the giant faces of the guards lean into view beyond them, peering down disdainfully at the audience, which might perhaps be quite visually startling if the audience weren't expecting it.

So, we have a blacked out stage, save for these two enigmatic barred design areas to the upper left and right. When the lights go up on the first seven-minute scene, then we presumably need only to light up the relatively tiny topmost stage, up at the apex of the triangle. The triangular structure of the whole stage will still probably not be apparent to the audience throughout this first opening scene, which just features the one illuminated spot with the eighty-year-old John Dee's deathbed musings in March 1609.

As the scene ends, immediately after the last, fiercely declaratory 'I was John Dee', the lights on the top stage dim just as the lights on the bottom-most stage are beginning to come up, showing us the figure of John Dee, aged 28 in the year 1555 and in prison at the Bishop's palace at Lambeth for the crimes of witchcraft, calculating, conjuring and plotting against the Queen, Mary Tudor. Dee is sharing his cell with a twenty-four-year-old man named Bartlett Green. Now, contrary to my notes for the first scene, I have since discovered no evidence for Bartlett Green being a leper. I'm reluctant to give up the idea of Dee's cellmate being disfigured in some way, as this gives him a somewhat more unearthly and perhaps prophetic aspect. As a compromise Green could be disfigured by a horrendous mask of acne, or perhaps pox-scars. I shouldn't have thought that this was unlikely, given the period.

As the lights come up on the bottom stage, we see that it is masked off to either side of the central illuminated area that represents the cramped and miserable cell in which Dee and Green are confined. The two cellmates sit facing each other in miserable silence for a moment, and then the face of our first guard looms suddenly into view on the projected screen image to our upper left of the stage. A few moments later he is joined by the second guard leaning into view to the upper right of the triangular stage. As the guards recount the details of Dee's life that have led him to his present circumstances, a pageant of hallucinatory fantasy imagery is reeled out across the middle tier of the stage to accompany this. The imprisoned figures of Green and Dee in the cell remain seemingly oblivious to the guards' dialogue or to the cavalcade of fantasy taking place on the stage just above their heads. When the lights go up, Dee is seated dejectedly on a cot, while Green stands with his back to a wooden support pillar in the middle of their cramped cell, idly picking his scabby face.

SCENE TWO

BISHOP BONNER'S PRISON AT LAMBETH PALACE, 1555.

FIRST GUARD: John Dee, you say? I take it he's the older of the two, the conjuror whose reputation's soiled, while Bartlett Green would be the slim and pretty-bottomed youth who stands and gazes into space, who stands and picks his seeping, weeping, poxy ruin of a face. He looks just like a bleeding angel what's been bleeding boiled.

And yet they languish here in lovely Lambeth for schemes against

Her Blessed Majesty: a cell of terrorisers, Protestants or sympathisers now enjoying Bishop Bloody Bonner's hospitality. I'd like to turk the younger cove if given half a chance, provided I need only see him from behind. I'm not so sure about his mate. He conjures and he calculates, works witchcraft with the stars and dates, he charms, and charts, and contemplates, and my knob loses stiffness over matters of the mind.

SECOND GUARD: I wouldn't let his cleverness dissuade you, and of his witchcraft you need have no fear. As for his reputation with math'matic calculation, well, I bet he never counted on his ending up in here. And conjuration is a thing that any man may do, whether we're bragging to the wife or telling lies. We conjure better things than he from naught but our vocabul'ry. Why, we could conjure Master Dee, his life in all its infamy, could summon it for all to see before their very eyes.

Born eight and twenty years since in the shadow of the Tower, where his own dad would later be reviled, he toddles off to Grammar School when but a tender flower then straight to Cambridge he departs where he becomes a dear old, fifteen-year-old Bachelor of the Arts; was reading bleeding Greek when he was just a bleeding child.

FIRST GUARD: You're never telling me that's fucking natural. If more proof of his sorcery you require, a college audience testified he made a massive beetle glide. You're never telling me he done that with some bits of fucking wire.

SECOND GUARD: If you ask me, that's more the work of demons, such as those bound by Solomon the King. To shift a thing of that size, well, then the assembled hordes of Hell are much more likely than some pulleys and some fucking bits of string.

FIRST GUARD: Next thing you know he meets our sixth King Edward, and does well by the wee Protestant lad. But Ed was dead by age fifteen which made his sister Mary queen and she's a howling Catholic nightmare and a lot more like their dad.

BOTH: God blind us, don't remind us of old Henry in his prime. Some of our rulers drool a bit, it's true. We've had some morons, maniacs or monsters in our time, but this is England. What's a man to do?

SECOND GUARD: Though even by our inbred national standard, then Scary Mary's fairly hard to beat when she's so desperate for an heir she's had her womb puff up with air and old Lord North's consid'ring pinching pauper babies off the street.

FIRST GUARD: Then there's her pretty sister kept at Woodstock, with Mary seeing plots at every turn. In such a fearful atmosphere it's little wonder matey here and his friend who's got vomit for a face will more than likely burn.

SECOND GUARD: But then, that's what you get for being clever, and possibly disloyal to the Pope. I can't speak for the younger whelp, but with friend Dee it didn't help that he wrote our beleaguered Queen such a beshitted horoscope.

Both: God love us when above us are the stars that guide our fate, be it a crib or shroud, for all to view. God keep the fool who serves a queen with news she's sure to hate, but this is England. What's a man to do?

First Guard: And so they languish here in lovely Lambeth, a stay which they're unlikely to survive. Their prospects would be clearer if they'd picked another era and not this year of our blessed Saviour, 1555. Their circumstances demonstrate that stars led them astray by failing to anticipate a Royal trend, which proves the future may not be determined by astrology, and that if your theology don't suit a change in monarchy your guardian angels may well be what gut you in the end.

Second Guard: And pissing 'round with sorcery is bound to let you down, especially with a Catholic on the throne. The spirits what you conjure up are no match for the Crown. They won't be with you in the dock. They won't be floating airy-fairy there above the chopping-block. They'll fly off and you'll bleeding end up on your bleeding own.

Both: God knows we don't suppose that it's a lesson what they'll learn, and we've a break for ale and mutton due. We should have more concern for those who may well shortly burn, but this is England. What's a man to do?

Some Intermediary Notes

At the conclusion of the guards' dialogue, their giant projected faces duck back out of site on the other side of their barred apertures and our attention moves to Dee and Green in their cell, a masked-off, relatively small area at the centre of the bottom stage. This is set up with Bartlett Green standing idly picking his scabs while he leans against the central wooden support post of the cell. I imagine Dee as sitting on a low prison bench that is placed so as to effectively mask Green's lower body from the audience. We reach a point later in the scene when the somewhat eerie figure of Bartlett Green starts to prophesy what is going to happen to them both. At this point, Green probably lets his previously active hands rest down by the post at his sides. Then, when he predicts that Dee will be released, we can pull back the curtains or whatever has been masking the sides of the wide bottom stage to show the free world outside the prison. We can also whisk the bench away to show that Green is standing at the post with faggots and firewood heaped around his feet. His hands now look as if they're tied behind his back around the wooden post, which is now the stake he is to be shortly burned at.

The outside world beyond the central cell where Green is singing his prophetic narrative could maybe be depicted with sliding scenery, Elizabethan landmarks amongst which Dee appears to wander lost for a while as Green predicts the demise of Queen Mary. Since this is Green's prophecy and thus in the realm of vision and imagination, we could also engage our middle stage, upon which the figure of Queen Mary with the inflatable pregnancy finally swells to a ridiculously huge size and bursts. All of this action, on both the bottom and central stages, is to briefly fill in the years between 1555 and 1558, which is roughly as follows: in 1556, while Dee is still wandering as if lost amongst the sliding landmarks of an immediately pre-Elizabethan world, Bartlett Green is burned for the imaginary Protestant plot against the Queen. I imagine we show this by having the pyre at his feet burst into flame at this point in Green's prophetic narrative. The flames (probably some sort of special effect, as I imagine these performers have a powerful union) can continue to rise and to devour the unfortunate Green as he continues to sing from the pyre, extending his prophetic narrative beyond the point of his own death as he burns.

Green prophesies that in 1558, Queen Mary dies, followed by Queen Elizabeth's rise to the throne, later in 1558, and the happy union between the new monarch and Dr Dee. We see this acted out upon the bottom stage, where perhaps one of the sliding pre-Elizabethan landmarks might be a kind of gilded cage with a beautiful twenty-five year-old red-headed woman inside it, even if the woman's full splendour is only glimpsed at first, with her turned from the audience as she sits pensively within her golden cage. This is to represent the young Elizabeth, kept under house arrest at Woodstock until after Mary's death. After Mary's balloon has burst, so to speak, we have the other sliding scenery hauled away to be replaced by items from the dazzling interior of an Elizabethan palace. The gilded cage opens, and Queen Elizabeth emerges for her splendid coronation, as astrologically charted by the loyal John Dee.

In order to distance our Elizabeth from previous portrayals and make her immediately striking and startling, as well as emphasising her otherworldly and erotic aspects, she might have some fabulous psychedelic pseudo-Elizabethan costume that leaves her chalk-white breasts exposed after the fashion of the women in Minoan Crete, a matriarchy where the exposed boobs were seen as exemplifying female power. This would be in keeping with the status of Elizabeth, ruling over what was effectively her own island matriarchy. The pair of them can perhaps be dancing at her coronation while the now almost-incinerated

Bartlett Green continues to sing from his blazing stake in the centre of all these lavish celebrations. The fireworks that accompanied the young Queen's coronation might perhaps burst up spectacularly from the wood and kindling at Green's feet as the blackened relic sings the final lines of his prophecy. At the end of the scene, we have the voice of Dee's daughter Katherine intruding upon our narrative, perhaps as if through the young Queen's lips. This is our cue to dim the lights on the lower stages and raise them on the topmost stage, where Dee's protracted reverie has just been interrupted by his daughter entering the dying-room, launching us into our next seven-minute interlude...

DEE: Did I miscalculate? Did I misread the portents writ upon the night's abyss? Did I mishear God's voice or misconstrue the role I thought set out for me by fate? When God commands, what is a man to do? Now He falls silent in my hour of need and leaves me to the stench of my own piss. How has my grand adventure come to this? Where did I err; did I miscalculate?

The angels counselled glory should be mine where I, too quickly, took them at their word and in my vanity believed it true that future days should hear my praises sung, almost as though t'were already occurred. Are angels not oblivious to time, with our tomorrows plain as yesterdays, our graves and cradles both within their gaze? Their wings beat once and dynasties decline. Who better knows our destinies than they? This was the slippery rock to which I clung, assured by immaterial spirits who see men's lives as a verse's single line. When God commands, what is a man to do? Have I misunderstood some fluttered word or mistranslated a celestial phrase for want of schooling in their crystal tongue? Or were they but hobgoblins of the mind, mere phantoms born of a deluded state? Was it naught save my own voice that I heard? In my belief, did I miscalculate?

GREEN: At last the burning issue is addressed, here where the truth we can no more evade. Were our prayers muttered to the empty air? For all our faith, was anybody there? How strange, then, that dawn finds me unafraid to see my pieties put to the test.

DEE: Sweet Bartlett Green, would thy strength were my own. Though young, thy bravery sets mine to shame. Thou art in truth more innocent than I of the concocted faults that land us here, of playing the conspirator or spy and eager to splash blood upon the throne. Without my learning you are without fear, and I know no more of thee than thy name.

GREEN: Souls such as I are strangers in your heart, fifth business passing back and forth like shades. We speak our messages, sound our refrains, leave softly and are never met again, slipping away into life's masquerade. Pale ghosts, we bring queer tidings, then depart.

DEE: Is this room colder than before you spoke? What is the draft that prickles at my nape? I know thee only as poor Bartlett Green, interrogator Phillpott's former friend, drawn in like him beneath a tainting cloak of accusations lacking form or shape, sprung from the night-fits of a tottering queen whose dark imaginings are without end.

Yet now I know thee in another light, thy ravaged face takes on a different shine. Is this room colder than before you spoke? Whence this chill feather stroking at my spine?

Green: Souls such as I know not continuum. We come and go at the Creator's whim and so see more of His design than thee, have glimpsed the props and scenery yet to be, and on my act the footlights now grow dim. I have a vision of the world to come.

Dee: Now am I lost. Is something happening? Attar of roses scents thy reeking sores and all of time falls open at my feet, where reason plunges and is swallowed whole. Pray, what unearthly atmosphere is yours? Why must I tremble at the news you bring as though at the Almighty's judgement seat? A mortal dread is roosted on my soul and sense is fled. Is something happening?

Green: My death treads near and brings death's clarity so that each dust-mote blazes like a sun, a morning light too savage to escape that blasts aside the future's threadbare drape: I have a vision of the world to come, a world where none save you remembers me.

Green: For thine own self, then, be ye unafraid. A week shall see thee quit this abject place, spared by a queen who frets she'll yet need thee, adrift on London's fraught and listing sea where none but thee recalls this blemished face, before September's russet hand is played.

Dee: Now am I lost on shifting panic streets where nervous and uncertain spectres teem. Which hound to back, which stall to try your luck when the missed guess invites a traitor's death? Mary, half-eaten by maternal dreams? At Woodstock under guard, Elizabeth? With history's sands sucked from beneath our feet the landmarks of the city come unstuck, lost in this ghastly twilight of regime.

Green: For sins neither committed nor confessed, inside these walls shall I receive small ease until they lead me out within the year unto a dismal yard not far from here, with logs and kindling heaped about my knees. At last the burning issue is addressed.

Then ringed about by vile and jeering men I am reduced to crackle, spark and flame. Freed from the charring flesh's heavy yoke I'm took to Heaven as a smudge of smoke where martyrs pierced by arrows know my name, for my complexion shall be flawless then.

And she who lit this pyre I stand upon and had the firewood about me piled, our barren Queen who drapes her realm in chains shall feel at last the longed-for labour pains. What grows within her womb is not a child, and after two more winters she is gone.

DEE: Now am I lost in expectations grand. The soul of carnival is everywhere. Is this a dead queen's funeral array, these bright and joyous ragamuffin tides, lanes hung with coloured lanterns from Cathay and bonfires jubilant throughout the land? At Woodstock fair Elizabeth abides, as though a fairy kingdom were declared.

GREEN: Those with more foresight will have guessed the rest: on fiery copper hair shall sit the crown, her coronation date yours to supply as her enchanter, though enchanted by her snowy teats, the sequins of her gown. At last the burning issue is addressed.

QUEEN: And how shall I reward thee, Doctor Dee? What might I grant these hands that drew my chart? What prize must I upon these lips bestow that told so well my starry destiny? My glamours are reflected in thine eyes, my swan's throat and my profile fit for coins. Come, tell to me each constellation's name, make me the ocean's mistress and the sky's, my name in curlicues on England's heart, and all my dearest favours thou shall know. I shall exhaust thee with my gratitude. White as the gates of Heaven are my thighs, my skin of tallow and my hair of flames. I am the candle burning at your loins. Forgive me, father, if I do intrude.

DEE: Now am I lost in eyes of melted jade. Now am I lost in opportunity both of the flesh and likewise the career, at suck on either alabaster breast. What glories might be mine, and at what cost? Is scholarship that is the all of me by hard cash and hard manhood both betrayed? What is the bargain I am striking here? 'Neath history's perfumed skirts now am I lost.

GREEN: Thine eyes upon her pearl-drenched bosom rest. At last the burning issue is addressed.

QUEEN: A codpiece surely gives away man's mood. You have an agile tongue and shapely knee and I should like to dance with Doctor Dee. Forgive me, father, if I do intrude.

FIRST GUARD: Outside the gates we guard Westminster Palace for our sins. We'll likely miss her Coronation dance. It's said she has six fingers like her mother, Anne Boleyn, and is as ruthless as her dad and has the seeming of one just as scheming and as screaming mad, but we'd all bleeding have her if we had the bleeding chance.

SECOND GUARD: And now we're fucking staunch Elizabethans, attendant on Her Majesty's desire. We torturers and brawlers are now sycophants and crawlers and we wouldn't piss on Mary's grave if it should be on fire. As for how long this one will last we neither know nor care, resigned in both our misery and mirth. We're under no illusion here. We have no cause to be of cheer. Her father's memory is too near. It's different Tudor, different year, and who knows what brute dreams of Empire here are given birth?

BOTH: God keep us should the sleepless giant of England cease to rest, embroiling us in foreign wars anew, where we'll end up with bleeding lances through our bleeding chest, but this is England. What's a man to do?

GREEN: A bloody star now rises in the west. At last the burning issue is addressed.

QUEEN: My sanguine light, of stellar magnitude. Forgive me, father, if I do intrude.

DEE: Now am I lost in recollection's trance, an old man in his memories regressed. Did I embrace her? Did we ever dance?

GREEN: At last the burning issue is addressed.

DEE: Now am I lost. Bright recall fades to gloom, and so ends my nostalgic interlude. I hear my daughter in another room...

QUEEN: Forgive me, father, if I do intrude. Forgive me, father, if I do intrude...

The Seventeenth Century

JESUITS:

Paranoid fantasies & strange realities

by SEAN WALSH

They were the devils of the seventeenth century: an order of cunning, utterly single-minded Catholics, who, with military discipline and psychotic dedication, gave themselves to the overthrow of legitimate government. The age begins, more or less, with their agents burned for a part in Britain's finest terror plot; a hundred years later they've been accused of assassinations, practising the dark arts, inventing sodomy, brainwashing young men, venerating the breast milk of the Virgin Mary, starting the Great Fire of London, impregnating the queen consort and worshipping Chinese ghosts. They were the Society of Jesus, better known as the Jesuits.

The order was founded by Ignatius Loyola, a Basque soldier who knew something of the world and women: as the man said, 'Up to my six-and-twentieth year I was entirely given to the vanities of this world'.[1] After the siege of Pamplona in 1521, however, Loyola found himself crippled and captured. A shattered leg, an amputated foot and weeks stretched on a surgical rack changed his life. He had a grand Damascene vision: an order of soldier-saints, ready to go out and push back the Protestant tsunami overwhelming Northern Europe

1. In 1515, before his conversion, a document from the Pamplona correctional court describes Loyola – 5′2″, incidentally – as 'cunning, violent and vindictive'.

The martyrdom of Jesuits in Japan, c.1597

and fight for a pure Catholic continent obedient to the Pope. After a brutally ascetic retreat at Manresa – sleep deprivation, hunger and hallucinations[2] – he became a peripatetic religious lunatic, wandering round Paris, Rome, Jerusalem, with a fake foot and stories of visions, a peculiar figure who'd duel anyone disputing the virginity of Mary.[3] He'd find converts to take up sackcloth and fasting, then lose them again. The Inquisition held him for a while: they thought he was one of the *Alumbrados*, or Illuminati, an inspired and heretical Spanish sect rumoured to be passionately promiscuous. But as he became firmer and smarter, The Society of Jesus began to take shape.

The order produced extraordinary figures over the course of

---

2. 'He could not make out very clearly what the thing was, but somehow it appeared to have the form of a serpent. It was bright, with objects that shone like eyes, although they were not eyes. He found great delight and consolation in looking at this thing.'

3. Loyola was a keen reader of those romances that would give us *Don Quixote*.

the sixteenth and seventeenth centuries: brave, clever and ingenious men whose dedication put them in places of power and expanded the empire of knowledge. That, of course, upset people. What follows will be a mixture of rumour, hearsay and the fantasies of a paranoiac century; nevertheless there are some truths at the bottom of all this, and truths that do credit to the order. The Jesuits offered counsel and knowledge to the rulers of Europe; and they went further into places where a man might end up scalped, seethed or crucified than any had gone before.

A Lump of wax

Jesuits were trained to have powerful minds. Loyola developed the Spiritual Exercises, visualisation training designed to strengthen and discipline the mind and will. The exercises relied on an exhaustive sensuous imagining of the Christian experience: what did the road to Calvary look like? Was there a slope? What would it feel like to pick up a chisel from Joseph's carpentry bench? You are in hell. Taste the tears of the damned and smell the rot of their flesh. Meditate; visualise; make it all concrete.

The inculcation of an insane obedience was the purpose of much of this training. In the words of the Exercises, 'I must let myself be led and moved as a lump of wax lets itself be kneaded, must order myself as a dead man without will or judgement.' The Jesuit-paranoiacs, though, said the training didn't end there. Take the testimony of Pierre Barrière, sent by the order, as the conspiracists believed, to undertake a hit on Henri IV of France. He admitted to studying at the College of Jesuits, and further he claimed to have seen 'the Chamber of Meditations, into which the Jesuites carry their greatest Sinners, to shew 'em several dreadful Portraitures of Devils, under various Figures, thereby Pretending to reduce 'em to a better Life, or rather to dislocate and disorder their minds, and prepare them by terrible Visions for some bloody Undertaking'.[4] Elsewhere it is claimed that an initiation

Dreadful Portraitures of Devils

4. *The Art of Assassinating Kings Taught Louis XIV. & James II. By the Jesuites*, [anon], (London, 1696), p. 79.

test involved darkened rooms, members of the order wearing horrific devil costumes and screaming from the murk at a new candidate. It is a peculiar cross between a provincial ghost train and a first reaching for behaviourist brain-washing mechanics, an entangling of science-fear and religion that is often a feature of the anti-Jesuit fantasia.

Some argued that the chamber of meditation, the devil costumes, all the psy-ops, were simply a test; that any young Jesuit terrified by this was simply destined to be a squaddie in the Jesuit army, but a young man unflustered by the fake devils would be introduced to the real work of the order, 'magick'. The young Jesuit who does not flinch will have propounded to them the 900 propositions of 'Picus, Earl of Mirandula', and they will then be introduced to the canon of magical writings: Trithemius, Cornelius Agrippa, Theophrastus, 'the *Steganographia* of I know not what abbott',[5] as well as studying the true meanings of the works of Saints Paul and John, and coming to admire Jesus's conjuring prowess.

This reputation for black magic haunted the order. In 1680s England, Father Edward Petre, spiritual advisor to James II, was believed to be consorting with devils; he was also believed to be the true father of James's son.[6] Petre had done little to deserve popular hatred and suspicion; his being a Jesuit was enough.

5. Mirandula is Pico Della Mirandola, humanist scholar and Platonic philosopher; his works laid the foundation for much in the later mystical and magical traditions; the *Steganographia* is a cryptological-magical work by the just-mentioned Trithemius. This is taken from a 1679 Popish Plot pamphlet, worked up from earlier sources, which claims to be *The Memoires of Mr James Wadswort, A Jesuit that Recanted*; but at no point do Wadswort's actual memoirs, *The English Spanish Pilgrime* (London, 1630), or his more discursive sequel, *Further Observations of the English Spanish Pilgrime* (London, 1630) spend ten pages raging against the supposed Jesuit belief that the breast milk of Mary is as spiritually efficacious as the blood of Christ.

6. The birth of this son – later James III to some, but The Old Pretender to most – was one cause of James's deposition from the throne in the Glorious Revolution of 1688.

Some device must be found out…

Why all the brainwashing? To what end the magic? Obvious questions with a simple answer: power and politics. The Jesuits wanted a Catholic Europe, with the order somewhere close to the centre. A typical mid-century scenario will begin with an explanation of how the Jesuits wish that 'some device must be found out, that the Duke of Bavaria may fall foul upon the Elector Palatine, or upon the Duke of Wittemberg…', and then explains how the Order plan to manipulate the Landgrave of Hess, the Marquises of Brandenburg and Pomerania, the Kings of Poland and Sweden, the Bishop of Wirtzburg, the Duke of Saxony, Elector of Colen and Duke of Weimar, in order to bring about their goal, which is slightly muddy by the end of this explanation, but most likely does involve the recatholicising of Northern Europe.

There is, as usual, something to this. The Jesuits were expelled from Bohemia, Silesia and Moravia before the Thirty Years War began

in 1618. By 1640, every Catholic ruler in Europe save the Doge of Venice and the King of Poland had a Jesuit confessor privy to their deepest secrets. In 1648, Jan Kasimierz, former Jesuit novice, would come to the throne of Poland. It's easy to see how a seventeenth century man, sizing up the politics of the continent, would think that something was afoot.

Further, all Europe knew that Jesuits believed one thing in particular: that it is perfectly legitimate to overthrow a heretical monarch by any means necessary.[7] While many thought these means were campaigns of classic diplomacy and an insinuation into the places of power, some suspected, and stated loudly, that they used a different sort of tactic: that, in fact, they used poison, delivered by brain-washed agents, to effect regime change.

They were blamed for most major political assassinations. In the sixteenth century, William of Orange was a favourite target of their

7. For example: 'The *jesuites* also teach it to be not only lawfull, but meritorious to lay hands upon the *Lords Annoynted*, and to murther hereticke Kings[…]' *Heresiography*, [Ephraim Paget] (London, 1645), p. 128.

attempts: one Jáuregui attempted to shoot him down in 1581, and after the attempt was found to be carrying a green wax candle with a cross on the base and a medal of the Virgin: proof enough for some that the Jesuits were behind this. When Balthazar Gérard succeeded in killing William three years later, he confessed that 'he liv'd privately with a *Jesuite*, whose Name he knew not, only that he was a Red hair'd man, Regent of the college of *Treves*.'[8] They'd also sent Edward Squire, a stablehand-turned-sailor imprisoned in Spain after being captured during Drake's final voyage, to kill Elizabeth I by poisoning the pommel of her horse's saddle.[9]

There were attempts on Henri IV of France at the start of the next century. Pierre Barrière, who informed us of the hell-chamber of the order, failed, but the Jesuits didn't give up. Next they sent John Châtel, another of their trainees, who stabbed Henri in the mouth, but again failed to kill him.

Jesuitical assassination plans were at the heart of the Popish Plot, one of England's greatest bouts of paranoia-hysteria. In brief, one Titus Oates, a pathological liar and clinical narcissist of the first water, claimed that he had discovered a Jesuit plot,[10] the complexity of which defies easy summary. The main points included the murder of the 'black bastard', Charles II, either by poison or stabbing, the assassin to

8. The accounts of assassination attempts are most fully recapped in *The Art of Assassinating Kings*. The attempt on Elizabeth I is fully chronicled in the *Authentic Memoirs of That Exquisitely Villainous Jesuit, Father Richard Walpole*, (London, MDCXXXIII)

9. The poisoned portraits and shirts of Jacobean drama were not perhaps so lunatic. John, King of Castile, had his boots poisoned by a Turk. Pope Clement VII met his end through the fumes of a poisoned candle carried before him in a procession. Truly a Golden Age of poisoners, graced by assassins like the remarkable Blessis, who claimed to be able to kill not only by poison, but by an arrangement of mirrors.

10. Oates claimed the Dominicans and Benedictines had also been approached for help. The latter promised the plotters £6,000; the former, sadly, had nothing they could spare. *Titus Oates*, Jane Lane, (Andrew Dakers; London, 1949) remains the fullest account of this peculiar figure.

More Jesuit martyrs in Japan, c.1597

receive around £10,000 and 300,000 masses for the health of his soul; the murder of his brother James, if he would not do the Jesuits' bidding; the fomenting of rebellions in Scotland, Ireland and Holland; and a concerted campaign of seditious sermons and tracts, some of which were to be delivered by Jesuits disguised as Dissenting ministers. His testimony included various other titbits on the Jesuits: he claimed to have heard an account of how, exactly, one Father Strange had started the Great Fire of London, but had failed to follow through on the plan of cutting every Protestant throat in the city in the aftermath.

As many shapes as Proteus

The story of the plot caught fire because people already believed that Jesuits were like that. They had a reputation for disguise: the Jesuit had 'as many shapes as Proteus had, and as many names as a Welshman'. How else to be everywhere, to watch without being seen? Their institutions had dressing-up rooms, according to some, and each Jesuit had several sets of costumes: soldier, sailor, merchant, whatever was necessary to infiltrate. There were also several sets of female clothes in these wardrobes, but they were only kept so Jesuit porters could lure in young women, who were to be used in the orgiastic rites taking place in the cellars.

As is the way of the order, you dismiss something, but then read a story about the protestant professor of Theology, Lorenz Nicolai, who preached in Stockholm during the reign of John III; he would summarise, clearly and effectively, Catholic attacks on Protestantism, then rebut them pathetically. King John entered the dispute at one lecture, with further weak arguments for the national religion. Classic Jesuit black ops: Nicolai was a Jesuit and the King, who'd come round to Catholicism, was in on the scheme.[11] Or how about the rumoured conversion strategy, where two Jesuits 'clad in gorgeous white' came to the bedside of Henry Fairfax with 'two good Disciplines in their hand' (a discpline's a whip) and beat him senseless, telling him in Latin that they were angels sent from the Virgin Mary to punish him for rejecting the Society of Jesus?[12]

Classic Jesuit black ops

How could an order of Catholic shapeshifters be trusted? Disguise and lies were taken as their two chief arts, though they of course would not call their lies 'lies'. They called them 'equivocation', and a remarkable treatise explained its principles. When a magistrate asks you if you swear to tell the truth, pull out a Latin answer: 'Juro', I swear; but say 'Uro', I sweat, which sounds just the same, and you won't be under oath.[13] Someone asks you if a priest they're hunting came this way? Say 'he came not this way' while discreetly pointing up

11. *The Power and Seceret of the Jesuits*, René Fülöp Miller (London, 1930).

12. They do have a talent for theatre: in the 1580s they performed public exorcisms in Buckinghamshire in front of crowds of hundreds, expelling demons such as Maho, Lustie Husse-Cap, and Hiaclito ('Prince & Monarche of the World') by means of the bloody girdle and bones of Edmund Campion, a Jesuit executed/martyred in 1581.

13. *A Treatise on Equivocation, [anon.]*, David Jardine, ed. (Longman, Brown, Green and Longmans; London, 1851).

your sleeve. It's true: no priest has climbed up your sleeve. A strange document, the treatise, with its explanations of why one can say in good conscience 'I will give you one hundred pounds', just as long as you silently add the rider 'if I find it in the street tomorrow'. It's a linguistic and semantic mare's nest of withheld propositions, secret signifieds, with an ugly divorce between intention and apprehension, and, all in all, is rather like spending time in the mind of a sociopath or scheming, fantasising child.

ANOTHER PART OF THE WORLD

There were more disguises. Those Priests who went on missions to India passed as Yogi and Brahmin, since this, they believed, was the only way to get the people to listen to you. It was much the same story in China: there they took up the head-gear of the Confucian literati and Catholic doctrine became the 'Heavenly Lord teaching'; God the Father picked up the names of the old Chinese gods: Shangdi ('Sovereign on high') sometimes; sometimes Tianzhu ('Lord of Heaven'); sometimes Shangzunzhe ('supremely honoured one'); sometimes Tiandi ('Sovereign of heaven'). They adopted Chinese names, too, Father Matteo Ricci, for instance, became Li Ma-teu and took up Buddhist robes.

These innovations horrified Catholics in the west, and in the great Chinese Rites controversy were used to discredit the order; Pope Innocent X banned the use of these titles. They had gone too far for Rome: members of the order were attending rites of ancestor worship – strips of paper burnt and given to the wind; food left out for the departed souls.[14]

They didn't go entirely native, though, fighting hard against Buddhism. How could it be right? As they explained, its homeland, India, 'is a small place, and not to be considered a nation of the highest standing'. It is easy to see that all those doctrines of emptiness and non-

14. *The Taiping Heavenly Kingdom*, Thomas H Reilly (University of Washington Press; Seattle and London, 2004).

being, the matter at the heart of Dao and Buddhism, do not make sense in the vigorous world of the Church militant.

However, their flexibility was a huge advantage as they tried to expand the Catholic empire East: while Dominicans patiently explained that all the Daoist-Buddhist-Confucians were going to hell, the Jesuits instead cast themselves as sages, and created marvels for the Emperor – complex clocks, intricate fountains, accurate orreries – to persuade the Chinese that this was a religion with power and knowledge worth cultivating. It culminated, perhaps, on the day when the Emperor K'ien-Lung met a lion in his garden; Brother Thibault, a watchmaker of some ingenuity, had turned his hand to the creation of automata.

Elsewhere, Jesuit trickery looked like old-fashioned lies and charlatanry. Stories of heinous misdeeds were coming out of Georgia, for instance, a part of the world that was alien to the West.[15] The Georgians had their own ancient branch of Christianity, so, to Jesuit eyes, they needed converting, and the country's ongoing conflict with Persia provided an ideal opportunity. The Queen Mother, Ketaban, had been captured after the Persian pillage of Cachetia in 1614; she was offered the chance to convert to the Persian religion, but, after the fashion of Christian heroines, refused; the Persian King, after the fashion of heathen villains, boiled her alive and threw her corpse 'upon the bare ground'.

Meanwhile, a band of Jesuits who were fruitlessly trying to convert the Persians decided to attempt Georgia instead, and, hearing the story of Ketaban's death, thought that her corpse would be the ideal prop for their campaign. They were unable, however, to locate it, so instead removed the head from a random carcass, anointed it, wrapped it up and went to visit King Teimurases, claiming to have the head of his mother. Refusing all rewards for their retrieval of her remains, they simply asked for a house where they could tend to this sacred relic.

---

15. Our source, *A Letter Relating the Martyrdome of Keteban, Mother of Teimurases, Prince of the Georgians & withall a notable Imposture of the Iesuites upon that occasion*, [Gregorius of Antioch] (Oxford, 1633), takes time to explain that the Georgians are 'a kind of Christians that live in another part of the world' (A2r).

Eighteenth century illustration of the flying boat, lifted by vacuum spheres of thinly beaten copper, imagined in the 1670 Prodromo of Lana Terzi SJ

Easily granted, of course, and the Jesuits set up shop. Large crowds gathered, miracles started to happen and the Brothers overcame their qualms about accepting gifts.

Ketaban's real body, however, had been recovered by her maid, Moachla, and when news reached Persia of the Georgian miracle head, she suggested to her captors that this wasn't really on. The Persian King gamely set up a truce with Georgia, and both sides tried to clear up the confusion; Ketaban's corpse was returned, and Teimurases was upset that some priests had set up a small fraudulent industry based around his mother's fake remains. The Jesuits vanish from the court and country shortly afterwards.

Money was believed to be the great motivator for Jesuit missions abroad, and the order were imagined to have wealth to shame Croesus. In fact, it was reputed that they kept their gold under the altar, so that their masses become a sacrifice to the God Mammon (it is unclear whether the gold was stored in the same vaults within which they had their orgies).[16]

The wealth came, it was believed, from their own little secular empire somewhere in South America, which pumped out gold to fund the fantastic ambition of the order. There were rumours of a Jesuit King called Nicholas who minted coins bearing his image. This is nonsense, of course, though the truth is more peculiar: they did have a secular empire in South America, the Jesuit Republic of Paraguay, which they managed to found off the back of a neat financial deal with Philip III of Spain, but this was not much of a goldmine, nor a giant jungle seminary. Rather it was like a country-sized conservatory, in which the newly converted tribespeople spent much of their time singing or learning to sing. Reports claimed that every Indian village had 'Four trumpeters, three good lutanists, four organists, as well as reed-pipe players, bassoonists and singers'.[17] While they forbade their subjects to learn Spanish or Portuguese, these Indians were at least saved from slavery and slaughter.

The Jesuit Republic of Paraguay

THESE ARE NOT IGNORANT SOTTS...

The Jesuits weren't idle travellers: they took careful note of the language and customs of the nations in which they proselytized. They recorded everything, accumulated information, became effective early anthropologists and linguists. They were *smart.*

Some of the fear and fog that surrounds them comes from this fact: 'These are not ignorant Sotts like the Anabaptists and others, educated and brought up in all manner of humane learning, and so

16. We have barely touched on Jesuits and sex. A curious topic: it is simultaneously believed that a) they are great seducers, to be found in Ladies' bedchambers, often hiding beneath the sheets and b) they invented sodomy and lead young men into depravity.

17. German sources, cited in *Power and Secrets of the Jesuits*, p287. The musical kingdom survives into the nineteenth century.

P. ATHANASIVS KIRCHERVS FVLDENSIS

able to do more mischief.'[18] Their mechanical ingenuity was obvious; we have already encountered the mechanical lion constructed for the Chinese Emperor; that was followed by Father Thibault building a tiger. Their authors turned out myriad volumes on the machines which fascinated the age – automata, fountains, microscopes, flying machines.[19] One of their reputed tools for the conversion of impressionable young men was a mechanical Virgin Mary which would lactate on Christmas morning.[20]

There was something terrifying about this Jesuit science, an accumulation of vast amounts of information with only a fuzzy link to empirical truth; it's a dark, disconnected sibling of the Enlightenment proper. Men of the time didn't trust the impulse:

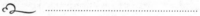

18. *Heresiography*, p128. The Anabaptists were the most radical of radicals, believing all things pure to the saved. They effectively turned the city of Münster into an anarchist commune before an extremely violent suppression.

19. The Jesuits were scientifically hamstrung: they were obliged to use a Ptolemaic version of the cosmos and tried to reconcile the new science to Aristotle. It meant mini-Kirchers like Caspar Schott and Lana Terzi could do little more than be anthologists, confusing fact and discovery with anecdote (a scorpion was generated in an Italian's brain because he had smelled too much basil) and folk science (lions are scared of cockerels because of tiny seeds that come from the birds' eyes).

20. *The Jesuits Discovered* (1652), cited in *The Jesuits*, Jonathan Wright (Harpercollins; London, 2004).

> *The truth is, this Jesuit [Athanasius Kircher], as generally most of his order, haue a great ambition to be thought the great learned men of ye world; & to that end write greate volumes on all subjects, wth gay pictures and diagrammes to sett them forth, for ostentation [...] But enough of those Mountebankes.*[21]

It would seem that in this world, where natural philosophy drifts into esoteric antiquarianism, and mechanical ingenuity sits alongside the decryption of abraxas jewels, the Jesuits are again far from the single truth of the Roman Catholic religion; but if these researches can show all religions are connected, that there is a single truth behind all things, that Christ's divinity is cyphered in the Egyptian teachings, then why not take up the Chinese names of God or the dress of a yogi?

The decryption of abraxus jewels

THE END

In the end, they created the creatures that would destroy them. Voltaire and Diderot, heroes of Enlightenment, were both educated by Jesuits, and the latter in particular had a deep hatred of the order. That the age of reason found the Jesuits egregiously troublesome is understandable; they were near kin. Like the Enlightenment, they also believed in the perfection of man; that the human spirit, however tainted by sloth, luxury and sin, could work – and work it would most definitely be, discipline and devotion demanded – towards a practical kind of purity. They both believed in a kind of Kingdom of Heaven on Earth, but where reason, liberty and truth were the watchwords of one, the other could only assent to submission, unity and faith.

The Philosophes, Ilustrados and Illuministi of the continent have their way: the order is expelled from most of Catholic Europe

21. British Library, London MS. Landsdowne 841, fol 33v. Cited p.300, 'Private and Public Knowledge: Kircher, Esotericism, and the Republic of Letters', Noel Malcolm, in *Athanasius Kircher: The Last Man Who Knew Everything*, Paula Findlen, ed. (Routledge; London and New York, 2004).

over the course of the eighteenth century and finally has its charter revoked in 1773. It survives underground, and is granted legitimacy again forty years later; however, there was a long history of expulsions and public vitriol to follow.

The Jesuit is still a figure to capture the imagination of writers – the shadow history and secret technologies of the order that run through Pynchon's 1997 novel *Mason & Dixon* offer one recent example – but they have lost the awful glamour of their sinister heyday, when the theologies and terror of the bloody and divisive wars that roiled Europe shook into life an imaginary sect of torturers and mechanics and stage-play poisoners, guarding their Piranesan carceri where the young of men of Europe were turned into regicidal automata.

The Jesuits remain an order of scholars, teachers and missionaries, respected, largely, around the world. They have a past, though: and it would be pleasing to believe that all the relics are around somewhere, that hidden in the fornices deep under the Gesu are the mechanical animals of Thibault, the pretend head of Queen Ketaban and the apotropaic bones of Campion; it would form a kind of museum to the devout politics and science of a counterfactual Catholic Empire, a doppelgänger Europe that can only exist in the imagination.

An Afterlife in ANOTHER PLACE

by STEVE MOORE

In his *Lives and Opinions of Eminent Philosophers,* written in the earlier half of the third century CE, Diogenes Laertius (of whom nothing is known, except that he followed the Epicurean school of philosophy and wrote very bad poetry) tells a curious tale of a young man called Epimenides who, apparently, lived c.600 BCE. Epimenides was a native of Crete who was one day sent into the country by his father, in search of a missing sheep. At noon, he turned aside and went to sleep in a cave, after which he didn't wake up for another 57 years. Thinking he'd only taken a short nap, he then went in search of the sheep, failed to find it and returned to the family farm. However, everything was different and a new owner had taken possession, so he returned to his home in the town, where he found much the same situation. No one there knew who he was, and it was only when he discovered his younger brother, now an old man, that he realised what had happened.[1]

Before we look at this story in a little more detail, there are a few other items from Diogenes Laertius' biography that are worth mentioning, for Epimenides became famous,

1. Diogenes Laertius, Vol. 1, pp. 115-121.

and is often included in lists of 'The Seven Sages of Greece'. When Athens was struck by plague in the period of the 46th Olympiad (595-592 BCE), Epimenides was summoned to the city to purify it. This he did by gathering a group of sheep, some black, some white, and letting them wander where they would. They were followed, and wherever each sheep lay down a sacrifice was offered to the local divinity. This story appears to explain why there were a number of stone altars in the area without the name of a divinity on them: they were thought to commemorate these sacrifices. The plague was abated, and Epimenides returned to Crete, where he died shortly afterwards. Various theological works and oracles were attributed to him in later days, as is the famous paradox 'All Cretans are liars (says Epimenides the Cretan).'

So, what are we to make of this? The first thing that should be said is that Diogenes Laertius' declared source for the story is Theopompus of Chios, a fourth century BCE historian who was notorious, even in antiquity, for his liking for strange and unlikely tales. Even so, while Diogenes Laertius gives us the fullest account, there are a number of other sources and, indeed, the 'Sleep of Epimenides' became proverbial. One problem, however, is that most of those sources are wildly at variance with one another beyond the basic element of the prolonged sleep.

Apollonius Dyscolus (second century CE), also allegedly quoting Theopompus, has Epimenides setting off for the country with a flock of sheep, and then losing one, rather than simply going off in search of a single beast.[2] Maximus Tyrius (also of the second century CE) places the sleep in the cave of Dictaean Zeus, a famous Cretan sanctuary high on Mount Dictae.[3] Elsewhere, while his father is variously named, all agree that Epimenides was Cretan, though in some sources he is said to come from Knossos, in others Phaestos. His age at death is variously given as 154, 157 or 299, while Plato's *Laws*, written in the early fourth century BCE, places his arrival in Athens not in

2. Apollonius Dyscolus, pp. 35-39.

3. Maximus Tyrius, p. 221.

the 590s BCE, but 'ten years before the Persian Invasion', c.500 BCE.[4] Worse, the length of his sleep is variously given. The most popular periods are 40 years (a number that will have some significance later on) and 57 years; but we also hear of 47, 50, 57 and 60 year naps.

Given this confusion, one has to ask whether Epimenides actually lived at all. This suspicion may increase when we actually look at his name, which would appear to derive from the Greek word *epimeno*, 'to abide still, to continue, to await', in turn deriving from *meno*, 'to abide, to linger, to continue, to be lasting, to await' ... particularly apt etymologies when we consider Epimenides' main claim to fame. There would seem to be two major possibilities here. First, that Epimenides was a real person, and that the legend has been constructed around him on the basis of the meaning of his name; secondly, that Epimenides may be more of a figurehead than a real person. But if he is more of an emblem than a historical figure, what exactly does he represent?

It's long been realised that noon is a symbolically 'timeless' moment: the sun is neither rising nor declining and, being directly overhead, casts little or no shadow. By entering the cave at noon, Epimenides effectively moves outside of time. Similarly, the excessive length of his sleep may not be intended to be taken literally, especially given the extreme variability of its duration in the source material. In the same way that the word *eternity* can be taken both to mean infinite duration and absolute timelessness, the sleep of Epimenides may be taken as indicating that he has, once again, stepped out of normal, linear time.

Infinite duration, absolute timelessness

In her recent book, *Caves and the Ancient Greek Mind*, Yulia Ustinova has shown that it was actually a fairly common practice for Greek seekers of wisdom to withdraw into caves or subterranean chambers, in quest of divine revelations. In effect, deep caves served as sensory deprivation chambers, devoid of light and sound, and under those conditions two things commonly occur: the experient develops a strong sense of timelessness, and hallucinations and dreams are

4. Plato, pp. 61-63.

regularly produced in a matter of hours.[5] It has to be noted that Epimenides only gained his reputation as a wise man after his sleep in the cave, not before it; and Maximus Tyrius tells us that while Epimenides was in the cave 'in a profound sleep for many years, he saw the gods, and the offspring of gods, together with Truth and Justice.'[6] This sounds very much like the sort of divine revelation (or hallucination, if you will) obtained through sensory deprivation, and we have tales of a number of other Greek sages seeking revelations in caves and chambers, including Pythagoras, Demosthenes and the Thracian Zalmoxis, as well as a number of lesser personages who carried out similar practices in caves dedicated to the Nymphs.[7]

Food of the nymphs

We're also told that Epimenides ate a special kind of food that he received from the Nymphs, but only in such small quantities that he was never seen to eat. Various recipes for this *alimon* have been preserved, all of which are vegetarian, the ingredients including cheese, honey, various seeds, and so on, and this may refer to the special diets and fasting practices known to have been used by seekers spending their time in caves;[8] it's extremely unlikely, however, that it refers to the use of hallucinogenic drugs, as the Greeks generally believed that dreams and visions were only valid if they were obtained in a state of complete sobriety.

It seems possible, then, that Epimenides was an archetypal

5. Ustinova, *passim*.

6. Maximus Tyrius, p. 221.

7. Ustinova, pp. 177–215.

8. Ustinova, p. 190.

and emblematic figure who represented, writ large, this sort of spiritual practice. Be that as it may, we're less interested here in discovering the "truth" behind the story, than in the story itself; for this has a very interesting afterlife, as we'll see. The reader may instantly think of Washington Irving's tale of *Rip Van Winkle*, but Rip was a mere stripling who only slept for 20 years, and not in a cave either.[9] The afterlife of Epimenides is rather stranger than that ...

Early in the fourth century CE, a Chinese Taoist called Ge Hong wrote a work called *Shenxian zhuan* ('Traditions of Divine Transcendents'). Ge lived from 283-343, and originally came from Jurong in Jiangsi Province, though he later travelled extensively throughout southern China, having opted to stay in the secular world and work in government administration. Numerous works are attributed to him, and the *Shenxian zhuan* is one of the earliest surviving works of Taoist hagiography.

Included in this fascinating collection of biographies is that of a certain Huang Chuping, a story that Ge seems to have taken from the *Lingbao wufu* ('Five Numinous Treasure Talismans'), a work that was near contemporary with Ge's own, but which was compiled from earlier traditions, possibly going back to the Han dynasty (206 BCE–220 CE). Huang, we're told, was a native of Danxi, near the Jinhua Mountain in Zhejiang Province. At the age of 15, he was made to tend sheep by his family. An unidentified Taoist passed by, noticed Huang's goodness, and took him to a cave on Mount Jinhua, where he stayed for more than 40 years. His elder brother, Huang Chuqi, searched for him in vain, until he came across a Taoist diviner in the nearby market. The diviner told him his brother was to be found on Mount Jinhua,

9. Irving, pp. 53-80.

and together they set off and found him. When reunited, Huang Chuqi asked what happened to the sheep. Huang Chuping told him they were on the eastern side of the mountain, but only white rocks were to be seen. Then Huang Chuping cried 'Sheep, get up!' and the white rocks stood up and became thousands of sheep. Afterwards the two brothers continued to practice together for another 5,000 days, eating pine resin and *fuling* fungus, after which they could disappear at will, cast no shadows in sunlight, and had the complexion of youths (i.e., they'd become immortal). Later they returned to their home village, but all their relatives had died, so they left. Eventually Huang Chuping changed his surname to Chi, and so became identified with Chisong zi ('Master Red-Pine'), although this is actually a much older figure who seems to have had a separate existence in the literature before Huang's story appeared.[10]

While some of the details have become garbled, the parallels with the Epimenides story should be obvious here. We have the sheep, the period in the cave of 40 years (corresponding at least to one of the more popular lengths for Epimenides' sleep), the brother, the return to the much-changed village and the obtaining of transcendent wisdom. We also have the special diet, and a curiously parallel tale of sheep and rocks. Where the wanderings of Epimenides' purificatory sheep in Athens were marked by anonymous stone altars, Huang's sheep are actually turned to stone, and then revived afterwards.

Of course, we have to consider the possibility that this could all be a gigantic coincidence; some form or other of the 'long sleep' story turns up not infrequently as a folklore motif, after all. Given that the correspondences between the two stories are actually quite numerous, however, it seems rather more likely that the core of the Epimenides story was transmitted to China, sometime between the fifth century BCE and the third century CE.

This is actually more plausible than one might think. We know that Alexander's Macedonians reached Bactria in the late 4th

10. Campany, pp. 309-311.

century BCE, and established colonies there; the story could then have been transmitted along the Silk Route at some point thereafter. Such a scenario isn't inherently unlikely. The eponymous hero of Tibet's great epic, Gesar of Ling, is also known as Gesar of Khrom; a direct transliteration into Tibetan of 'Caesar of Rome'.[11] And there's also the possibility that the story could have been carried directly from the classical Mediterranean world by sea. For example, Chinese histories record an embassy, arriving by sea in 166 CE, sent by the Roman 'king', An-tun (i.e., Marcus Aurelius Antoninus), with the implication that intercourse was continued thereafter (though the Chinese complained about the amount of jewels the embassy brought in tribute).[12] So at least channels were open by which the Epimenides story could have reached China prior to Ge Hong's time, even if we can't actually prove direct transmission.

Even so, there's still another twist in the tale, which brings it right up to date.

Huang Chuping was worshipped as a Taoist immortal in the area around Mount Jinhua, with temples established possibly as early as the Jin dynasty (265-420 CE). This worship, which never spread beyond the Jinhua area, continued until the seventeenth century and then, apparently, died out. He was, though, to make a remarkable comeback toward the end of the nineteenth century, in a completely different location, a long way to the south.[13]

Leung Yan Ngam was the son of a dealer in medicinal herbs, who was born in 1861 at Rengang village, not far from Guangzhou

11. Snellgrove & Richardson, p. 49.

12. Hirth, p. 42.

13. Lang & Ragvald, *passim*. The final section of this article is largely dependent on Lang & Ragvald's history of Wong Tai Sin.

(Canton). He grew up steeped in medicinal lore and Taoist practices, and in his early twenties joined the Customs Service, where he remained for 15 years. However, in 1894 there was an epidemic of bubonic plague in Guangzhou, with at least 20,000 dead within a few months. As the cause of the plague was not yet understood, people naturally turned to the gods.

Spirit writing

One method of consulting the gods, especially among the aristocracy, was by 'spirit-writing' (*fuji*). This is a form of automatic writing where the medium uses either a bamboo stylus or a brush, sometimes attached to a hoop. The brush, of course, writes on paper; the stylus (which is rather more common) writes in a tray of sand, which is smoothed after each Chinese character has been written and recorded. Leung and his friends formed a spirit-writing circle in Guangzhou, and were particularly impressed by the messages and medical prescriptions transmitted by a Taoist immortal called Wong Cho-ping … the Cantonese pronunciation of Huang Chuping.

There seems to be no reason to suppose that Leung had any prior affinity with Wong Cho-ping, though being a practising Taoist he would almost certainly have had access to Ge Hong's *Shenxian zhuan*, or one of the epitomes or encyclopaedias deriving from it. By spirit-writing, Wong dictated an autobiography which is remarkably similar to Ge Hong's account, except that it's in the first person and contains a few more homely details. Readers may decide for themselves whether Leung was either consciously or subconsciously aware of Ge Hong's account as he wielded the *fuji*, or whether the immortal's autobiography is a remarkable confirmation of the original tale. All that really matters here is that, in a time of plague, Wong Cho-ping re-emerged into public consciousness and began dictating medical prescriptions. As the section of Epimenides' story about his cure of the Athenian plague doesn't seem to have carried over fully into the Ge Hong account, this is a rather remarkable coincidence.

The rest of the tale can be briefly told. In 1899, Leung and his associates established a temple to Wong, now known as the 'Great Immortal Wong', Wong Tai Sin (Huang Daxian), not far from

Guangzhou. This was followed by another in Rengang, Leung's place of birth, and then in 1915, Leung moved to Hong Kong to escape the chaos of post-revolutionary China. There he established another temple (*above*) to Wong Tai Sin in 1921, at a location in Kowloon that had been prescribed by Wong Tai Sin via *fuji*, before dying shortly after it opened. The temple has survived Japanese occupation, colonial interference, and the transfer of sovereignty to the People's Republic, and is now one of the largest and most popular places of worship in Hong Kong.

Fuji is no longer practiced at the temple, although thousands visit to pray and consult the 'fortune-sticks' (*qiu qian*), where a numbered stick is shaken from a small drum, the number referring to one of a hundred divinatory poems. Such are the numbers of visitors that those in difficulty can take their messages to one of up to a hundred fortune-interpreters plying their trade in booths in the temple grounds, and the temple raises thousands of dollars each year for charity. The surrounding area of Kowloon is now known as Wong Tai Sin, as is the nearest underground railway station, a somewhat ironic turn of events, considering Wong's association with caves.

And if that doesn't seem enough of a claim to fame, 1986 saw Hong Kong's TVB channel produce a lengthy drama series about the (largely non-canonical) life of Wong Cho-ping, while 1992 brought the movie, *The Legend of Wong Tai Sin*, an entertaining piece of popular hagiography starring local actor Lam Ching-ying (1952-1997), which locates Wong Tai Sin firmly in the slightly-pantomimic pantheon of Taoist/Buddhist folk mythology. The temple, moreover, has now joined the internet age, and has its own website offering, among things, an extremely slow-loading on-line prayer facility.[14] Sometimes it seems to take, well, 40 years or more.

All of which, of course, is a very long way from an uncertainly-identified cave in Crete, at an uncertain period around the sixth century BCE. But what a very strange trip it's been…

BIBLIOGRAPHY

APOLLONIUS DYSCOLUS. *Historiae*. (Ed. Guilielmi Xylandri & Joannis Meursii & Ludovicus Henricus Teucherus). Lipsiae: Bibliopolio Gleditschiano, 1792.

CAMPANY, ROBERT FORD. *To Live as Long as Heaven and Earth*. Berkeley: University of California Press, 2002.

DIOGENES LAERTIUS. *Diogenes Laertius* [Trans. RD Hicks]. Cambridge, MA & London: Harvard/Heinemann, 1925.

HIRTH, F. *China and the Roman Orient* (1885). Rpt. Chicago: Ares Publishers Inc, 1975.

IRVING, WASHINGTON. *The Sketchbook of Geoffrey Crayon, Gent.* (1863). Rpt. Philadelphia: JB Lippincott & Co., 1875.

LANG, GRAEME & LARS RAGVALD. *The Rise of a Refugee God*. Hong Kong: Oxford University Press, 1993.

MAXIMUS TYRIUS. *The Dissertations of Maximus Tyrius* [Trans. Thomas Taylor] (1805). Rpt. Frome: Prometheus Trust, 1994.

PLATO: *Plato* [Trans. RG Bury]. Cambridge, MA & London: Harvard/Heinemann, Vol. 9, 1926.

14. Sik Sik Yuen.

Sik Sik Yuen. *www.siksikyuen.org.hk*

Snellgrove, David & Hugh Richardson: *A Cultural History of Tibet* (1968). Boulder, CO. Prajna Press, 1980.

Ustinova, Yulia. *Caves and the Ancient Greek Mind*. Oxford: Oxford University Press, 2009.

Science and Spectacle ❧ *Stories from the*

MEDICAL MUSEUM

Text and photos by
JOANNA EBENSTEIN

In the middle of the entrance to the Museum was a woman who was the cashier, then on one side there was a man's skeleton and the skeleton of a monkey, and on the other side there was a representation of Siamese twins. And in the interior one saw a rather dramatic and terrifying series of anatomical casts in wax which represented the dramas and horrors of syphilis, the dramas, deformations. And all this in the midst of the artificial gaiety of the fair. ❧

PAUL DELVAUX
on the Musée Spitzner[1]

There is nothing more fascinating to me than the secret world of the medical museum. These liminal spaces illustrate – in the most visceral of ways – the permeable boundaries of early science and medicine, combining spectacle and education, the popular and the academic, beauty and horror, theatre and sobriety, popular and professional, sacred and profane, fact and metaphor, eros and thanatos. The museums and their curious denizens – anatomical Venuses, horsemen of the apocalypse, slashed beauties and anatomical Adonises – are tangible artifacts of a worldview in which the disciplines once mingled with intriguing narrative promiscuity. Here magic and science, superstition and positivism, body

1. Ronald Alley, *Catalogue of the Tate Gallery's Collection of Modern Art other than Works by British Artists*, Tate Gallery and Sotheby Parke-Bernet, London 1981.

Venus endormie *(breathing model). Collection Spitzner : Musée Orfila, Paris. Courtesy Université Paris Descartes*

and soul held equal sway and provided the balance at the heart of the grand inquiry into the mysteries of humanity, and the secrets of the universe.

The professional and academic medical museums have, however, long been shadowed by a more spectacular, less sober cousin – the popular anatomical museum. These museums – in displays that were equal parts fairground midway and sober medical display – exhibited medical models and specimens for a popular audience, with a focus on hygiene, curiosities and anomalies, embryology, sexually transmitted diseases, and the unclothed female body. The divisions between these two institutions – the popular and professional medical museum – were often blurred, and artifacts that began their museological lives in one would often wind up on display in the other.

Sexually transmitted diseases & the unclothed body

Although largely forgotten today, these popular anatomical museums – close cousins of the popular Dime Museum – were a ubiquitous phenomenon of the nineteenth and early twentieth centuries; most major cities throughout Europe and the United States boasted at least one, if not many, such establishments, which were patronised by a broad cross-section of society. Today, artifacts from popular anatomical museums often reside in academic medical museums, their surprising former lives completely undetected.

The displays crowded into a typical popular anatomical museum might seem an odd mix to the contemporary viewer. Public hygiene and anatomical knowledge were popular themes, and museums typically featured displays about embryological development, waxworks of distressed genitalia riddled with sexually transmitted diseases, models and skull collections depicting racial science as it was then understood, and medical and anatomical curiosities of all sorts. Typically, the centerpiece was a full-length recumbent (and often nude) extremely lifelike female wax figure called an Anatomical Venus, Parisian Venus, Florentine Venus, or a Sleeping Beauty. Her role was to act as both a lure to the possible visitor and as a promise of the revelation of the secrets of the female body. Lectures would be given on the premises, and 'ladies nights' were held so that the gentler sex could learn about the mysteries of anatomical knowledge without the presence of gentlemen.

Counter-balancing the ladies' nights was a sort of science-age Chamber of Horrors: these spaces, often open to 'gentlemen only', were filled with horrifyingly graphic waxwork depictions of diseased genitals, educating men about the dangers of the excesses of spermatorrhea[2] (excessive ejaculation) and sexual indulgence, serious concerns at a time when syphilis was still a fatal mystery and spermatorrhea an ardently

2. Spermatorrhea was regarded as a real and terrifying medical disorder in the nineteenth century, caused by over indulgence of the sexual appetite and onanism. Its symptoms included, as a 1895 medical guide describes, 'loss of nervous energy, dull-ness of the mental faculties, and delight in obscene stories... the face bloated and pale, and the disposition is fretful and irritable; the appetite is capricious... pains in the chest, wakefulness, and during the night lascivious thoughts and desires. The relish for play or labor is gone, and a growing distaste for business is apparent... and the face becomes blotched and animal-like in its expression. The victim is careless of his personal appearance, not unscrupulously neat, and not unfrequently a rank odor exhales from the body.' (*Pierce's The People's Common Sense Medical Adviser in Plain English; or, Medicine Simplified*, 1895, Buffalo, New York.

Femme à barbe *(real skin). Musée Orfila, Paris. Courtesy Université Paris Descartes*

feared phantom. Some museums even provided a 'doctor' on the premises who was on hand (for an additional fee, of course) to provide counsel and prescribe patent medications, usually with a mercury base, to gentlemen worried that their own 'night with Venus' might, as the popular maxim warned, have led to 'a lifetime with Mercury'.

The fabled Musées d'Anatomie Delmas-Orfila-Rouviere or, as it is usually referred to, the Musée Orfila, of Paris, France, is a perfect example of just such a collection. Combining enlightenment restraint with frank titillation, this collection is a wonderful hodge-podge of amazing objects amassed over several centuries, with provenances ranging from eighteenth-century private anatomical curiosity cabinets to popular anatomical museums to the collections of refined gentleman doctors. A few of the amazing things you will find here: a breathing, full length wax Venus, called 'The Sleeping Beauty' (see page 292); a nineteenth-century collection of criminal, ethnic, and comparative anatomical brain casts; skulls from asylums for the mentally ill; a wax model of the Hottentot Venus; a life-sized wax model of the conjoined Tocci Twins; a full-length wax Caesarian section attended to by phantom floating gentleman hands; crumbling mummies; a dizzying array of venereal waxes; a display illustrating comparative female genitals before and after defloration; handsome be-coiffed women undergoing terrifying surgeries; a profusion of human preparations,

Phantom floating gentleman hands

bottled and wax-injected; a poignant 'femme à barbe' under a bell jar (*previous page*). All these, and many more, are housed in a darkened, almost inaccessible gallery on the eighth floor of a Parisian university, with a sense of scale and constrained exuberance more appropriate to a surrealistic World's Fair pavilion than a museum.

The collection had its genesis in an anatomical cabinet assembled and established in 1794 by the infamous anatomical artist Honoré Fragonard – cousin of the well known rococo painter Jean-Honoré Fragonard. Honoré was quite different to his better-known painter-of-pastel-romps-of-the-aristocracy cousin, and his work had a somewhat more macabre bent, at least to the contemporary eye: in the styling of allegorical tableaux, Honoré Fragonard used actual flayed and preserved human bodies as his medium.[3] Most of his surviving works – such as his 'Horseman of the Apocalypse', 'Human foetuses dancing a jig' and 'The Man with a Mandible' (inspired by Samson attacking the Philistines with an ass's jaw) – are still on display at the Musée Fragonard d'Alfort outside of Paris, while an assortment of other pieces from his vast oeuvre are housed in medical museums around the world.

Over the years, the Musée Orfila vastly expanded its holdings under the directorship of various keepers, each adding important and spectacular collections, including a collection of brain casts of birds, mammals, children, criminals, and representatives of various races modelled by Paul Broca; specimens displaying the comparative anatomy of reptiles and birds; casts of the heads of criminals executed during the nineteenth century; and, perhaps most notably, a beautifully restored (and remarkably intact) set of objects once displayed in the Grand Musée Anatomique Ethnologique du Dr. P Spitzner, or the Musée Spitzner, one of the best known and cited popular anatomical museums of the nineteenth century.

3. 'Bodyworlds' impresario and self-styled artist/anatomist Gunther von Hagens explicitly refers to Fragonard as his inspiration and pays homage with more than one creation.

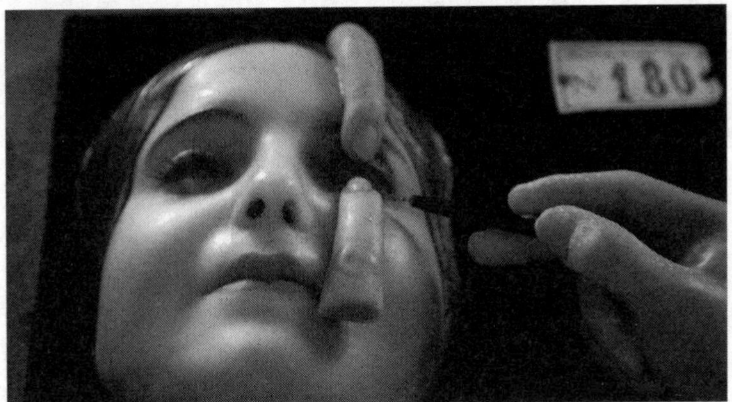

Opération de la cataracte. *Collection Spitzner : Musée Orfila, Paris. Courtesy Université Paris Descarte*

The Musée Spitzner was in many ways a typical popular anatomical museum. Opened in Paris in 1856 by self-styled doctor Pierre Spitzner under the banner 'Science, Art, Progress!', it remained in its original Paris location until the 1880s when, after a devastating fire, it went on the road, travelling the great fairgrounds circuits of France, Britain, Germany, Holland and Belgium until finally closing its doors during World War II. The collection is unique in that it remained a viable business for so long, and that it still exists – as part of the Musée Orfila – in a relatively intact state with many of its remarkable pieces in excellent repair, having recently undergone an expert restoration.

The Spitzner Collection is also special for being the cited inspiration for a number of artists and writers, most notably the surrealist Paul Delvaux, who painted the museum a number of times in works like 'The Musée Spitzner' and 'La Vénus Endormie' (both 1943). In interviews, he repeatedly cited his visits to the museum as being the single greatest influence on his work. The Sleeping Venus was a particular fascination for Delvaux, and it appeared repeatedly as a theme in his work:

> *All my Sleeping Venuses originate there... [They are] an exact transcription of the Sleeping Venus of the Spitzner Museum, but with Greek temples or with models – anything you like. It is different, but the understanding is the same.*[4]

Until late 2009, the wonders recounted by Delvaux and other visitors to this enchanted collection were still on view, if extremely difficult to access, on the eighth floor of the Faculty of Medicine, René Descartes University, in the heart of Paris, where they had resided since the 1950s. The Reclining Venus – then in the curators' office in the shadow of the gorgeously restored full-length Tocci Twins and a smattering of diseased genitalia and foetal abnormalities – still breathed at the flick of a switch, looking uncannily like Duchamp's *Étant Donnés* come to mysterious and mesmerizing life.

A walk through the darkened museum would take you face to face with the extremely poised woman enduring a Caesarian section, rows of brain casts, a series of diseased eyes rendered beautifully in wax, a beatific young waxen boy undergoing a tracheotomy, a fashionable Parisian lady having her eye sliced by phantom hands (uncannily like the famous scene in Buñuel and Dalí's *Un Chien Andalou*), a wax man undergoing a surgery for hernia, a wall full of coloured hands behind a skeleton and so, enchantingly, on.

Unfortunately The Musée is now no longer accessible at all. The entire collection has been moved from the museum that housed it since 1953 to unknown basement rooms. This future of this fragile, historic, and remarkable collection is now uncertain.

This article is indebted to the work of scholar Kathryn Hoffman; particularly influential was her essay 'Sleeping Beauties in the Fairground: The Spitzner, Pedley and Chemisé Exhibit' as published in *Early Popular Visual Culture*, Volume 4, Issue 2 July 2006.

4. Delvaux, quoted in *Paul Delvaux 1897–1994*, exh.cat., Brussels, 1997.

Arthur Machen's

LITTLE MYSTERY

Was he M?

by ROGER DOBSON

WITH MYSTERY lying at the heart of nearly all his fiction it seems appropriate that the cult author Arthur Machen (*pictured overleaf*) is himself involved in an eighty-year-old literary mystery which may be fated to remain unsolved. The riddle relates to the discovery of eleven short fictional 'Little Fables'. The fables were published in *John O'London's Weekly* between October 1929 and February 1930. No author was credited but the sketches appeared under the initial 'M'. Was Machen 'M'? He was friendly with *John O'London's* editor Wilfred Whitten and was a regular contributor to the journal.

Some members of the Friends of Arthur Machen,[1] amongst whom the question has stirred lively debate, are convinced the fables are Machen's work and others are equally certain they are not. Other Macheniacs seem to be reserving judgement until the puzzle can be solved either way – if it can ever be solved, which seems unlikely. The situation is akin to the discovery of a series of Renaissance sketches: whether the sketches have any value rests on whether they can be authenticated as the work of Leonardo da Vinci.

The principal problem for the advocates of Machen as author is that some of the fables, which are only around one hundred and forty words at their longest, are feeble and ineffective. They include elements which Machen, as the grand master of suggestion and the sinister, would surely have rejected as subject matter. Yet they may possibly date from a period before Machen evolved into the polished and painstaking author of *The Great God Pan* (1894) and *The Three Impostors* (1895), both published by John Lane in the 'Keynotes' series,

1. A modern-day society of Machen scholars and enthusiasts.

with Aubrey Beardsley's decorations. Jerome K Jerome gave Arthur Conan Doyle a copy of the book, and Doyle endured a sleepless night. 'Your pal Machen is a genius right enough,' he told Jerome, 'but I don't take him with me to bed again.'

The decade ended with Machen producing his masterpiece *The Hill of Dreams*, unpublished until 1907 partly through the furore over the Wilde scandal. *The Hill of Dreams* has been variously called 'the most beautiful book in the world' and 'the most decadent novel in all of English literature'. Henry Miller wrote of it: 'I will not say it is the greatest book written in the English language (that for the idle critics) but I can say that it has bereft me of emotion.' Could the author of the lapidary prose of *The Hill of Dreams* have perpetrated such trivial vignettes as the fables?

Most of the story elements lack the characteristic Machen stamp. In 'The Unalterable Man' a character who has unshakeable opinions puts a 'mental bowler' on his head, takes up an 'intellectual umbrella' and ends as a scarecrow in a field. Such ingredients seem un-Machenian; yet the sketch does have some relevance. Machen may be parodying his own unwavering opinions. He claimed he largely held the same views in middle age as he did as a young man; though in one essay he admits to having been a Gladstonian Liberal in his early years until government reforms of the 1880s led him to unrepentant High Toryism.

The Broadway singer and Machen researcher the late Edwin Steffe originally disinterred the 'Little Fables' in the 1960s, sending them to one of the founders of the Machen society, Godfrey Brangham, who was unimpressed by them: he did not think they were by Machen.

The 'Little Fables' were unearthed again by Arizona booksellers Richard Russell and his wife Elaine Gross Russell (www.sangraal-books.com), the authors of *Antique Trader Vintage Magazines Price Guide* (2005). Richard Russell also found a series of fables by Robert Louis Stevenson, published in *Scribner's Magazine* and *Longman's Magazine* in 1895, which may have influenced whoever wrote the *John O'London's* sketches. One of these RLS fables, 'The Citizen and the Traveller', runs:

'Look around you,' said the citizen. 'This is the largest market in the world.'

'Oh, surely not,' said the traveller.

'Well, perhaps not the largest,' said the citizen, 'but much the best."

'You are certainly wrong there,' said the traveller. 'I can tell you . . .'

They buried the stranger at the dusk.

Were the fables Machen copying RLS just as in *The Three Impostors* he imitates *The Dynamiter* (1885), Stevenson's sequel to the *New Arabian Nights* (1882)?

Richard Russell knew bookseller Bill Koshland, the archivist of Alfred A Knopf, Machen's US publishers, who had a fund of stories about authors and how some books were sold to Knopf. In the 1920s Machen sold some experimental pieces, his *Ornaments in Jade* sequence (1924), written in the late 1890s, to Knopf. 'So just at this time I knew Machen was selling pieces like "Little Fables" to his publishers,' said Richard. It is logical to assume, Richard argues, that as a regular contributor to *John O'London's* the journal bought some, just as Knopf did. *John O'London's Weekly*, which ran from 1919-54, published fiction by authors such as Max Beerbohm, Joseph Conrad, Thomas Hardy, Somerset Maugham and Rebecca West.

Elaine Gross Russell said: 'When JOLW used new writers, they featured them and always had their full name. The "regulars", on the other hand, were not always easily identifiable. Machen was indeed a "regular" during certain periods. The magazine always had the highest praise for him and his work.' Elaine adds that the magazine's fiction, though eclectic, was generally realistic. The fables' brevity and odd tone suggest that the editor would have published such atypical work only from an established contributor such as Machen.

When the final fable, 'The Stairs', appeared in *John O'London's* it was printed in the midst of a Machen essay. Though hardly definitive proof, this hints that Machen was 'M'. He sometimes, though rarely, used the initial in journalistic pieces. Machen occasionally used pseudonyms or disguised his authorship. His first publication, the poem *Eleusinia* (1881), was anonymously issued as a pamphlet by 'A Former Member of H. C. S.' – Hereford Cathedral School. *The Anatomy of Tobacco* (1884), his first book, appeared under the pseudonym Leolinus Siluriensis. Machen enthusiast Barry Humphries writes from 'the deepest Australian Outback' to say that 'to my recollection the fables are kosher'.

As with Aesop's fables, some of the sketches point a moral, but this was uncharacteristic of Machen's fiction. In his introduction to *The House of Souls* (1906) he satirized the tendency for English fiction to contain 'useful doctrine and information'. 'How plain, for instance, is the warning in the tale of "The White People", where we see the necessity of the careful supervision of young females; while in "The Great God Pan" the dangers of unauthorized research are clearly and terribly indicated.' In 'Trouble' two men encounter a fierce dragon. One man flees but finds for the rest of his life 'dragons swelling like balloons on every side'. The second man advances 'and took the dragon of sorrow by its nose, and lo, not only did it become the size of a moderate dog, but he found it was sitting on jewels'. Confront your fears and you may profit by them might be the moral here. Machen may have felt that introducing a moral in the short compass of the fables was acceptable.

Several of the 'Little Fables' do exhibit a certain wit. In 'The Peril of Success' a famous lion hunter sits for weeks admiring his latest kill, but the lions become familiar with this practice. 'They came up one day just as he was contemplating his last and greatest success; and he was seen no more.' In 'The Generous Grocer' a rich grocer gives away harmoniums as presents. A fairy presents him with a magic mortar-board rendering him invisible. 'But, at the end of his first night, he had heard such dreadfully true things said about him that he returned the mortar-board and went to live with an aunt in Australia under an assumed name.'

Harmoniums and a magic mortar-board

In 'The Saint and the Lion' a holy man and a lion take long walks in the desert. One day the lion returns alone, 'with his waistcoat undone, and looking rather stout'. The lion explains: 'I'm very sorry in some ways, but you see he began to give me more, and more, and still more good advice.' Machen was a devout Christian but disliked sanctimonious moralizing, and so the tale may reflect this attitude.

Contrasted with the few impressive fables there are those which seem ludicrous. In 'Alphonse' a goldfish, Alphonse Tichicoco, living in a Japanese river, is captured in a bowl, putting an end to all his splendid dreams. His family mount a rescue, letting down a rope into the bowl, but the fish reacts angrily, saying: 'Whatever are you talking about? I am not in a globe.' If the tale is meant to be an allegory or parable about imprisonment and lost dreams the meaning seems very obscure. Although nearly all his work celebrates mystery, in acknowledgment of the universe's unfathomable enigmas, Machen was customarily transparent with his meanings.

Unless it contains some hidden significance, 'Fashions' is the most bizarre vignette. Performing circus horses rest in a field in summer, showing all their tricks to an Unadulterated Ass, who also has a party piece to reveal, but this is simply his crying 'Hee Haw'. Impressed, the horses copy the ass. 'And when the winter came they all rushed into the arena, but, instead of doing their lovely tricks, they stood in a circle and kept on saying, "Hee Haw".' And that, believe it not, is the end.

The Machen Friends would probably be able to dismiss the 'Little Fables' were it not for one darkly sinister gem. 'The Pedlar' does seem very much like Machen, having the genuine stamp of terror:

> *He came with masks to sell — they were hanging over his shoulder, masks of every kind. He walked all through the fair, along the passage ways between the stalls. And he stopped at corners and played upon a little flute, and sold the masks to the gathering crowds, cheap; and, under the flares, he fastened them on — on men and women and children. And they went running, crying with strange joy, until they stopped and shrieked out in the night, for the pedlar man.*
>
> *But he had gone, and the masks were fastened for life.*

All the elements in the fable recur in Machen's other works: masks, pedlars, fairs, flutes and flares. The line 'crying with strange joy' has an authentic Machenian ring. This has led to the suggestion that only this one tale was by him, while the rest are by lesser mortals, authors unknown and perhaps deservedly forgotten: a round-robin effort. But if this was the case why was the single initial 'M' used? What does it stand for? 'M' for mystery perhaps?

In 'The Stairs' the narrator writes of people who are lonely and feeling wretched. A magician waves his wand revealing a flight of stairs on which thousands of people sit like birds on telephone wires. The magician explains: 'Instead of going on a step at a time to the top and so to all the discoveries of Truth and Goodness, and Beauty which await them there, they will stop on the draughty steps half-way up.' Gwilym Games, the editor of the Friends' newsletter *Machenalia*, says that '"The Stairs" could be viewed as exhibiting Machen's philosophy. This is the type of thing he might well have written'.

Gwilym has theorized that the fables, a few of which can be viewed as slightly reminiscent of Machen's decadent style, may be experiments written in the 1890s. By the late 1920s the extraordinary vogue for Machen's work in the US had faded: he had not felt able to create new fiction to capitalize on his renaissance. Strapped for money, his good relationship with Wilfred Whitten may have encouraged Machen to sell them 'as a set of curiosity pieces' to *John O'London's*. Alternatively, Gwilym says that if they are by Machen they may have been written directly to commission in the 1920s to fill a gap as Machen, having passed through Fleet Street, could produce copy at great speed which varied in quality and tone. This might explain why so many Machen experts discount the fables completely.

A few Machen touches do occur here and there, such as the use of quasi-biblical lines which occur in Machen's prose, such as 'And they looked upon him and wept' and 'And [the dragon] sat right in the midst of the way', but the overall effect of the tales seems un-Machenian.

In 'Clever Dogs' two duellists sharpen themselves on a grindstone until their tongues resemble steel rapiers. They fence in a

Little Fables.—III.

CLEVER DOGS.

AND in a certain town there lived two gentlemen who were rather able. And, in their back gardens every morning, they used to sharpen their tongues on grindstones, until they became a couple of steel rapiers. And then they used to think of clever things to say and go out in the evening and fight with each other in the city square.

And large numbers gathered to see two people fencing with their tongues, and to marvel at the flash of them under the arc lamps. And they were such clever fellows, and wore so much padding, that they hardly ever hurt each other. But the people standing by got sparks and bits of steel in their eyes, so that at least half the inhabitants of the city had only one eye, or were blind, or had a dreadful squint.

M.

city square, wearing so much padding that they rarely hurt themselves. 'But the people standing by got sparks and bits of steel in their eyes, so that at least half the inhabitants of the city had only one eye, or were blind, or had a dreadful squint.' And so it ends. What does it signify? Why should onlookers be injured by duellists? Is this an allegory of Machen's heated occult and mystical arguments with his old friend, the author and Golden Dawn magus AE Waite? But no one was ever injured in their debates.

Heated occult & mystical arguments

If some of the fables are allegories or parables it is near impossible to decode them today. 'The Three Prisoners' (shades of *The Three Impostors*) is at least entertaining. Three men captured by giants are held in nasty cells. One man, after moaning and hooting, lies down and dies. The second man papers the walls and ceiling of the cell in a light blue and pretends he is on Hampstead Heath. 'But the third man picked his prison lock.' A parallel exists here with Machen's late tale 'The Cosy Room' (1929), in which a chamber with 'a gay flowering paper on the walls' turns out to be the condemned cell. And one can perhaps detect in the second man's delusion a common theme with *The Hill of Dreams*, where the hero Lucian Taylor, mortified by society's philistines, takes refuge in an imaginary realm, recreating in his mind the ancient Roman city of Caerleon-on-Usk, Machen's birthplace in South Wales.

Machen developed an idiosyncratic punctuation style using the semi-colon for emphasis as in 'Ah; if one only had the courage to be truly wise!' and 'For; I firmly believe . . .' If any of the fables contained this unusual use of the semi-colon this would almost conclusively prove him the author. Alas, the punctuation provides no clue.

Other ironic Machen pieces, such as *Spoof Tennis* (1912), which anticipates Beckett's *Waiting for Godot* and is far more entertaining, and the title essay in *Dog and Duck* (1924), about a venerable but bogus game of boules – some readers failed to realize that Machen had invented the game himself – contain flashes of artistic genius. By contrast, the 'Little Fables' seem largely devoid of this.

Machen biographer Mark Valentine is convinced that Machen was not the author because 'they are not his style, not his form, not particularly his philosophy, and not his practice (on the whole and except when young) to publish anonymously. The other important point is that *John O'London's Weekly* had innumerable contributors and to guess that M – a very common initial – must of all these relate to Machen is very tenuous, without supporting evidence.

'I have some bound copies of *John O'London's Weekly*, and they would print any old thing in the middle of people's stories and essays, completely unrelated. If anything, in fact, this argues against it being by Machen, since it was the standard practice to have unrelated boxed items.'

Bob Mann of the Friends found some similar fables by TWH Crosland, the journalist and poet, published in an anthology *The White Wallet* (1928), the year before the first of the *John O'London* series

Little Fables.—I.

TROUBLE.

NOW, upon a bright spring day two men did walk along the road, and, suddenly, from down a side path, there came unexpectedly a most disagreeable dragon. And it sat right in the midst of the way, and its eyes were as big as tea-trays, and, every time it roared, it swelled.

And one man took to his heels, and for the rest of his life he was running this way and that, with dragons swelling like balloons on every side.

But the other man advanced, and took the dragon of sorrow by its nose, and lo, not only did it become the size of a moderate dog, but he found it was sitting on jewels. *M.*

appeared. That Machen was imitating Crosland – they disliked one another – seems unlikely but not impossible. Crosland wrote a parody of 'The Bowmen', *Find the Angels: The Showmen – A Legend of the War* (1915). Ironically, some of the Crosland fables are superior to the *John O'London's* efforts. In one of them an undertaker sees a tree 'blossoming in billowy white, like a bride' while a yellow butterfly floats by. 'And the undertaker remarked that he never had pretended to understand this world.' Could Machen, master of language, be outshone by Crosland? This seems almost beyond belief.

A precedent for the fables may exist. In the early 1890s Machen produced several rather weak 'society' stories for vanished journals such as *The Whirlwind, The World* and *St James's Gazette*. These potboilers, such as 'An Underground Adventure', 'Sir John's Chef', 'A Wonderful Woman', 'A Remarkable Coincidence' and 'Jocelyn's Escape' (available in *Ritual and Other Stories*, Tartarus Press, 1992), would have been long forgotten if he had not acknowledged his authorship decades later, when his work began to be collected and studied by enthusiasts such as Vincent Starrett from 1917 and John Gawsworth in the 1930s. If Machen students did not know otherwise, no one would have believed him to be the author of such works. The contrast with the powerful

Little Fables.—II.

FASHIONS.

NOW in a certain field there lived during the summer months a number of performing horses. And they were the most delightful creatures resting after the winter circuses.

And in the next field to them there resided a plain and Unadulterated Ass.

And every summer morning when no one was looking, they showed him all their lovely tricks.

And the Unadulterated Ass looked through a hole in the hedge and watched.

And then one day he said : "I have a trick," and he gave the most terrific "Hee Haw."

And all the horses marvelled and set to work to learn it.

And when the winter came they all rushed into the arena, but, instead of doing their lovely tricks, they stood in a circle and kept on saying "Hee Haw." ***M.***

first chapter of *The Great God Pan*, published as a self-contained short story in *The Whirlwind* in 1890, is astonishing.

Machen's other tales from the early 1890s, such as 'The Lost Club' and 'A Double Return', hint of the genius that was to emerge later that decade. 'A Double Return' caused a scandal, because it involves an impostor who impersonates a painter, managing to spend an illicit night with the artist's uncomprehending wife. The wife expires from shame a few months later. 'Are you the author of that story that fluttered the dovecotes?' Wilde asked Machen. 'I thought it very good.' The tale ended Machen's relationship with the *St James's Gazette*.

These lesser stories, which are of great interest simply because they are by Machen, were tracked down by his loyal disciple and biographer John Gawsworth and published in *The Cosy Room and Other Stories* (1936). 'There are things in it, dating from 1890, that make me sick to look at,' Machen wrote to a friend at the time. 'It is a strange and – to me, at all events – an appalling thing to be confronted with the casual, temporary stuff of 1890,' he complained to Waite. Gawsworth, he wrote, had gone grubbing in dustbins of 45 years ago. More than a century on, this 'temporary stuff' is still enchanting readers: *Ritual* is now in its fourth edition. The fables may belong to the same category.

Machen was a fervent Dickensian, yet even Dickens produced work that he was later heartily embarrassed by. He wrote of his sentimental burletta *The Village Coquettes*, written in 1836 at the same time as *The Pickwick Papers*, that 'if I knew it was in my house and if I could not get rid of it in any other way, I would burn the wing of the house where it was'. Machen may have felt similarly about the fables. Even literary titans find maintaining high standards difficult. If one did not know otherwise, who would believe that the author of that unconvincing crime melodrama 'Hunted Down' (1859) was also the creator of those undoubted masterpieces *David Copperfield* (1849-50) and *Great Expectations* (1860-1)?

Harold Billings, biographer of Machen's nineties associate MP Shiel, has examined some of Machen's notes dating from the mid-1890s held by the Humanities Research Center at Austin, Texas. It was hoped that the jottings might contain some reference to the fables, or even the fables themselves. If Machen was the author they surely must have been early rather than mature work. No allusions have been found so far.

No Machen scholar has gone through all of his extant letters – mostly held by US universities – so references may exist there. Perhaps *John O'London* editor Wilfred Whitten's papers are also held somewhere.

The fables are without the brilliance of the story synopses from the 1890s which Machen included in his memoir *The London Adventure* (1924). Of the eleven fables, only 'The Pedlar' seems to strike the sinister Machen note recognisable from *The Great God Pan* and *The Three Impostors*. They lack the magic Machen was able to bring even to minor work. Harmoniums; a magic mortar-board conferring invisibility; a lion in a waistcoat; a goldfish called Alphonse waxing his moustache; a man with a mental bowler: such things seem alien to the type of imaginative elements that figure in Machen's works. They seem more akin to Hans Christian Andersen's fairy tales or to Lewis Carroll's whimsy, but perhaps that is why he signed them 'M'. Could it be that the hypercritical Machen was ashamed of them? Yet it seems strange that the fables, if they are Machen's work, escaped John Gawsworth's eagle eye over the years. The great bookman does not appear to refer to them anywhere. They are just the type of material Gawsworth would delightedly have resurrected to mark Machen's centenary in 1963.

The American HP Lovecraft scholar ST Joshi is currently compiling a Machen bibliography, so it would be useful for the Friends to confirm whether Machen was the author. Unless the question can be resolved it will present a dilemma for any future editor of a collected Machen edition. Should the fables be included or not?

As a devotee of insoluble mysteries Machen would perhaps have enjoyed the Friends' problem. As he wrote: 'man is made a mystery and exists for mysteries and visions'. The office-boy who bets a half-crown on a horse 'is really only an example of the love of man for the unknown; the half-crown is a venture into mystery', he declared. Machen said that he did not want to know the explanation for the *Mary Celeste* riddle or have the words and music of the legendary sirens' song revealed. 'The more mysteries the better,' he wrote.